Gillian Tett is the US managing editor and columnist at the *Financial Times*, the world's leading newspaper covering finance and business. In 2014 she was named Columnist of the Year in the British Press Awards, and was previously named Journalist of the Year (2009), Business Journalist of the Year (2008) and Wincott Financial Journalist of the Year (2007). In 2011 she was awarded the British Academy's President's Medal. Tett is the author of *Saving the Sun* and *Fool's Gold*. She lives in New York City.

@gilliantett

'Engagingly written, this is also a history of our need to classify the world and how that can be our downfall' Hazel Davis, *The Times*

'A profound idea, richly analyzed' *Wall Street Journal* (Europe)

'Highly intelligent, enjoyable and enlivened by a string of vivid case studies. It is also genuinely important . . . her prescription for curing the pathological silo-isation of business and government is refreshingly unorthodox and, in my view, convincing' Felix Martin, *Financial Times*

'Gillian Tett is a gifted, innovative and informative writer . . . Tett writes beautifully and her book is full of insights. Those who do not know her work should make up for the oversight' Vince Cable, *New Statesman*

'Here's a piece of advice: read *The Silo Effect*, if only because your boss may already be immersed in Gillian Tett's latest study on how organisations can go badly awry. You would not want to be caught unawares, now, would you? Also, you might be missing something rather brilliant. Yes, honestly . . . Tett's anthropological approach adds academic rigour and richness' Anne Ashworth, *The Times*

'Supremely wise' Rohan Silva, *Evening Standard*

BY GILLIAN TETT

Saving the Sun

Fool's Gold

The Silo Effect

THE
SILO
Effect

Why Every Organisation Needs
to Disrupt Itself to Survive

GILLIAN TETT

ABACUS

First published in Great Britain in 2015 by Little, Brown
This paperback edition published in 2016 by Abacus

1 3 5 7 9 10 8 6 4 2

A CIP catalogue record for this book
is available from the British Library.

ISBN 978-1-84408-759-4

Printed and bound in Great Britain by
Clays Ltd, St Ives plc

Papers used by Abacus are from well-managed forests
and other responsible sources.

MIX
Paper from
responsible sources
FSC® C104740

Abacus
An imprint of
Little, Brown Book Group
Carmelite House
50 Victoria Embankment
London EC4Y 0DZ

An Hachette UK Company
www.hachette.co.uk

www.littlebrown.co.uk

For Romaine Joy Carley Tett,
in grateful, loving memory

Contents

Note from the Author

This book started during the Great Financial Crisis of 2008. But it is not a book about finance. Far from it. Instead, it asks a basic question: Why do humans working in modern institutions collectively act in ways that sometimes seem stupid? Why do normally clever people fail to see risks and opportunities that are subsequently blindingly obvious? Why, as Daniel Kahneman, the psychologist, put it, are we sometimes so 'blind to our own blindness'?[1]

It was a question I often asked myself in 2007 and 2008. Back then, I was working as a journalist in London, running the markets team of the *Financial Times*. When the financial crisis erupted, we threw ourselves into trying to understand why the disaster had come about. There were lots of potential reasons. Before 2008 bankers had taken some crazy risks with mortgages and other financial assets, creating a gigantic bubble. Regulators had failed to spot the dangers, because they misunderstood how the modern financial system worked. Central bankers and other policymakers had given the wrong economic incentives to financiers. Consumers had been dangerously complacent, running up huge credit card debts and mortgage loans without asking whether they could be repaid. Ratings agencies misread risks. And so on.

But as I dug into the story of the Great Financial Crisis as a journalist (and later wrote a book about it, *Fool's Gold*[2]) I became convinced that there was another reason for the disaster: the modern financial system was surprisingly fragmented, in terms of how people organized themselves, interacted with each other, and imagined the world. In theory, pundits often like to say that globalization and the Internet are creating a seamless, interlinked world, where markets, economies, and people are connected more closely than ever before. In some senses, integration is under way. But as I dug into the 2008 crisis I also saw a world where different teams of financial traders at the big banks did not know what each other was doing, even inside the same (supposedly integrated) institution. I heard how government officials were hamstrung by the fact that the big regulatory agencies and central banks were crazily fragmented, not just in terms of their bureaucratic structures, but also their worldview. Politicians were no better. Nor were the credit rating agencies, or parts of the media. Indeed, almost everywhere I looked in the financial crisis it seemed that tunnel vision and tribalism had contributed to the disaster. People were trapped inside their little specialist departments, social groups, teams, or pockets of knowledge. Or, it might be said, inside their silos.

That was striking. But as the 2008 crisis slowly ebbed from view, I realized that this silo effect – as I came to call it – was not just a problem at banks. On the contrary, it crops up in almost every corner of modern life. In 2010, I moved from London to New York, to run the American operations of the *Financial Times*, and when I looked at the corporate and government world from that perch, I saw a fragmented pattern there too. The silo syndrome cropped up at gigantic companies such as BP, Microsoft, and (later on) General Motors. It plagued the White House and Washington agencies. Large universities were often beset with tribalism. So were many media groups. The paradox of the modern age, I realized, is that we live in a world that is closely integrated in some ways, but fragmented in others. Shocks are increasingly contagious. But we continue to behave and think in tiny silos.

So this book sets out to answer two questions: Why do silos arise? And is there anything we can do to master our silos, before these silos master us? I tackle this partly from the perspective of someone who has spent two decades working as a financial journalist, observing global business, economics, and politics. That career has trained me to use stories to illustrate my ideas. So in this book you will hear eight different tales about the silo effect, ranging from Michael Bloomberg's City Hall in New York to the Bank of England in London, Cleveland Clinic hospital in Ohio, UBS bank in Switzerland, Facebook in California, Sony in Tokyo, BlueMountain hedge fund in New York, and the Chicago police. Some of these narratives illustrate how foolishly people can behave when they are mastered by silos. Others, however, show how institutions and individuals can master their silos. Some of these are stories of failure. But there are also tales of success.

But there is a second strand to this book. Before I became a journalist (in 1993), I did a PhD in the field of cultural anthropology,* or the study of human culture, at Cambridge University. As part of this academic work, I conducted fieldwork, first in Tibet, and then down on the southern rim of the former Soviet Union, in Soviet Tajikistan, where I partly lived between 1989 and 1991 in a small village. My research was focused on marriage practices, which I studied as a tool to understand how the Tajik had retained their Islamic identity in a (supposedly atheist) communist state.[3]

When I first became a financial journalist, I was often wary about revealing my peculiar past. The type of academic qualifications that usually command respect on Wall Street, or the City of London, are MBAs or advanced degrees in economics, finance, astrophysics, or another quantitative science. Knowing about the wedding customs of the Tajiks does not seem an obvious training to write about the global economy or banking system. But if there is one thing that the Great Financial Crisis showed it is that finance and economics are *not* just about numbers. Culture matters too. The way that people organize institutions, define social networks, and classify the world has a crucial impact on how the government, business, and economy function (or sometimes do *not* function, as in 2008). Studying these cultural

---

* In the United States this is known as cultural anthropology. In the U.K. it is known as social anthropology. Either way, cultural/social anthropology is about the study of how people live, think, and interact, not how they function in a biological sense. The study of human biology and evolution is normally called physical anthropology. These branches of anthropology often blur. But cultural anthropology does not usually place great emphasis on science.

aspects is thus important. And this is where anthropology can help. What anthropologists have to say is not just relevant for far-flung non-Western cultures, but can shed light on Western cultures. The methods I used to analyze Tajik weddings, in other words, can be helpful in making sense of Wall Street bankers or government bureaucrats. The lens of anthropology is also useful if you want to make sense of silos. After all, silos are cultural phenomena, which arise out of the systems we use to classify and organize the world. Telling stories about the silo effect as an anthropologist-cum-journalist can thus shed light on the problem. These tales may even offer some answers about how to deal with silos, not just for the bankers, but government bureaucrats, business leaders, politicians, philanthropists, academics, and journalists too.

Or that, at least, is my hope.

Introduction

BLOOMBERG'S SKUNKWORKS

'We can be blind to the obvious, and we are also blind to our blindness.'

—Daniel Kahneman, *Thinking, Fast and Slow*[1]

IN THE EARLY HOURS OF APRIL 25, 2011, A BRUTAL FIRE BROKE OUT IN A POOR neighborhood in the Bronx, New York.[2] Within minutes, flames engulfed the building, at 2321 Prospect Avenue. Dozens of firefighters rushed to the scene. But it was too late for Juan Lopez, thirty-six, a soccer-loving Mexican construction worker, his wife, Christina Garcia, forty-three, and her son, Christian, twelve.[3] As the flames spread, they were trapped by a maze of illegally constructed walls inside their tiny apartment. On the street outside, firemen and bystanders could hear their desperate screams.[4] Nobody could rescue them.

In the days after their deaths, the press angrily hunted for scapegoats. Some pointed the finger at the New York government in City Hall. The building at 2321 Prospect Avenue had been illegally subdivided many times,[5] to enable the landlord to extract more rent; but though the neighbors had reported the dangerous conditions to city officials, nothing had been done. Other observers blamed a gang of local drug dealers,[6] who were using the basement of the building as a den. Still others pointed to bankers.[7] The registered owner of 2321 Prospect Avenue – Dominic Cedano – had taken out a subprime loan to buy the building during the credit boom, but later defaulted.[8] The house had duly been tossed into legal limbo by the banks, and the local utility cut off the electricity. Relatives of the Garcia family begged them to move. But Juan Lopez was finding it tough to get construction work, and since a room at 2321 Prospect Avenue was only $100 a week, the family stayed on, using candles for light. 'We don't know what happened, we're really sad,' Katia Garcia, a relative, told the newspaper. Rosemary Pagan, a neighbor, said: 'Katia kept telling Christina, "You have to move from there." [But] financially, they didn't have the money to move.'[9]

For a few days recriminations flared. Then they died down, as the media's attention moved to the next scandal. But a few miles away, inside the majestic City Hall building in downtown Manhattan, the tragedy sparked debate. When the news of the Garcia fire first broke, the mayor, Michael Bloomberg, asked some of his staff if there was anything that could be done to prevent this type of fire. At first glance, it seemed not. One of New York's dark secrets is that house fires have been tragically commonplace: in the decade before 2011, about 2,700 structural fires broke out each year,[10] on average killing about eighty-five people,[11] and these typically occurred in subdivided buildings in poor neighborhoods, or places where poor immigrants, such as Juan Lopez, tend to live, crammed together. In theory, New York had teams of inspectors who were supposed to combat this fire risk. But the inspectors faced fearsome odds: each year the Department of Buildings received about 20,000 complaints about dangerous housing, which the building and fire inspectors were both supposed to chase up.[12] But New York only employed 200-odd inspectors, who were supposed to monitor four million properties in one million buildings. The city did not have more funds to expand the department.[13] The odds were hopelessly stacked against anybody hunting for firetraps. Even when the inspectors looked at buildings that had attracted specific complaints, they only found unsafe conditions 13 percent of the time.

But though the problem seemed daunting, two men on Bloomberg's team, Mike Flowers and John Feinblatt, thought they might, just possibly, have a solution. This did not involve anything to do with firefighting equipment, but something else: thinking about 'silos.' City Hall sat atop a very large organization, which employed roughly 150,000 people.[14] Like most government bodies, the New York government was run as a bureaucracy, subdivided into more than three dozen agencies, which ran a wide variety of services, ranging from firefighting to cultural affairs to urban planning to education. Most of these different agencies were independent in spirit and function.

Communication between these teams was patchy, at best. The Fire Department was a case in point: the firemen worked in a unit that was revered by New Yorkers, particularly after the

bravery that firemen displayed during the attack on the World
Trade Center in 2001. But the department was also profoundly
independent, semidetached from everyone else. So much so, that
when emergency workers rushed to the World Trade Center in
September 2001, they discovered that the radios and walkie-
talkies used by the fire, policy, and health departments could
not tune into the same communication channels.[15] Nobody had
noticed this before, precisely because these different teams were
so disconnected.

But what would happen, Flowers and Feinblatt asked, if somebody tried to break those specialist silos down? Was it possible
to take a joined-up view of the problem of fire risk? Could silo-
busting change how people imagined firetraps – and even save
lives? It was a novel idea. Indeed, it seemed so alien to the City
Hall culture that Feinblatt and Flowers initially kept their project
secret, christening it 'skunkworks' (a reference to the hidden military programs that the U.S. defense company Lockheed Martin
has long organized to design military planes).

But in the months after the Garcia deaths, this skunkworks
ended up producing some surprising results. What Flowers and
Feinblatt discovered is that if you start thinking about silos, and
even breaking them down, this endeavor can produce big wins.
And not just in relation to handling fire risks, but almost every
other area of the modern world.

MIKE FLOWERS NEVER EXPECTED to be a silo-buster. His journey
toward that role started a long way from New York, in the unlikely
place of Iraq. A burly, cheery man who grew up in Philadelphia,

he initially trained as a lawyer, and during the 1990s he worked as a government prosecutor in the tough jungle of the Manhattan district attorney's office.[16] The role suited him: with his balding head and rapid-fire speech, Flowers has a passing resemblance to James Gandolfini, the actor who played Tony Soprano on the television show – albeit with a slimmer physique and more affable manner.

But after a few years of the gritty Manhattan beat, Flowers tired of the daily battles and moved to Washington to work in a high-paid private legal job. Then he swerved again, after deciding that corporate law was just too dull for his taste, and signed up for a job in postwar Iraq. There he started working as government prosecutor for the American military, which had taken control of the country a year before and was starting to conduct trials of officials linked to the former regime of Saddam Hussein. One of his first tasks was to bring witnesses from across Baghdad into the courtroom in the military zone to testify against Hussein.

It was a difficult job, since the Baghdad traffic was constantly being snarled by car bombs or roadblocks. 'It was a war zone, then, obviously, and I was trying to get my witnesses in and out for the trial,' he recalled. 'We had a problem moving them about, and not getting shot at.' Initially Flowers accepted this unpredictability. One day, however, he got chatting to a young marine, and realized that an innovative piece of research work was being conducted by a part of the military that went under the unwieldy name of the 'Joint Improvised Explosive Device Defeat Organization,' or JIEDDO. This initiative pooled data from the traffic flows and matched it up with an analysis of where the roadside bombs were exploding. Nobody had tried to link these pools of data before. But when they were combined, they illustrated a pattern: whenever a car bomb was about to go off in a certain quarter of town, the traffic in that area would die down. So Flowers started watching the JEIDDO data to get clues about when violence might erupt – and when the traffic lulls suggested that he should *not* move his witnesses around. 'I guess that was because there was local intelligence, people knew that an attack was planned and got out the way,' Flowers observed. 'But to be honest I didn't care about the cause – all I wanted to know was if I should bring my witnesses in on a Tuesday or Wednesday, say.' Either way, it taught him a simple lesson: sometimes it paid dividends to connect seemingly unconnected bits of information.

In 2009, Flowers returned to Washington to work with the Senate team conducting investigations into the 2008 financial crisis. But then officials at the City Office of New York offered him a job investigating financial fraud in New York. He was wary, not wanting to get sucked into the never-ending task of grappling with financial reform. So he presented an alternative idea: if he came to New York, could he conduct investigations by using some of the data-crunching – or connecting – techniques that he had witnessed in Iraq? 'I am a lawyer by training, not a math geek, but my experience of Baghdad had shown me what you do with data,' he explained. 'And I knew that New York City is the ultimate collector of information – it collects data on *everything*. Traffic tickets, building codes, tax liens, you name it! So I reckoned that if anyone could ever get all their arms around that information, it could completely change how we investigate fraud. And from that it's a gradual step to say that the information is not just used for fraud, but for anything the city does.'

Flowers's timing was perfect. At the start of the decade, Bloomberg had been voted in as mayor after a career spent in finance and then as an entrepreneur running a successful financial data company. He had arrived in his post determined to change how City Hall worked, and had two particular obsessions. One was an interest in how organizations managed information flows; or more often *mis*managed it. 'If you cannot measure it, you cannot manage it,' was one of his favorite slogans.[17] His second obsession was breaking down internal silos: he was convinced that the best way to run an office was with open plan office spaces that forced employees to intermingle. This was not how government was usually laid out: City Hall – which dates from 1812, making it the oldest municipal building in America[18] – had traditionally been divided into dozens of tiny offices, separated by thick walls, marble halls, and pillars. But when Bloomberg arrived he demanded that the officials move out of their marble rabbit hutches and into the only large space that available – the historic speakers' hall. There he placed dozens of desks under the oil paintings and statues to create an open plan office. He called it the 'bullpen.' 'Everyone has the same size desk, the same size computer,' explained Robert Steel, deputy mayor. 'The mayor sits in the middle, along with everyone else.'

Bloomberg tried to apply the same silo-busting principles in a much wider sense. He declared that the different departments needed to work together far more closely than before, breaking down the long-established barriers. Indeed, he was so determined to promote change that he appointed a non–New Yorker, Stephen Goldsmith, as deputy mayor for operations. Before coming to New York, Goldsmith had worked as mayor of Indianapolis, where he had earned acclaim by overhauling how its city bureaucracy functioned, breaking down silos to make the system more efficient. Bloomberg was eager to replicate that in New York.

However, Goldsmith quickly discovered that it was much harder to promote a revolution in New York than in Indianapolis. Shuffling around furniture in the bullpen was one thing. Persuading bureaucrats to change their working habits was quite another still. 'The unions are really strong in New York and they want to protect everyone,' explained Goldsmith. 'It's a huge place. There are 2,500 different job categories in the New York government – yes, 2,500! – and all these different silos are so entrenched.' But even if the rhetoric of Bloomberg's plans did not play out as he hoped, everybody in City Hall knew the direction of Bloomberg's ambition. That appealed to Flowers and in 2010 Flowers agreed to join the New York government, hoping to try some experiments.

THE FIRE AT 2321 Prospect Avenue in Bronx presented the first big chance for Flowers to test some ideas. Soon after he arrived, Flowers placed an advertisement on Craigslist, the online advertising and brokerage site, seeking young data crunchers. Nobody in City Hall usually recruited staff that way. But Flowers quickly assembled a team of recent college graduates: Ben Dean, Catherine Kwan, Chris Corcoran, and Lauren Talbot.[19] 'I wanted somebody fresh out of college with skills in mathematical economics, someone who could give me a fresh pair of eyes.'

Then he installed the 'kids,' as he called them, in a downtown warehouse.

A few days after the Garcia family death, Flowers asked the team to comb through the data that New York was collecting about fire risk. He wanted to see if there was anything that might predict when fires would break out. At first glance, there did not appear to be any obvious clues. The Fire Department had extensive information about previous fires and reports about illegally converted buildings that had been logged via the 311 telephone line that was normally used when people wanted to complain to the government. But – oddly enough – although most calls about illegal conversions emanated in lower Manhattan, that was *not* the place with most fires, nor where most illegal conversions were found. Those happened in the outer boroughs, such as the Bronx and Queens. That was because many poor immigrants (like the Garcia family) were too scared of the authorities to actually report problems. Those 311 calls were not a good predictor of fires.

So was there a better way to guess where fires might break out? What would happen, Flowers asked, if you looked at data from other sources – *outside* the Fire Department? Flowers asked his kids to leave their computers for a few days and go on 'ride-alongs' with the inspectors from the different Sheriff's Office, Police, Fire, Housing, and Building Departments. What, he asked, were the essential features of fire traps? How could you spot them?

Many of the inspectors were initially suspicious. The New York Fire Department, for example, has a long, proud history, and the inspectors did not like outsiders meddling in their operations.

They tended to be scornful of City Hall, and there was a plethora of rules that stipulated that buildings inspectors could only look for some types of problems – while fire inspectors hunted for others. But Flowers was determined to break down these boundaries, and his time in Baghdad had left him convinced that if you wanted to understand a problem there was no substitute to getting out and watching real life unfold. Life could not be put into neat, predefined boxes or just observed from an office or computer program; you had to be willing to watch, listen, and rethink your assumptions.

So he sternly told his kids to be humble – and keep an open mind about what might help predict fires. 'We listened to firemen, to policemen, to inspectors from the Buildings Department, from Housing Preservation and Development, the Water Department. I asked them: "When you go to a place that's a dump, what do you see?" What are the clues? We listened, listened, listened.' Gradually, a pattern emerged. Dangerous buildings, the kids learned, tended to have been built before 1938, when the building codes were tightened in New York. They were usually located in poor neighborhoods, their owners were often delinquent on their mortgages, and the buildings had generated complaints about issues such as vermin before.[20]

So Flowers's kids hunted for data on those issues. It was surprisingly difficult. In theory, New York was a gold mine for data-loving geeks, since the forty-odd agencies that sit directly under City Hall's control have long collected extensive records of their activity. City Hall officials were so proud of this data stash that when Bloomberg created his bullpen in City Hall, he installed computer screens on the walls, between the historic oil paintings, to display these beloved statistics. But there was one big catch: the data was held in dozens of different databases, since not only were the agencies separated from each other, but there were subdivisions within the agencies. The numbers as crazily fragmented as the people.

However, the kids used a database of properties known as 'PLUTO' (the Primary Land Use Tax Lot Output)[21] to isolate a subset of 640,000 houses in the New York district that were registered with City Hall to hold one to three families. Due to a peculiar quirk of New York law, the Fire Department was only allowed to inspect about half of these; the rest fell under the control of the Department of Buildings. However, the kids tracked through all the different – separate – records from the Fire and Building Departments for data about house fires and illegal conversion complaints. They also scoured the Department of Finance and Department of Investigations – separate bodies that dealt with tax and fraud respectively – for information about previous tax and mortgage defaults, and checked with the Building Department for a list of properties built before 1938. Finally they combined those data pools in a single statistical model. Slowly, a pattern emerged. Whenever all four of the risk factors cropped up together at an address, there was a dramatically higher incidence of house fires and illegal conversions, *even if nobody had ever complained about problems*. Or to put it another way, if you wanted to predict which houses were likely to be fire traps, the best clue came not from 311 calls or specific complaints about fires, but by combining disparate data on mortgage defaults, violation of building codes, data on the age of structures, and myriad indicators of neighborhood poverty.

So Flowers went to the Building Department inspectors, with the support of Goldsmith, and asked them to inspect the houses that were violating the building code and looked dangerous on the aggregated data. 'At first they didn't like this idea at all – they said we were nuts!' Flowers recalled. But eventually the Building Department backed down and used his data. The results were stunning. Traditionally, when the inspectors had looked at buildings, they had only uncovered actual problems in 13 percent of the places. With the new method, problems were uncovered 70 percent of the time.[22] At a stroke – and without spending any more money – the fire detection process had become almost *four* times more effective.

Was that just a lucky fluke? The team tested the same technique with larger buildings. Initially, the results were poor. So Flowers dispatched some of his young data scientists out on the rounds with the inspectors again, and told them to do more on-the-ground research: was there something that made big buildings different from small buildings? Days passed without any clear clue. But then one of the data crunchers heard a veteran inspector remark by chance, as they drew up outside a large building: 'This building is fine – just look at the brickwork!' The computer scientist asked why the brickwork mattered, and the inspector explained that years of inspections had shown that landlords who paid to install new bricks did not tolerate fire hazards. So the kids changed tack – and looked at some data on brick deliveries across New York, another unnoticed data pile in another corner of the

New York bureaucracy. When that was plugged into the statistical map, the accuracy of their predictions surged. In isolation, those records about bricks were not revealing; joined up with other data points, it was dynamite.

Then the kids applied the same silo-busting approach elsewhere. Cigarettes were a case in point. In previous decades, the city had suffered a big problem with tobacco smuggling since cigarettes cost twice as much in New York as Virginia (due to tax) and the city only had fifty sheriffs to inspect 14,000 news dealers.[23] But by cross-checking business licenses against tax fraud data, Flowers's team dramatically increased the detection rates. They performed a similar trick with illegal sales of OxyContin, the oft-abused prescription drug. Since the city had thousands of pharmacies it had traditionally been hard to spot illegal OxyContin sales by random inspections. But after combining fragmented databases, Flowers's team determined that just 1 percent of all the pharmacies accounted for around 24 percent of Medicaid reimbursements for the most potent types of OxyContin prescriptions.[24] Detection rates soared.

The kids even dove into the unpleasant problem of 'yellow grease' fat used in restaurant deep-fryers. There are an estimated 24,000 restaurants in New York, and many deep-fry their food. 'Just think of those fries, spring rolls, whatever!' Flowers liked to say, pointing at his belly. Under New York law, restaurants are supposed to get rid of this grease by taking out contracts with a waste disposal company. However, many have traditionally flouted that law and just tipped the fat down manholes into the New York sewage system instead.

For years it had been almost impossible to prevent these illegal dumps, since the grease was usually thrown down the manholes late at night. But the skunkworks kids collected reports from the environmental department about yellow grease pollution, and compared it to separate pools of data on business licenses, tax returns, kitchen fires. They plotted out restaurants that had *not* applied for waste disposal licenses – and created a list of likely grease dumpers. Then the team approached a separate department of the City Hall bureaucracy that was trying to promote biodiesel recycling, and asked if they might collaborate with the health and safety inspectors, and the fire services, to persuade restaurants to stop dumping yellow grease into manholes, and sell it to recycling groups instead. 'When the inspectors go into a restaurant now and find yellow grease dumps, they don't just go in there and say: "Hey, knock it off! Pay us a $25,000 fine!"' Flowers later recalled. 'Instead they say: "Don't be dumb – get paid for getting rid of this stuff! Sell it to the biodiesel companies! There is a whole industry out there that actually wants to *buy* yellow grease!"'

Indeed, the benefits of silo-busting were so obvious and powerful that Flowers often wondered why nobody had thought of it before. After all, statistical geeks have been using advanced data-sampling techniques for years, and are trained to look for correlations. Why had nobody tried combining the databases before? Flowers knew the answer to his own question even before he asked it: New York's government was marred by so many silos that people could not see problems and opportunities that sat just before their noses. The story of the skunkworks, in other words, was *not* really a story about statistics. It was a tale about how we organize our lives, our data, our departments, our lives, and our minds. 'Everything here is arranged in a fragmented way. It's tough to join it all up. When you do, it's obvious that you get much better outcomes,' Flowers observed.

'But somehow [this joined-up approach] doesn't happen much. You just gotta ask: *why?*'

THE PARADOX OF AN INTERCONNECTED WORLD

The story of New York's City Hall is not at all unusual. On the contrary, if you look around the world today, our twenty-first-century society is marked by a striking paradox. In some senses, we live in an age where the globe is more interlinked, as a common system, than ever before. The forces of globalization and technological change mean that news can flash across the planet at lightning speed. Digital supply chains link companies, consumers, and economies across the globe. Ideas – good *and* bad – spread easily. So do people, pandemics, and panics. When trades turn sour in a tiny corner of the financial markets, the global banking system can go topsy-turvy. We live, in short, in a world plagued by what the economist Ian Goldin has dubbed the 'Butterfly Defect': a system that is so tightly integrated that there is an ever-present threat of contagion.[25] 'The world has become a hum of interconnected voices and a hive of interlinked lives,' as Christine Lagarde, head of the International Monetary Fund, observes. '[This is a] breakneck pattern of integration and interconnectedness that defines our time.'[26]

But while the world is increasingly interlinked as a system, our lives remain fragmented. Many large organizations are divided, and then subdivided into numerous different departments, which often fail to talk to each other – let alone collaborate. People often live in separate mental and social 'ghettos,' talking and coexisting only with people like us. In many countries, politics is polarized. Professions seem increasingly specialized, partly because technology keeps becoming more complex and sophisticated, and is only understood by a tiny pool of experts.

There are many ways to describe this sense of fragmentation: people have used words like 'ghettos,' 'buckets,' 'tribes,' 'boxes,' 'stovepipes.' But the metaphor I find useful is 'silo.' The roots of this come from the ancient Greek term *siros*, which literally means 'corn pit.'[27] Even today, the word retains that original sense: according to the *Oxford English Dictionary*,[28] a silo is a 'tall tower or pit on a farm used to store grain.'[29] However, in the middle of the twentieth century, the Western military adopted the word to describe the underground chambers used to store guided missiles. Management consultants then imported the phrase to describe a 'system, process, department, etc. that operates in isolation from others,' as the *Oxford English Dictionary* says. The word 'silo' today is thus not just a noun, but can be employed as a verb (to silo) and adjective (silo-ized). And the crucial point to note is that the word 'silo' does not just refer to a physical structure or organization (such as a department). It can also be a state of mind. Silos exist in structures. But they exist in our minds and social groups too. Silos breed tribalism. But they can also go hand in hand with tunnel vision.

This book is not 'anti-silo.' It does not argue that silos are always bad, or that we should just issue a moratorium and 'abolish all silos!' (Although that might sometimes seem tempting.) On the contrary, a starting point of this book is that the modern world needs silos, at least if you interpret that word to mean specialist departments, teams, and places. The reason is obvious: we live in such a complex world that humans need to create some structure to handle this complexity. Moreover, as the flood of data grows, alongside the scale of our organizations and complexity of technology, the need for organization is growing apace. The simplest way to create a sense of order is to put ideas, people, and data into separate spatial, social, and mental boxes. Specialization and expertise usually deliver progress. After all, as Adam Smith, the eighteenth-century economist, observed, societies and economies flourish when there is a division of labor.[30] Without that division, life is far less efficient. If those 150,000 staff working in New York's government were not organized into expert teams, there would be chaos. A dedicated team of trained firefighters is likely to be better at fighting fires than a random group of amateurs. Silos help us to tidy up the world, classify and arrange our lives, economies, and institutions. They encourage accountability.

But silos can also sometimes cause damage. People who are organized into specialist teams can end up fighting with each other, wasting resources. Isolated departments, or teams of experts, may fail to communicate, and thus overlook dangerous and costly risks. Fragmentation can create information bottle-necks and stifle innovation. Above all else, silos can create tunnel vision, or mental blindness, which causes people to do stupid things.

The world around us is littered with examples of this. One of the reasons the Great Financial Crisis of 2008 erupted, for example, was that the financial system was so fragmented that it was almost impossible for anyone to take an interconnected view of how risks were developing in the markets and banking world. Gigantic financial companies were split into so many different departments, or silos, the leaders who were supposed to be running the groups did not understand what their own traders were doing. But this is not just a problem affecting banks. In 2010, BP revealed that one of its rigs had suffered an explosion in the Gulf of Mexico. As oil spurted out into the sea, causing terrible pollution, recriminations flew around. Then, as investigators dug into the issues, a familiar pattern started to emerge: BP was a company beset by numerous bureaucratic silos, with technocratic geeks scurrying around in specialized fields. Though the oil company had a technical team monitoring safety, that group was not connected with the team that handled the day-to-day operations on the Macondo oil rig. Messages did not get passed across, or not until it was far too late.[31]

In the spring of 2014 General Motors admitted that some of its compact cars, such as the Chevrolet Cobalt and Pontiac G5, had been fitted with a faulty ignition switch that could flip from the 'run' position to the 'accessory' position while driving, cutting the engine power and disabling the airbags. The company admitted that some engineers had been aware of this fault since 2001 and had known that it would have cost a mere 90 cents per car to fix it. However, they had not changed the switch, even as people died in car crashes, because the information about the switches sat in one tiny, bureaucratic silo. Worse still, the engineers who handled the switches had minimal contact with the legal team that was worrying about reputational risk. General Motors, in other words, was a company that was riddled with silos – and where staff had little internal incentive to collaborate in a proactive way. Like the bankers, or the safety managers at BP, the individual teams protected their own interests, even when this threatened to damage the company as a whole.[32] 'We have to find a way to break these silos down,' Mary Barra, the newly appointed CEO, lamented to staff after the damning report came out.[33]

Similarly, when investigators dug into the reasons that the CIA and other intelligence services failed to foresee the threat posed by al Qaeda in 2001, they found a pattern where individual departments hoarded data and did not share it across the group.[34] When reporters in Britain investigated why the National Health Service has made so many disastrous decisions over the procurement of IT systems between 2008 and 2011, it emerged – once again – that the managers who were ordering IT systems in one department had not consulted with anyone else.[35] When there was an outcry over the computing glitches that dogged the launch of healthcare.gov, the insurance website that the administration of President Barack Obama launched in late 2013, a similar pattern emerged. Although individual computer experts working for the program had been aware that the website faced severe problems for a long time, their messages had not been passed across to the teams managing the political campaign. Nobody in the White House had fully understood what the specialist 'geeks' were doing, because the work seemed so technical and complex.

Perhaps one of the most striking – and sad – examples of silos, however, emerged when the Obama administration launched a program in 2009 to offer homeowners help with their mortgages after the Great Financial Crisis. The theory behind the plan sounded sensible: the banks were supposed to offer struggling homeowners a reduction in the monthly mortgage payments if they met certain criteria (say, having a job). But there was a crucial, tragic catch: the financial companies were so fragmented in how they organized themselves that when some bank departments started trying to help a mortgage borrower by reducing their monthly payments, the team offering mortgage relief often failed to inform the department that was in charge of implementing foreclosures. That had terrible consequences. When the banks' foreclosure teams saw that mortgage borrowers had reduced their payments, they sometimes assumed that the borrower had defaulted and seized the house. In those situations, instead of *helping* mortgage borrowers, the White House plan sometimes ended up harming them – because of the silos. 'It was terrible,' Austan Goolsbee, a key Obama adviser, later explained. 'No one imagined silos like that inside banks. The silos were so strong they did the exact opposite of what [everyone] expected. It was completely crazy.'

CULTURE VULTURES

So is there any way to avoid the 'craziness' – or blindness – that silos can create? This book argues that the answer is: yes.

And in the pages that follow, you will read a series of stories that show both the perils and promise of silos, drawn from government, corporate, and nonprofit sectors. The narrative is divided into two parts. The first section covers three tales of individuals and institutions that have been overwhelmed by silos in slightly different ways. Chapter Two relates the story of Sony, a company that once enjoyed wild success, but then became so fragmented that it missed chances to innovate, triggering its decline. Chapter Three recounts the tale of UBS, a gigantic bank that was so beset with silos that the top managers completely failed to see that a timebomb was ticking inside its books, because some traders had been buying securities linked to subprime U.S. mortgages. Chapter Four explains how a sense of tunnel vision and tribalism among economists working in places such as the Bank of England and the Federal Reserve prevented bright people from seeing how the financial system was spinning out of control before 2008. In numerous professional fields and institutions, people become trapped by the silos they inherit, not just in terms of how organizations are structured but also, most importantly, how people think. What happened to the economics profession before 2008 illustrates that trend.

But the second part of the book is more optimistic, since it narrates the stories of some individuals and institutions who are trying to overcome silos in their minds, lives, and organizations.

In Chapter Five, I tell the story of how one computer geek in Chicago embarked on a dramatic career change, jumping across professional silos in a manner that inspired him to launch a striking experiment inside the Chicago Police Department.

Chapter Six turns to Facebook, and explains how the social media company has tried to prevent itself from succumbing to the silo curse with some fascinating experiments in internal social engineering. This story can be read as a good counterexample to the tale of Sony, not least because the Facebook staff have developed their internal silo-busting experiments *precisely* because they did not want to end up in the same situation as Sony or other giants such as Microsoft.

Chapter Seven explains how doctors in Cleveland Clinic, the gigantic medical center, have tried to fight the curse of silos with another tactic: encouraging specialists to deliberately question how they classify the world, and imagine different taxonomies. Instead of just accepting the normal classification system in medicine, these doctors have turned their taxonomies upside down. In that sense then, the chapter is a good counterpoint to the story about the economics profession in Chapter Four, since one problem that beset economists (like most specialist professions) is that the experts did *not* examine how they mentally organized the world, but just assumed that their taxonomies were self-evidently correct.

Chapter Eight takes a different tack. It tells the story of how one hedge fund, BlueMountain Capital, has made money by taking advantage of the silos in the financial system around it. That illustrates a key point: one person's silo can be another's opportunity, and one institution's loss can be another's gain. The tale of BlueMountain, then, is a good counterpoint to the tale of UBS and other big banks, since it shows that individuals who are willing to take a joined-up view, or look at silos in perspective, can enjoy big advantages compared to rivals. Silo-busters can be innovative. They can sometimes spot new business opportunities. Savvy silo-busting investors can make money.

These stories are not meant to be comprehensive. I know there are innumerable other examples I could have chosen to illustrate the perils and pitfalls of silos. However, I focused on these particular eight tales to streamline the narrative and make it as easy as possible to follow. It is important to stress, though, that these narratives should not be read as fully finished tales of 'success' or 'failure,' but just as snapshots of stories that are still in progress. The perils associated with silos can never be permanently defeated. Mastering silos is a constant battle, because the world around us is constantly changing, pulling us in two directions. We need specialist, expert teams to function in a complex world. But we *also* need to have a joined-up, flexible vision of life. Mastering silos requires us to walk a narrow line between these two contradictory goals. It is hard.

So how do we deal with this challenge? One place to start is to recognize that silos exist and to think clearly about their effects. And I believe that a discipline that can help us to frame the analysis and debate is anthropology. This is not a field that normally springs to mind when people think about silos. On the contrary, when people have written about silos, they have usually done so by drawing on two bodies of research: management consultants, who offer advice on how institutions can organize themselves better; or psychologists, who study how our minds work. However, silos are fundamentally a cultural phenomenon. They arise because social groups and organizations have particular conventions about how to classify the world. Sometimes these classification systems are explicitly defined. New York's City Hall has official, formal structures that stipulate how each department and team is organized and sits in relation to each other, in a hierarchy. However, the conventions that we use to classify the world are often *not* officially defined or spelled out. Instead, they arise out of a dense set of rules, traditions, and conventions that we have absorbed from our surroundings, often in an unthinking way. Many of the really important patterns we use to classify the world, in other words, are inherited from our culture. They exist at the borders of conscious thought and instinct. They seem natural to us, in the same way our culture appears 'normal.' So much so, that we rarely even notice them at all, or even think about the fact that we have formal and informal classification systems that shape how we respond to the world.

However, cultural anthropologists do think about these classification systems – a great deal. That is because anthropologists know that the process of classification is fundamental to human culture; indeed, our taxonomies *are* our culture. Sometimes anthropologists study these cultural patterns in non-Western settings. Indeed, the anthropologists who are famous in popular culture today tend to be those who did their research in places that seem exotic to modern Westerners: people such as Margaret Mead (who studied youth and sexuality in the Samoan Islands),

Franz Boas (Eskimos), Claude Lévi-Strauss (Amazonian myths), or Clifford Geertz (cock fighting rituals in Java), and so on. But not all anthropologists work in non-Western contexts. On the contrary, many modern anthropologists now work in complex industrial settings, too, where they also study the cultural patterns that shape twenty-first-century societies. 'Anthropologists are culture-vultures; but not in the way this phrase is usually used,' as Stephen Hugh-Jones, a British anthropologist, explains. 'For anthropologists "culture" is not a matter of refinement of tastes or the intellectual side of civilization; it is the commonly-held ideas, beliefs and practices of any society of any kind.'[36] In that sense, the discipline can help to shed light on how we classify the world, and why we create silos.

So before we turn to the stories of how some institutions have been mastered by silos, and mastered them, this book starts with a detour. Chapter One explains why anthropology can be useful in terms of making sense of the modern world – and its silos – by telling another story, that of Pierre Bourdieu, a French anthropologist-cum-sociologist. Bourdieu started his life doing research in Algeria during the horrors of the Algerian Civil War. But he later switched tack and did a series of provocative analyses of modern France and other aspects of the Western world. At first glance, this may not seem to be obviously connected to the tales that I relate in this book about complex institutions. (And if readers just wish to read about tales of institutional failure or success they should skip this part and go straight to Chapter Two.) But Bourdieu's research illustrates some of the defining traits of cultural anthropology and shows why using an anthropological lens can be useful, irrespective of whether you define yourself as an 'anthropologist.' Even – or especially – in places such as New York's City Hall, UBS, the Bank of England, or Sony.

PART ONE
SILOS

1

THE NONDANCERS

How Anthropology Can Illuminate Silos

'Every established order tends to make its own entirely arbitrary
system seem entirely natural.'

—Pierre Bourdieu[1]

IT WAS A DARK WINTER'S EVENING IN 1959 IN BÉARN, A TINY VILLAGE IN A
remote corner of South West France. In a brightly lit hall, a
Christmas dance was under way. Dozens of young men and
women were gyrating to 1950s jive music. The women wore full
skirts that swirled around them, the men sharp, close-cut suits.[2]
On the edge of the crowd, Pierre Bourdieu, a Frenchman in his
thirties with an intense, craggy face, stood watching, taking
photographs and careful mental notes. In some senses, he was
at 'home' in that dancehall: he had grown up in the valley many
years earlier, the son of peasants, and spoke Gascon, a local dia-
lect of French that was impossible for Parisians to understand.

But in other senses, Bourdieu was an outsider: as a precociously brilliant child, he had left the village two decades earlier on a scholarship, and studied at an elite university in Paris. Then he traveled to Algeria, serving as a soldier in the brutal civil war, before becoming an academic.

That gave him an odd insider-outsider status. He knew the dancers' world well, but he was no longer merely a creature of this tiny environment. He could imagine a universe beyond Béarn and a different way of arranging a dance. And when he looked around at that hall, with that insider-outsider vision, he could see something to which his own friends were blind. In the center of the hall, there was light and action: the dancers were doing the jive. That was the only thing that the villagers wanted to watch, or would ever remember from that night. Dance halls, after all, are supposed to be all about *dancing*. But 'standing at the edge of the dancing area, forming a dark mass, a group of older men look[ed] on in silence,' as Bourdieu later wrote. 'All aged about thirty, they wear berets and unfashionably cut dark suits. As if drawn in by the temptation to join the dance, they move forward, narrowing the space left for the dancers ... but do not dance.'[3] That part of the hall was *not* what people were supposed to watch; it was being ignored. But it was nevertheless present, as much as the dancers. 'There they all are, all the bachelors!' Bourdieu observed. The people in that hall had somehow divided themselves and classified each other into two camps. There were dancers and *non*-dancers.

But why had that separation occurred? Bourdieu had received a clue to the answer a few days earlier, when he met up with an old school friend. At one point, the man had produced an ancient prewar photo, depicting their classmates as children. 'My fellow pupil, by then a low-ranking clerk in the neighbouring town, commented on [the photo], pitilessly intoning "un-marriageable!" with reference to almost half [the pictures],'[4] Bourdieu wrote. It was not intended as an insult, but as a description. Numerous men in the village were finding it impossible to find wives, because they had become unattractive – at least as culturally defined by local women.

This 'unmarriageable' problem reflected radical economic change. Until the early twentieth century, most of the families around Béarn were farmers, and their eldest sons were typically the most powerful and wealthy men, as they inherited the farms according to local tradition. Eldest sons were thus considered catches for local women, particularly compared to the younger sons who often had to leave the land in search of a living. But in postwar France, the pattern had changed: agriculture was declining and the men who could leave the farms were seeking better paid jobs in town. Many young women were moving to the cities in search of work. The older sons, who were tethered by tradition to the farms, were being left behind. On a day-to-day basis, the villagers did not articulate that distinction. But the classification system was constantly being expressed and reinforced in a host of tiny, seemingly mundane, cultural symbols that had come to seem natural. To the villagers in Béarn it seemed obvious that 1950s jive music, full skirts and tight male suits, were a cool, urban phenomenon; if you could dance, that signaled that you were part of the modern world, and therefore marriageable.

What really intrigued Bourdieu, though, was not just *why* this economic change had occurred, but why anyone accepted this classification system and the unspoken cultural norms. This distinction between marriageable and unmarriageable men – or people who could or could not jive – had not been imposed in any formal manner. Nobody had conducted a public debate on the matter. There were no official rules in 1950s France that *banned* farmers from doing the jive or stopped them from learning the dance steps, buying a few suits, and just jumping into the ring. But somehow those men were banning themselves: they had voluntarily placed themselves in a social category that indicated they 'could not dance.' And the implications for those men were heartbreaking. 'I think of an old school friend, whose almost feminine tact and refinement endeared him to me,' Bourdieu observed, noting that his friend 'had chalked on the stable door the birthdates of his mares and the girls' names he had given them' as a sad protest against his 'unmarriageable' state and lonely life.[5]

So why didn't the men protest against their tragic state? Why not just start dancing? And why didn't the girls realize that they were ignoring half the men? Why, in fact, do any human beings accept the classification systems we inherit from our surroundings? Especially when these social norms and categories are potentially damaging?

*

A POSTWAR DANCE HALL in Béarn lies a long way from Bloomberg's City Hall, in terms of geography and culture. Marriage strategies do not have much in common with banks. But in another sense, French peasants and New York bureaucrats are inextricably linked. What these two worlds share in common – along with every society that anthropologists have ever studied – is a tendency to use formal and informal classification systems and cultural rules to sort the world into groups and silos. Sometimes we do this in a formal manner, with diagrams and explicit rules. But we often do it amid thousands of tiny, seemingly irrelevant cultural traditions, rules, symbols, and signals that we barely notice because they are so deeply ingrained in our environment and psyche. Indeed, these cultural norms are so woven into the fabric of our daily lives that they make the classification system we use seem so natural and inevitable that we rarely think about it at all.

Insofar as anyone can tell, this process of classification is an intrinsic part of being human. It is one of the things that separate us from animals. There is a good reason for that: on a day-to-day basis, we are all surrounded by so much complexity that our brains could not think or interact if we were could not create some order by classifying the world into manageable chunks. The seemingly trivial issue of telephone numbers helps to illustrates this. Back in the 1950s, a psychology professor at Harvard named George Miller studied how short-term memory worked among people who operated telegraph systems and telephones. This research showed that there is a natural limit to how many pieces of data a human brain can remember when it is shown a list of digits or letters.[6] Miller believed that this natural limit ranged between five and nine data points, but the average was 'the magic number seven.' Other psychologists subsequently suggested it is nearer to four. Either way, his conclusion also contained a crucial caveat: if the brain learns to 'chunk' data, by sorting it into groups – akin to the process of creating a mental filing cabinet – more information can be retained. Thus if we visualize numbers as chunks of digits we retain them, but not if they are a single unbroken series of numbers. 'A man just beginning to learn radiotelegraphic code hears each dit and dah as a separate chunk. [But] soon he is able to organize these sounds into letters and then he can deal with the letters as chunks ... [then] as words, which are still larger chunks, and [then] he begins to hear whole phrases,'[7] Miller explained. 'Recoding is an extremely powerful weapon for increasing the amount of information that we can deal with.'

This process applies to longer-term memory too. Psychologists have noted that our brains often operate with so-called mnemonics, or mental markers, which enable us to group together our ideas and memories on certain topics to make them easy to remember. This is the neurological equivalent, as it were, of creating files of ideas inside an old-fashioned filing cabinet, with colorful, easy-to-see (and remember) labels on the topic. Sometimes this processing of clustering is conscious. More often it is not, as the psychologist Daniel Kahneman has noted.[8] Either way clustering ideas into bundles enables us to create order and arrange our thoughts. 'You can't think or make decisions, let alone create new ideas ... without using a range of mental models to simplify things,' argue Luc de Brabandere and Alan Iny, two management consultants. 'Nobody can deal with the many complicated aspects of real life without first placing things in such boxes.'[9]

This need to classify the world, however, does not just apply to our *internal* mental processes. Social interaction requires shared classification systems too. This, after all, is what a language is at its core: namely a commonly held agreement between people about what verbal sounds will represent which buckets of ideas. However, societies or social groups have cultural norms too, which shape how people use space, interact with each other, behave, and think. A crucial part of those shared social norms – if not the central element of a 'culture' – is a commonly held set of ideas about how to classify the world, and impose a sense of order. Just as our brains need to classify the world to enable us to think, societies need to have a shared taxonomy to function. Back in the seventeenth century, the French philosopher René Descartes observed 'I think, therefore I am' (or, to cite what he actually wrote in Latin and French respectively, '*cogito ergo sum*,' or '*je pense, donc je suis*').[10] But it is equally true to say 'I classify, therefore I think and am a social being.'

But while the act of classification is universal, the way we do it is not: different societies use a wide range of classification systems to organize the world. These vary even when dealing with issues that seem to be universal, such as natural phenomena. In theory, the way humans experience colors should be consistent. We all live in the same universe, with the same spectrum of light, and most of us have similar eyeballs (except for individuals prone to color blindness). But in practice, human societies do not classify colors in the same way. For decades Brent Berlin, an anthropologist, worked with Paul Kay, a linguist, to study how languages around the world described the color spectrum.[11] They found at least seven different patterns: some groups in Africa seemed to divide the world into merely three color buckets (roughly, red, black, and white), but some Western cultures used five times as many categories. That finding prompted Caroline Eastman and Robin Carter, two cognitive anthropologists (or people who work in a subset of the discipline analyzing culture and the mind), to conclude that while the color spectrum may be a universal, the way we classify it is not. 'Colors can be represented as a grid showing a variation of wavelengths (hues) and brightness,' Eastman and Carter wrote. 'Each color term represents a region on this grid containing a focal point which is generally agreed to be described by that color term. [But] although there is general agreement on the foci both across cultures and within cultures, there is much less agreement on the boundaries.'[12]

The way that other parts of the natural world are classified varies as well. Birds are found almost everywhere around the world. But some cultures consider birds to be an animal, and do not differentiate between birds; others make precise distinctions. The English word 'seagull,' for example, is not a category that translates easily into other languages. Similarly, different animal categories can have different associations in different places. Jared Diamond, for example, has looked at how different cultures around the world define their fauna and flora. (Diamond sometimes defines himself as an 'environmental anthropologist,' which is a another subset of the discipline.) He points out that while the concept of a 'horse' is associated with meat in France, and a 'cat' viewed that way in China, those categories of animals are not classified as 'edible' in a place such as America.[13]

The taxonomy of social relationships varies even more. Sexual reproduction is universal. However, anthropologists and linguists have discovered at least six different systems for 'mapping' kin in different societies around world (in cultural anthropology courses at universities these are known as the 'Sudanese,' 'Hawaiian,' 'Eskimo,' 'Iroquois,' 'Omaha,' and 'Crow' systems). There is even greater variation in how societies organize their space, define jobs, imagine the cosmos, organize economic activities, or track time. In some cultures, 'cooking' is classified as a uniquely female job, performed by women inside the domestic sphere. But in suburban America, when cooking entails a barbecue and meat, it is often classified as a 'male' pursuit. Similarly, in Jewish culture, Saturday is classified as a holy day; however, in Muslim culture it is Friday, while in Christian cultures it is Sunday. In many non-Western societies – such as tribes in the Amazon – there is no sense of a seven-day week at all, far less a weekend. So too with dance. Numerous societies have rituals for dancing. However, in some societies dancing is classified as a religious activity. In others it is considered profane, or the very opposite of sacred. In some places, men do not dance with women, but in other cultures the whole point of dancing is that men and women should dance together. The only element that is absolutely common to all these diverse situations is that wherever and however people dance, eat, cook, arrange their space or family lives, they tend to assume that their own particular way of behaving is 'natural,' 'normal,' or 'inevitable' – and they usually consider that the way that *other* people dance (and classify the world) is not. This variety illustrates a simple, but crucially important, point: the patterns that we use to organize our lives are often a function of nurture, not nature. That makes them fascinating to analyze. And one person who had a particularly interesting perspective on them was the man who stood watching the dancers – and nondancers – in the Béarn hall, namely Pierre Bourdieu, one of the fathers of modern anthropology.

BOURDIEU NEVER SET OUT to be an anthropologist. He spent the early years of his life assuming that the best way to make sense of the world – if not the only way – was to study philosophy. It seemed a natural assumption, given that he came of age in postwar France, at a time when philosophers such as Jean-Paul Sartre commanded extraordinary popular prestige. 'One became a philosopher [then] because one had been consecrated and one consecrated oneself by securing the prestigious identity of a "philosopher," Bourdieu explained.[14] And Bourdieu was hungry for an identity. He was born in 1930 in Denguin, a tiny hamlet close to Béarn, and his father was a sharecropper-turned-postman who never completed his education. At the age of eleven Bourdieu won a scholarship to attend a boarding school in Pau, a city down in the valley. But it was a scarring experience. As a rural peasant in a sea of wealthier, urban children from Pau, Bourdieu felt inferior. 'I think that Flaubert was not entirely wrong in thinking that "someone who has known boarding school has learned, by the age of twelve, almost everything about life,"'[15] he observed. 'I lived my life [at boarding school] in a state of stubborn fury ... caught between two worlds.'

In an effort to fit in, he excelled at his lessons and played rugby with ferocious passion; the sport was wildly popular in South West France. But French society was a stratified, class-ridden place, where people were classified into groups though numerous subtle signals, embedded in language, demeanor, culture, and posture. Bourdieu felt an outsider and he constantly rebelled against the ferocious discipline. 'The old seventeenth century [school] building, vast and rebarbative, with its immense corridors, the walls white above and dark green below, or the monumental stone staircases ... left no secret corner for our own solitude, no refuge, no respite,'[16] he recalled. 'The adult man who writes this does not know how to do justice to the child who lived through these experiences, his times of despair and rage, his longing for vengeance.'

At seventeen, Bourdieu escaped by winning a scholarship to the elite Ecole Normale Supérieure in Paris to study philosophy. After graduating with a high mark, he embarked on a postgraduate research program to explore the epistemology (or knowledge system) of Maurice Merleau-Ponty, another revered early-twentieth-century French intellectual giant, who worked as a phenomenological philosopher. But then his life took an unexpected turn. In 1955, at the age of twenty-five, Bourdieu was called up to perform military service. Usually, elite students just served as officers in pleasant rural locations. But when Bourdieu was summoned, a bloody civil war had started to loom to the south. Although France had ruled Algeria for over a hundred years, Algerian rebels were demanding independence. Bourdieu told his military superiors that he strongly opposed the Algerian War on principle, since (like many young French intellectuals), he loathed colonialism. The army punished him by assigning him to the front line. 'I first landed in the Army Psychological Service in Versailles, following a very privileged route reserved for students of the Ecole Normale,' he explained. 'But heated arguments with high-ranking officers who wanted to convert me to [support] 'L'Algérie Française' [French-run Algeria] soon earned me a reassignment.'[17]

In the summer of 1955 Bourdieu traveled south across the Mediterranean on a boat, in a military unit 'made up of all the illiterates of Mayenne and Normandy and a few recalcitants.'[18] On the ship he 'tried in vain to indoctrinate my fellow soldiers' to oppose the war. But the soldiers already had a strong set of prejudices about Algeria and deeply held views about how the Algerians should be classified. 'Even before setting foot in Algeria, they had acquired and assimilated the whole vocabulary of everyday racism [with] extreme submissiveness towards the military hierarchy,' he lamented. Isolated, Bourdieu spent months in a desert town called Orléansville, defending an ammunition dump against guerrilla attacks, before being reassigned to Algiers, the capital.

As the war escalated, Bourdieu doggedly worked on his doctoral project out of a tiny bunk room in a military garrison in Algiers. Academic reflections offered one welcome escape from the horrors of a war that Bourdieu considered unjust. But he steadily became disillusioned with philosophy too. Back in the rarefied, safe, intellectual atmosphere of Paris, Bourdieu had believed – like many young French intellectuals – that the abstract philosophy of thinkers such as Sartre or Merleau-Ponty offered the perfect key to understanding the world. But amid the horror of Algerian War, it seemed ridiculous to think that abstract philosophy alone could explain real life. By late 1955 Algerian rebels were not just mounting attacks on ammunition dumps, but slitting the throats of French military personnel and civilians. The French army was using brutal tactics to fight back. They staged house-to-house raids, arrested thousands of suspected rebels, tortured captives, bombed villages, and resettled tens of thousands of people, out of their mountain villages into sterile, quasi-camps. So Bourdieu changed tack, and decided to write a book about real life in Algeria, instead of the philosopher Merleau-Ponty. '[I wanted] to tell the French people . . . what was really going on in a country of which they knew next to nothing . . . in order to be some use, and perhaps also to stave off the guilty conscience of the helpless witness of an abominable war.'[19] And to do so, he turned to a discipline that was just starting to become fashionable, due to the writings of French academic Claude Lévi-Strauss: the world of anthropology.

TO SOME PEOPLE, BOURDIEU'S interest in anthropology might have seemed baffling. Anthropology has often been considered a strange discipline: difficult to define and for outsiders to understand. It is simultaneously everywhere in modern intellectual thought, but nowhere. The word comes from the Greek (*anthropos*

literally means 'the study of man') and the first recorded example of somebody trying to study human culture in a systematic
way probably appears in the writings of the Greek historian
Herodotus in 450 BC. (When he wrote about the battles between
the Greeks and Persians, Herodotus devoted a considerable
amount to an analysis of the cultural differences that he saw,
comparing and describing them as distinct social systems and
patterns.)[20] Then, during the seventeenth and eighteenth century,
the concept of anthropology reappeared when men such as David
Hume declared a desire to 'study the nature of mankind.'[21] But in
the nineteenth century, this endeavor turned into a full-fledged
academic discipline. 'When anthropology was born, shortly
after the middle of the nineteenth century, two factors, above all
others, determined its form,' as Ernest Gellner, an anthropologist,
notes. 'Darwinism and colonialism.'[22] The nineteenth-century
elite in Europe and America felt a need to understand the 'alien'
peoples that they were encountering in Africa, Asia, and the
Americas (usually because they wanted to control them, tax
them, or convert them to Christianity, or all three). Meanwhile,
the emergence of Charles Darwin's ideas about evolution was
sparking a passionate debate and interest in the question of
what it meant to be human. Just as biologists and zoologists
were trying to understand how the animal kingdom evolved,
historians and social scientists became interested in studying
how 'primitive' peoples had developed over the centuries into
'advanced' societies. One facet of this inquiry revolved around
the physical evolution of humans. Another, though, focused
on the social and cultural evolution. 'The European and North

American conquests of extensive regions previously inhabited only by simpler societies inevitably inspired the idea that these populations could be used as surrogate time machines,' Gellner notes. 'Anthropology was born out of an intense curiosity about the past, about human *origins*.'[23]

One of the first men who blazed a path on this intellectual road was James Frazer, a nineteenth-century Scottish intellectual. He collected extensive data on myths and legends from around the world, and collated these into a highly influential book, *The Golden Bough*, which explored how human consciousness and culture had moved from being 'primitive' to 'civilized.' Numerous other anthropologists took a similarly evolutionary approach. But at the turn of the century Franz Boas embarked on a similar project with the Native Americans. Boas had started his academic career as a botanist, but during a trip to the Arctic he became fascinated by how the Eskimos classified snow, and dove into cultural anthropology instead. He then switched his attention to the Native Americans, gathering artifacts and material about their customs and 'primitive' minds, which he plotted into groups. But then he floated a striking idea: maybe it was wrong to assume that humans always evolved in a social sense along a single path. Perhaps culture should be studied on its own terms.

As the nineteenth century turned into the twentieth, this anti-evolutionary idea spread: anthropologists gradually moved away from their earlier assumptions that non-Western cultures were always inferior, or less developed than the cultures of Europe or America. They could not always be squeezed into patronizing historical models.

Bronislaw Malinowski exemplified this shift. An ethnic Pole who was born in the former Austro-Hungarian empire, he studied at the London School of Economics, he started his academic career doing old-fashioned anthropology, studying the indigenous people of Australia. Then, when World War I broke out, he realized he could be interned in Australia as an enemy national. To avoid that, he headed for the Trobriand Islands, near Papua New Guinea, and ended up staying there far longer than expected due to the war. As a result, instead of just swooping in and out, gathering artifacts, which would later be analyzed from the comfort of a faraway library, he ended up pitching his tent among the Trobriand villagers and living there for many months. That enabled him to watch the villagers for an extended period, as a fly on the wall, leaving him convinced that it was quite wrong to label the Trobriand Islanders as 'primitive.' On the contrary, Trobriand culture had a certain beauty and rhythm of its own that needed to be understood *in its own terms*. This was epitomized by a ritual known as the Kula, which involved the elaborate exchange of shells between different islands. To a casual observer, this practice might have seemed quaint, bizarre, and pointless, particularly since the shells did not appear to have any immediate value or use. However, Malinowski pointed out that the Kula was not just a sophisticated and elaborate system, but it had a crucial social function, since the exchange of shells not only defined who was in the social group, but also created ties of obligation and trust linking the archipelago.

In 1922 Malinowksi published a book, *Argonauts of the Western Pacific*, that described his findings.[24] It changed the discipline. Around the world, young anthropologists started to conduct what they called 'participant observation' and 'ethnography,' or the process of watching the people they studied and then writing thick descriptions. British anthropologists such as Evans Pritchard went to Sudan, and John Radcliffe-Brown went to the Andaman Islands, Margaret Mead, an American anthropologist, went to Polynesia, and Ruth Benedict went to Australia and then studied Japan. Clifford Geertz, another American luminary, went to Bali, and Maurice Bloch left France for Madagascar. And as this new breed of anthropologists conducted their research, the discipline of anthropology effectively split into two. One stream, known as 'cultural anthropology' in America (or 'social anthropology' in Europe) looked at culture and society; the second stream, called 'physical anthropology,' studied human evolution and biology. Initially, these endeavors had been entwined. But when anthropologists started looking at social systems in the present, the study of human evolution began to seem less connected to modern culture, and some anthropologists started to find more affinity with other disciplines, such as linguistics.

Claude Lévi-Strauss, a French anthropologist, is a case in point. He started his career as a linguist and philosopher, in the classic French intellectual style. But Lévi-Strauss (like Bourdieu) eventually tired of abstract musing. 'Since I was a child, I have been bothered by, let's call it the irrational, and have been trying to find an order behind what is given to us as a disorder,' he later observed. 'It so happened that I became an anthropologist ... not because I was interested in anthropology, but because I was trying to get out of philosophy.'[25] In the late 1940s he became fascinated with myth and legend. He believed that if you analyzed myths around the world, you could understand how human cognition worked. His theory, called 'structuralism,' posited that the human brain has a tendency to organize information in patterns, marked by binary oppositions (not dissimilar to how computers code data), and these patterns are expressed and reinforced in cultural practices, such as myths or religious rituals. It was a theoretical construct that did not draw directly on much participant observation of the type that Malinowski had pioneered. However, Lévi-Strauss supported his argument with extensive data drawn from communities around the world, and when he published his ideas in the 1950s in books such as *The Elementary Structures of Kinship, Tristes Tropiques*, and *The Savage Mind*,[26] the books earned widespread plaudits. They also provoked a new wave of interest in the then little-known discipline of anthropology among European intellectuals. Such as the ambitious would-be philosopher Pierre Bourdieu.

BY 1957, A FULL-BLOWN war had erupted in Algeria and Bourdieu's military service had come to an end. But he remained haunted by a desire to 'explain' the world around him, and to understand the *anthropos* of Algeria. So after being discharged from the army, he applied for a teaching post at the University of Algiers, and set out on an intellectual crusade. 'The simple desire to observe and witness led me to invest myself ... in frenzied work,' he explained.[27] His methods were the opposite of philosophy or any other armchair disciplines such as economics. He journeyed in buses to the most remote corners of Algeria, hitched rides on French military cavalcades, or traveled furtively with Algerian friends. He sat down among the local people, quietly sitting, observing, asking questions, and living among them.[28] It was a crazily dangerous endeavor. The countryside was teaming with rebels and French soldiers. In remote villages, elderly Algerians sometimes pulled him aside and recounted 'in places where no one would hear us, of the torture the French army had inflicted on them.'[29] French officers would describe how extremist Algerians were cutting the throats of French children and women, or planting roadside bombs. In high mountains, Bourdieu would see guns hidden under the men's flowing white robes, or djellaba, and 'along the whole shoreline, the mountains were in flames,' and the 'doors of all the cafés were protected with wire mesh to prevent grenade attacks.'[30] But Bourdieu pressed on. '[My] disregard for danger owed nothing to any sort of heroism but, rather, was rooted in extreme sadness and anxiety.'[31] Like Malinowksi, Bourdieu was determined to taste and see real life, at the grass roots. He wanted to understand the mental map that Algerians used to order their world.

It was up in the high mountains of Algeria that Bourdieu first turned this fascination into a full-blown theory. During his research, he spent time with a group of Berber tribesmen, known as the Kabyle, and discovered that they had strong ideas about the best way to build a house. Their dwellings were always rectangular, the front door facing west, with a giant weaving loom placed opposite this door. Inside the house, the Kabyle always separated the space in two, divided by a low internal wall. Half of the house – which was typically raised a bit higher, and larger and lighter – housed a weaving loom, and was used to entertain guests and stage formal meals. Men slept there. However, the second half of the house was smaller, darker, and lower. That was where animals lived, children and women slept, and the Kabyle stored everyday goods, along with anything that was wet, green, or damp.

When Bourdieu asked the Kabyle villagers why they arranged their houses in this pattern, they found his question bizarre. To them, it seemed normal to classify space, objects, and people in this way. They had grown up dividing their homes like this and to do anything else felt strange. If somebody had suggested that the Kabyle should store wet, green, or damp items in the place where men slept they would have laughed or winced, just as an American suburban family might recoil if you suggested storing shampoo in the car, or putting the fridge under the bed. To the Kabyle, this pattern was simply how the world worked.

But Bourdieu, as an outsider, could see that the pattern was not inevitable. He could also see that the way the Kabyle arranged their house echoed how they organized other aspects of their life. In Kayble culture, men were considered separate (and superior) to women, and public space was distinct from the private sphere. Similarly, their religion distinguished between 'damp' and 'fertile' activities, and those that were 'dry.' The spatial map of a Kabyle house thus reflected a social and mental map too, and this created a subtle, mutually reinforcing interplay of space, mind, and body. The Kabyle built their houses that way because of their cultural norms about how women, say, should interact with men, and these norms were reinforced whenever they stepped into their houses, to a point where the patterns seemed entirely natural.

The Kabyle are not unique. This interplay is found in all human societies. Take New York's City Hall. As Bloomberg discovered when he became mayor, the layout of the government offices reflected local ideas about how people should work. The fact that firefighters sat in dedicated departments reflected the idea that firefighters were a specialist team, separate from others. But precisely because firefighters sat apart from teachers, say, it seemed natural they should be separate. Architecture is driven by our mental vision of the world. But the way we design offices, say, ingrains our classification systems as well. We all tend to be creatures of our own environment, in a physical, social, *and* mental sense, although we usually do not notice this at all. Habits matter.

IN 1961, PIERRE BOURDIEU left Algeria. By then, the French military had used such brutal tactics against the rebels this had sparked a widespread backlash. (Indeed, the aggressive policies were so counterproductive that when America went into Iraq fifty years later, the Pentagon staged screenings of the film *The Battle of Algiers* to its officers as a cautionary tale of what *not* to do in the Middle East.) Eventually, the backlash became so intense that the French government decided to withdraw. Angry local French settlers took revenge against some of the French intellectuals who had opposed the war, and Bourdieu fled for his life.

He returned to Paris to a comfortable academic post, working with Raymond Aron, a prominent sociologist. The next natural career step for Bourdieu would have been to build on his reputation as an expert in Algeria, as an anthropologist. After all, anthropologists were expected to study exotic, non-Western cultures, like the Kabyle Berber. But once again, Bourdieu refused to conform. Back in 1959, while he was based in Algiers, he had visited his family in the French Pyrenees and become fascinated by what he could see unfolding there. When Bourdieu looked at his old hometown, he could see that the French villagers had just as many rules, patterns, and social maps as the Kabyle. To Frenchmen, their rules seemed natural, if not obvious. But to outsiders they did not. So Bourdieu concocted a bold plan. He asked a young Algerian sociology student, Abdelmalek Sayad, to travel with him out to the Pyrenees. Bourdieu had worked with Sayad to conduct his research in Algeria and they made a good team: Sayad, as a local insider, understood how Algerian culture worked; but Bourdieu, the French outsider, could spot patterns in Algerian culture that Sayad did not see. Bourdieu reckoned that this same principle could work in reverse: Abdelmalek would be an outsider in France, so he would spot oddities that French people ignored.

This was not anthropology in the way that Victorians like James Frazer had first imagined the craft. For one thing, Bourdieu was turning the colonial power structures upside down, treating

French villagers on the same level as the Kabyle. But Bourdieu was convinced that the best way to understand any society was to take an inside-outsider view, and to flip perspective. So Sayad and Bourdieu repeated exactly what they had done in Algeria: they tramped around the hills of South West France, measuring things, watching everyday life, talking to people. Sometimes Bourdieu took his father with him, to help him become a real insider in local French culture. On other occasions, Bourdieu deliberately positioned himself as an outsider from his subjects. 'The most visible sign of the conversion of the gaze [from insider to observer] was the intensive use I then made of photographs, maps, ground plans and statistics,' he later explained.[32] But as he kept flipping his perspective he gained new insights into the *anthropos* of France. It was unexpectedly liberating in a personal sense too. Twenty years earlier, Bourdieu had been furious over the way he felt excluded from the snobbish culture of élite France. Now he realized that his childhood anger had produced an unexpected benefit, teaching him to notice cultural patterns. Instead of just wanting to destroy the hierarchy, he now wanted to understand it.

IN SUBSEQUENT YEARS, BOURDIEU broadened his gaze into the Western world way beyond his hometown. He analyzed the French elite, studying how their seemingly mundane choices in relation to food, art, furnishings, and so on helped to define modern French society – and stratify it into different social groups. In one of his most famous books, *Distinction*, he analyzed how a mundane action, such as deciding to order bouillabaisse in a restaurant (or not) creates social labels and markers that sort people into different groups. The tiny decisions that people constantly make in their lives are never irrelevant or meaningless. Small signals constantly express and reinforce power relations. Our ideas about what is pretty, ugly, tacky, trendy, or cool classify people (and things) into particular mental and social buckets.

Then Bourdieu turned his lens to the world of American arts funding, the nature of photography, the operations of the modern media, and behavior of political groups. He peered into the French education system and different academic tribes that dominated the universities in Paris. He also looked at the poorest parts of French society, seeking to make sense of how the 'dispossessed' people lived in the infamous *banlieue* – suburbs – of Paris. Wherever he went, he obsessively watched, listened, and tried to flip his analytical lens back and forth from insider to outsider, seeking to uncover patterns that people inside a society could not always see, blending the participant observer principles of Malinowski with the vision of Lévi-Strauss. 'I spent hours listening to conversations, in cafés, on *pétanque*, or football pitches, in post offices but also at society receptions or cocktail parties or concerts,' he recounted. 'I have been able to participate in universes of thought, past or present, very distant from my own ... the aristocracy or bankers, dancers at the Paris Opera or actors at the Théâtre-Française, auctioneers or notaries, and work myself into [their world].[33]

This research eventually produced some fifty-seven books, and gave birth to numerous theories. It is worth spelling out five of his most important ideas (out of a long list of his concepts), since these five points provide an intellectual framework for this book.

- First, Bourdieu believed that human society creates certain patterns of thought and classification systems, which people absorb and use to arrange space, people, and ideas. Bourdieu liked to call the physical and social environment that people live in the 'habitus,' and he believed that the patterns in this habitus both reflect the mental maps or classification systems inside our heads *and* reinforce them.
- Second, Bourdieu also believed that these patterns help to reproduce the status of the elite. Since this elite has an interest in preserving the status quo, it also has every incentive to reinforce cultural maps, rules, and taxonomies. Or to put it another way, an elite stays in power over time not just by controlling resources, or what Bourdieu described as 'economic capital' (money), but also by amassing 'cultural capital' (symbols associated with power). When they amass this cultural capital, this helps to make the status of the elite seem natural and inevitable. The wealthy French pupils at Bourdieu's boarding school, for example, exuded a 'natural' sense of authority and power by wrapping themselves in dozens of tiny, subtle cultural signals, which nonelite people such as Bourdieu lacked.
- Third, Bourdieu did not believe that the elite – or anyone else – created these cultural and mental maps deliberately. Instead, they arose as much from semiconscious instinct as conscious design, operating at the 'borders of conscious

and unconscious thought.' The habitus does not just reflect our social patterns, but it ingrains them too, making these seem natural and inevitable. The elite and nonelite are both creatures of their cultural environment.

- Fourth, Bourdieu believed that what really matters in a society's mental map is not simply what is publicly and overtly stated, but what is *not* discussed. Social silences matter. The system ends up being propped up because it seems natural to leave certain topics ignored, since these issues have become labeled as dull, taboo, obvious, or impolite. In any society, Bourdieu argued, there are ideas that are freely debated, and there can be differences of views about this (or a clash between the orthodoxy and heterodoxy). But outside that space of acceptable debate (or the 'doxa') there are many issues that are never discussed at all, not because of any clearly articulated plot, but because ignoring those issues seems normal. Or as Bourdieu said: 'The most powerful forms of ideological effect are those which need no words, but merely a complicitous silence.'[34] The *non-dancers* in a village hall matter.

- But a fifth key point that is implicit in Bourdieu's work is that people do *not* always have to be trapped in the mental maps that they inherit. We are not robots, blindly programmed to behave in certain ways. We can also have some choice about the patterns we use. How much choice humans have to reshape their cultural norms was – and is – an issue of hot dispute. When Bourdieu was first embarking on his academic career, Sartre, the French philosopher, declared that humans did have free will, and could develop their thoughts as they chose. Lévi-Strauss took another view: he thought that humans were doomed to be creatures of their environment, since they could not think out of their inherited cultural patterns.

Bourdieu, however, rejected both of these ideas; or, more accurately, he steered a middle ground between these two extremes. He did not think that people are robots, programmed to obey cultural rules automatically. Indeed, he did not like the word 'rules' at all, preferring to talk about cultural 'habits.' But he also believed these habits and the habitus shaped how people behave and think. Social maps are powerful. But they are not all-powerful. We are creatures of our physical and social environment. However, we need not be blind creatures. Occasionally, individuals can imagine a different way of organizing our world, particularly if they – like Bourdieu – have become an insider-outsider by jumping across boundaries.

BY THE TIME BOURDIEU died in 2002, his work had made him famous in France. So much so that his death was marked by the main French paper, *Le Monde*, with a huge headline on its front page declaring '*Pierre Bourdieu est mort!*' Outside France, he was not as well known by the public. But his life had become a very powerful symbol of how the study of *anthropos* had developed across the West. Anthropology was no longer just a study of the 'other,' or exotic, alien, non-Western cultures. It had also become a study of the 'self,' or the place where the

Western anthropologists who (still dominated) academic debate lived. The ideas advanced by Bourdieu had blended with the work done by numerous other anthropologists to create a new approach.

Kate Fox, a British anthropologist, is one such descendant. Her father, Robin Fox, was an anthropologist at London University, then Rutgers in America, and he pursued a career that seemed typical of anthropology at the time. He studied the Cochiti Indians of New Mexico, taking his family with him to live there as he strode around dusty villages. 'Unlike most infants, who spend their early days lying in a pram or cot . . . I was strapped to a Cochiti Indian cradle-board,' Kate Fox recalls.[35] This boundary-hopping created such an impression on her that she eventually chose to become an anthropologist herself. (A notable trait of the discipline is that many of the people who choose to study anthropology have been exposed to cultural dislocations at some point in their childhood or young adult lives; myself included.) But when Kate did her own research she decided that she did not want to study 'exotic' peoples, but her own English society instead. 'The human species is addicted to rule making. Every society has food taboos, rules about gift-giving, rules about hairstyles, rules about dancing, greetings, hospitality, joking, weaning, etc.,' she wrote in *Watching the English*, which analyzes English rituals, ranging from horse racing rituals to conversations about the weather. 'I don't see why anthropologists feel they have to travel to remote corners of the world and get dysentery in order to study strange tribal cultures with bizarre beliefs and mysterious customs. The weirdest, most puzzling tribe of all is right here on our own doorstep.'[36]

Numerous other anthropologists have followed a similar path, studying not just the Western world but some of the most modern and complex parts of it. In the late twentieth century Karen Ho (at the University of Minnesota) spent several years studying the habitus of Wall Street banks, using the same intellectual framework that Bourdieu developed among the Kabyle to understand the mind-set of bankers.[37] Caitlin Zaloom, another American anthropologist, has studied financial traders in Chicago and London.[38] Alexandra Ouroussoff, a British anthropologist, has studied credit rating agencies.[39] Douglas Holmes (at Binghamton University) has analyzed central banks and explored how institutions such as the European Central Bank and Bank of England use words and silences to shape markets.[40] Annelise Riles (from Cornell Law School) has explored how international lawyers treat finance.[41] Geraldine Bell (an anthropologist employed by Intel) has analyzed computing culture. Danah Boyd, a self-styled 'digital anthropologist' employed by Yahoo, has explored how social media has shaped American teenagers.[42] These are just a tiny sample of the work that thousands of anthropologists have done, and are still doing, in companies, government departments, urban communities, rural villages, and so on. However, wherever anthropologists work, the research tends to share particular traits: a focus on watching real life, usually through participant observation; a desire to connect all parts of society, rather than just concentrate on one tiny corner; a commitment to analyzing the gap between rhetoric and reality, or the social silences that mark our lives; and, above all else, a passion for *anthropos*, or understanding the spoken and unspoken cultural patterns that

shape human existence, or the intellectual endeavor that drove
Bourdieu.

However, by the time that the brilliant Frenchman died, his
heritage was marked by a profound irony: though he had been
highly influential for anthropology in the last couple of decades
of his career, Bourdieu stopped calling himself an 'anthropologist,' and started describing himself as a 'sociologist' instead. He
did that partly because he was offered a juicy job as 'Professor
of Sociology' in a Paris university. Another factor, however,
was that as the twentieth century wore on the disciplines of
anthropology and sociology increasingly blended into one. As
anthropologists started to study complex Western societies and
sociologists conducted more on-the-ground research, it became
harder to draw distinctions between the academic fields. In any
case, Bourdieu believed that it was ridiculous to fret too much
about academic boundaries or labels. He did not want to put any
discipline into a specialist box, and he hated the way that universities tended to classify academics into different, competing
tribes. To Bourdieu, 'anthropology' was not really an academic
label or self-contained discipline, but an attitude toward life. It
was an intellectual prism, or mode of inquiry, that anyone could
use to get a richer understanding of the world, in combination
with other fields such as economics, sociology, among others. To
be an anthropologist you did not need to sit inside a university,
or have a doctorate. Instead, you needed to be humbly curious,
ready to question, criticize, explore, and challenge ideas; to
look at the world with fresh eyes and think about the classification systems and cultural patterns that we take for granted.

'Anthropology demands the open-mindedness with which one must look and listen, record in astonishment and wonder that which one would not have been able to guess,' as Margaret Mead, the former doyenne of the American anthropology world, once observed.[43]

That carries wide lessons, not least because it means that anthropology can be applied to many fields. In my case, for example, I started my career doing a PhD in anthropology in a classic manner. I traveled to Soviet Tajikistan, and spent many months in a remote mountainous village engaged in participant observation of the type pioneered by Malinowksi. I wore Tajik clothes, lived with families, helped them in their daily chores, and spent hours observing the villagers, studying how this community used marriage rituals to express ethnic identity. (Essentially I concluded that the villagers maintained their Muslim identity in a supposedly atheist communist system by juggling these marriage rituals and symbols, subdividing their space and using marriage ties to define their social group.) However, like Bourdieu, I later became frustrated with what I saw of the world of academic anthropology. Although the discipline promotes the idea of taking an interconnected perspective on the world, university departments of anthropology can be surprisingly introverted and detached from the wider world. (That is partly because the discipline tends to attract people who are better at listening and observing than thrusting themselves into the limelight. Its adherents also tend to be antiestablishment, and wary of dealing with the institutions of power, perhaps because they analyze them so extensively.) I on the other hand was eager to interact with the world in a more dynamic manner. So when an opportunity arose to move into journalism, I grabbed it; it seemed a place I could use some of my training in observation and analysis. Writing stories felt like the anthropological equivalent of being on a speed date.

But once you have conducted anthropology research, as I did, you never lose that perspective. Studying anthropology tends to change the way you look at the world. It leaves a distinctive chip in your brain, or lens over your eye. Your mind-set becomes instinctive: wherever you go or work, you start asking questions about how different elements of a society interact, looking at the gap between rhetoric and reality, noting the concealed functions of rituals and symbols, and hunting out social silences. Anyone who has been immersed in anthropology is doomed to be an insider-outsider for the rest of their life; they can never take anything entirely at face value, but are compelled to constantly ask: *why*? Anthropology, in other words, makes you permanently curious, cynical, and relativist. Adding that perspective to other fields of inquiry enhances your analysis, just as salt adds flavor to food.

I certainly would not pretend that studying anthropology is the only way to get this insider-outsider perspective, or to question the cultural patterns around us. We all know some individuals who have an innate ability to question cultural rules, pierce social silences, see the story *behind* the story, and analyze social patterns but have never studied anthropology. But we also know many people who do not question the world; in fact, most people never analyze or question the cultural patterns – or habits – that guide them. Most of us are unthinking creatures of our environment, in the sense that we rarely challenge the ideas we inherit. But the key point is this: with or without a formal training in anthropology, we all do need to think about the cultural patterns and classification systems that we use. If we do, we can master our silos. If we do not, they will master us.

Moreover, when people are mastered by rigid silos this can cause debilitating problems. As I shall now explain in the following chapters, starting with the story of Sony – and its peculiar 'octopus pots.'

2
OCTOPUS POTS

How Silos Crush Innovation

'I came to see, in my time at IBM, that culture isn't just one aspect of the game. It *is* the game.'

—Lou Gerstner, former CEO of IBM[1]

THE MOOD IN THE VAST, MAJESTIC VENETIAN BALLROOM IN THE SANDS Expo and Convention Center in Las Vegas was hushed and excited. Hundreds of technology journalists and electronics experts sat before a huge video screen, suspended on a stage between ornate pillars and red velvet curtains. The lights went down and a giant animated mouse appeared on the screen, whiskers twitching; it was a character from *Stuart Little*, a hit children's film of 1999.

With a squeaky voice, the mouse announced some of the recent creative triumphs of Sony, the Japanese electronics and media group. 'But you don't just want to hear from me! Oh no! I gotta get out of the way for Nobuyuki Idei – Ideeeeiiiiii,' the mouse squeaked, as he leapt around a cartoon kitchen. 'The CEO of Sony, Soniiiiiiii!'[2] A tall, solemn, distinguished Japanese man stood up. The laughter died away. Once a year in November, the titans of the computing and electronic world gathered in Las Vegas for the Comdex trade fair for the computing industry. Just the day before, on November 13, 1999, Bill Gates, the legendary founder of Microsoft, had declared in a speech that the world was on the verge of an innovation revolution.[3]

Now Idei was due to make the second big keynote. The audience was eager to hear how Sony would respond to this upheaval. Twenty years earlier, the Japanese group had earned extraordinary success by launching the popular Sony Walkman. The device had changed how millions of consumers listened to music, and earned Sony a reputation for being a hotbed of innovation. In the 1960s and 1970s it had produced radios and televisions, in the 1980s there were camcorders, digital cameras, and video recorders, and in the 1990s Sony had jumped into computers and developed a vast music and film empire based out of America, generating hits such as *Star Wars* and *Stuart Little*.

But could this successful corporation adapt to the Internet? Could it produce another hit like the Walkman? Idei knew that expectations for his speech were sky-high. He was determined not to disappoint. 'The Internet and high-speed connection networks are both a threat and opportunity for us all,' he solemnly told the audience, likening the digital revolution to 'the giant meteor that destroyed the dinosaurs' many millennia ago, in terms of its potential impact on traditional companies. 'What we are and will be is a broadband entertainment company,'[4] he added in careful, precise English. He had spent his life rising through the ranks of the giant Sony global edifice both in Japan and America.

Next to Idei, on the Venetian Ballroom stage, sat George Lucas, the film director. 'I am playing hooky from writing *Star Wars* Episode 2!' he declared, sparking laughter across the ballroom, before explaining that Sony's new products were transforming how *Star Wars* and other films were made. 'Whatever I can imagine, I know I can put on the screen somehow. This is it. This is the revolution, and I'm in the middle of it. It's a great time to be alive.'[5]

The excitement in the hall mounted. The Sony executives unveiled more gadgets, such as a new PlayStation console. 'Just the fact that Lucas came on stage was impressive,' said Timothy Strachan, sales manager of Sydney-based Total Peripherals. 'Having been in the industry for 13 years, it's great to see Sony bring a game machine like the PlayStation 2 into the world of computing.'[6] Then Steve Vai, a wild-haired guitar virtuoso, appeared on stage. He cut a sharp contrast to the impeccably neat, white-shirted Japanese executives. But Idei turned to Vai and asked him to play something. Chords ripped through the hall from his guitar. Then Vai casually pulled out a little device, the size of a packet of chewing gum, and revealed that this was yet another Sony invention: a digital music player called the 'Memory Stick Walkman.'

Howard Stringer, a British man with a cherubic face, who was running Sony's operations in America, stood up and took the device. 'Listen!' he said, speaking with a clipped, upper-crust British accent that was sometimes dubbed 'BBC English.' The device was tiny. However, the chords were crystal clear. The audience applauded. The watching journalists and technical experts suddenly understood what was going on: the same company that had changed how the world listened to music back in 1979 by launching the Walkman was attempting to repeat the same trick. This time, however, it was producing a digital version of the Walkman, suitable for the Internet age.

Would it work? On that exuberant day in the Venetian Ballroom in November 1999, most observers would have said yes. After all, Sony seemed to have everything that a company might need to build a twenty-first-century successor to the Walkman: creative consumer electronics engineers, slick designers, a computing division, expertise with video games, *and* it owned 50 percent of BMG, a music label bursting with famous artists such as Michael Jackson and Vai. No other company had so many advantages under one roof: not Samsung, Microsoft, Panasonic, or Steve Jobs's Apple.

But as the audience sat, gazing in awe, something peculiar occurred. Idei stepped forward and waved a *second* device. It was a Vaio MusicClip, a pen-size digital audio player. He explained that this device had also recorded the guitar music. The chords from Vai's guitar pierced the hall again.

By the standards of normal corporate strategy, this profusion of devices was profoundly odd. When consumer companies unveil new products, they tend to keep the presentation simple, to avoid confusing customers (or their own salesmen). Typically, they only offer one technology at a time in each specific niche. That was what Sony had done with the original, iconic Walkman.

But now Sony was unveiling not one, but two different digital Walkman products, each of which used different proprietary technology. Indeed, soon after the company produced a third offering too, known as the 'Network Walkman.' The devices competed with each other. The company seemed to be fighting itself.

To the audience, the risks of that strategy were not immediately clear. The plethora of devices was taken as a sign of the company's eclectic, creative genius. But years later, when some of Sony's own leaders looked back on that day in Las Vegas, they realized that all those devices had been an ominous signal of disaster. Why Sony unveiled not one, but *two* different digital Walkman devices in 1999 was because it was completely fragmented: different departments of the giant Sony empire had each developed their own – *different* – digital music devices, with proprietary technology, known as ATRAAC3, that was not widely compatible. None of these departments, or silos, was able to agree on a single product approach, or even communicate with each other to swap ideas, or agree on a joint strategy.

This had debilitating consequences. Within a couple of years Sony had dropped out of the digital music game, paving the way for Apple to storm the market with the iPod. But the only thing that was more startling than the presence of these silos at the time was that so few people inside Sony could see just how crazy the situation had become, far less change this sense of fragmentation. Sony was a company sliding into tribalism, but its employees were so used to this pattern that they had failed to notice it at all.

In some sense, this makes Sony no different from any other social group. As I explained in the previous chapter, humans always assume that the way that they organize the world around them is entirely natural and inevitable. The Kabyle Berber whom Bourdieu studied considered it normal to put men in one part of the house and women in the other. The employees in New York's City Hall took it for granted that the Fire Department should sit in a different section from other staff, or that government statistics be kept on separate databases. So too most of the employees at Sony assumed it was natural that the people developing computers in one department were separate from the part of the company that was handling music.

Some of the managers and staff could see that this pattern had drawbacks. Stringer, the British man running the Sony American operations, was worried. Indeed, in the years after Sony unveiled its different – competing – digital Walkman devices, Stringer threw himself into the task of fighting the silos, with sometimes comical results. 'What went wrong at Sony? Silos were a big part of it all,' Stringer later observed.

However, on that heady day in 1999, the Sony staff felt too excited about their new gadgets to start questioning their cultural patterns. They were flush with success, and could not see disaster in front of their noses. Or the threat to the company that was symbolized by those competing gadgets on the Las Vegas stage.

SONY DID NOT START as a bureaucratic behemoth. When the company first sprang to life after World War II,[7] the Japanese group had an unusual spirit of flexibility and creativity. Traditionally, Japanese society has been marked – or marred – by a sense of rigid hierarchy and corporate discipline. Employees generally do not move between companies and juniors do not challenge their seniors or take risks by overturning established patterns. This sense of hierarchy and conformity was particularly strong during the militarist period of the 1930s. However, after Japan lost the war in 1945, the country became more open to change for a few years. So many senior men had been killed or discredited in the conflict that it was possible for young men to challenge the status quo.

It was in these conditions that Sony was born. The group was founded by two young men, Akio Morita and Masaru Ibuka, who had first met on a military base in 1944. They were each working on an Imperial Army engineering project to develop a heat-seeking missile. They did not appear to have much in common: Morita was a young, well-bred scientist and heir to his family's ancient sake-brewing business; Ibuka a gruff, antisocial engineer who hailed from a humble background. But the two men shared a passion for engineering and an iconoclastic view. So when Ibuka decided to use his engineering skills to set up a workshop in a bomb-damaged department store in central Tokyo, he persuaded Morita to leave his ancestral sake business and join the entrepreneurial venture.[8]

The new company started with a dozen employees and the equivalent of $500 of capital, and tried ventures ranging from the production of electric rice cookers to selling sweetened miso soup and building a miniature golf course on a burned-out tenement lot. But then the group started performing radio repairs, and tried to copy a type of tape recording devices that American soldiers were bringing into Japan.[9] It was a challenging venture: Japan was so short of any tools at the time that the only way to make magnetic tape for cassettes was to grind down magnets and glue the powder onto plastic, using chemical mixes cooked over a stove. '[We] made those first tapes by hand,' Morita recalled. 'We would cut enough tape for a small reel and then we would lay out the long strip on the floor of our laboratory. [But] our first attempts to get a magnetic material were failures ... the magnets we ground into powder were too powerful. ... We ended up painting the coating on by hand with fine brushes made of the soft bristles from a raccoon's belly.'[10] But by 1950, Morita and Ibuka had found a way to copy those America tape recorders on a large scale and were selling them inside Japan, under the name Tokyo Tsushin Kogyo (Tokyo Telecommunications Engineering). Then Ibuka visited the United States and persuaded Western Electric, the parent company of Bell Laboratories, to sell him a license for the manufacture of transistor radios for $25,000. The company started making a tiny new portable radio for the Japanese market. They called this the 'pocketable radio,' and it quickly sold on a massive scale, under a new brand name, 'Sony' (chosen since it was easy to pronounce). 'Miniaturization and compactness have always appealed to the Japanese,' Morita explained.[11]

By the end of the 1950s Ibuka and Morita's entrepreneurial venture had changed beyond all recognition. Its revenues had grown to more than $2.5 million and it employed 1,200. Then it swelled further as it moved into numerous products. Initially, it focused on radios and recorders. Then, in the 1960s it developed the pathbreaking Trinitron color technology for televisions. It moved into video recorders and cameras. However, its most memorable hit was the Walkman.

'The [Walkman] idea took shape when Ibuka came into my office one day with one of our portable stereo tape recorders and a pair of our standard-size headphones,' Morita recounted.[12] '[Ibuka] looked unhappy and complained about the weight of the system ... [so] I ordered our engineers to take one of our reliable small cassette tape recorders we called Pressman, strip out the recording circuit and the speaker, and replace them with a stereo amplifier. I outlined the other details that I wanted, which included very lightweight headphones, which turned out to be one of the most difficult parts of the Walkman project.' Initially, Morita's own staff thought that he was mad; nobody could believe that a tape player would sell without a recording device. Some of the staff also hated the Walkman name, since it was ungrammatical. 'I thought we had produced a terrific item and I was full of enthusiasm for it, but our marketing people were unenthusiastic,' Morita admitted.

The group of engineers duly debated the idea, with voices from across the company pitching in; ever since the company had first sprung to life in a bomb-damaged basement of a Tokyo department store, Morita and Ibuka had taken pride in the idea that their company was a place for creative, boundary-free brainstorming. However, Morita and Ibuka were not willing to let debate drag on. They went with their gut. When the gadget went on sale, in 1979,[13] it stormed the market, selling more than twenty million units within a few years. 'I do not believe that any amount of market research could have told us the Sony Walkman would be successful, not to say a sensational hit that would spawn many imitators,' Morita said. 'And yet this small item has literally changed the music-listening habits of millions of people all around the world.'[14]

IN THE LATE 1990S, four long decades after Morita and Ibuka had created their entrepreneurial experiment in the bombed-out basement of a Tokyo department store, and twenty years after Sony had stormed the market with its innovative Walkman, the company appointed a new man as president and co–chief executive officer: Nobuyuki Idei. His appointment symbolized a bigger shift. Until the early 1990s, the company was effectively run by Ibuka and Morita. However, in 1992 and 1993 the two men suffered strokes within months of each other and ended up in the same nursing home. There they spent long hours sitting next to each other in their invalid chairs, holding hands, in silence, unable to speak.

Back in the Sony headquarters, the company announced that Norio Ohga, Morita's protégé, would take the helm. Ohga had been appointed chief executive officer in 1989, but, as so often in Japan, the formal title did not correspond to the real power. Though Morita was supposedly retired, he had exerted enormous influence over Sony until the point where he could no longer talk. But with Morita incapacitated, power had passed on, and to the outside world Ohga seemed an impressive and charismatic figure. Not only was he skilled in engineering, but he was also trained as a concert pianist.[15] But he was not popular. And he arrived at a time when Sony was starting to face headwinds. In the early 1980s, the West had been hit by recession, sparking a fall in consumer purchases of electronic goods. The company responded by cutting prices and investing in more research. But this strategy caused a decline in its profit margins and a rise in debt.

Ohga knew that he needed to make the company more dynamic. But he faced a problem that besets almost every successful company: size. In the 1950s and 1960s, Sony had been a tightly run, relatively small, and flexible operation. By the late 1990s, it employed 160,000 people and was involved in activities ranging from radios to television to computers to home insurance to movies, as well as those famous Walkmans. A close-knit boutique had become a sprawling, complex behemoth. Ohga's solution was to use his own person to knit the company together, and enact policies. He was often autocratic and was not afraid to take bold decisions. In the early 1990s, for example, some of the Sony engineers started tossing around the idea of creating a games console. They suggested calling it PlayStation. Initially, there was great internal skepticism about the concept, just as there had been over the Walkman. But Ohga overrode that. 'Ohga pushed Sony to pursue the games business on its own, ignoring all objections,' observed Sea-Jin Chang, a Korean business analyst, in a seminal study on Sony. 'He often said that 'Ibuka contributed to Sony with the Trinitron TV, Morita with the Walkman, and me with the PlayStation.'[16]

This autocratic approach drove the company forward. But it stoked considerable resentment inside Sony. And the man who succeeded Ohga as president a couple of years later, Nobuyuki Idei, was from a different mold. Unlike the founding fathers, Idei was not an engineer by training. He had spent his career in Sony's corporate management. Unlike Ohga, Idei was not an autocrat, preferring to lead in a more consensual style. And as he looked at Sony's challenges, he became convinced that the best way to handle the swelling size and complexity of the company was to divide the company into specialist, self-standing units – or what management consultants like to call silos.[17]

Idei's inspiration for this decision partly came – oddly enough – from Swiss giant Nestlé. Idei sat on the board of the confectionary and food giant, and had noticed that Nestlé had a distinctive way of running its operations. During the decades immediately after World War II, most large multinational companies were run as giant bureaucracies, all operating on a single grid. But by the 1990s, a new thinking, or fashion, was taking hold among Western business schools. Management consultants and experts had become convinced that it was better to run big companies not as a single grid, but as a collection of distinct, self-enclosed, accountable units. The idea was that having separate units, or silos, would create more transparency, accountability, and efficiency. Nestlé had embraced this idea in a particularly striking way. During the 1990s, the Swiss food giant implemented a restructuring program that forced each department – say, chewing gum or chocolate – to operate like distinct businesses, with separate 'profit and loss' (P&L) accounts. Management was held responsible for meeting specific targets on profits, margins, sales, and managing their own investments, and their success or failure could be easily tracked since each department had its own balance sheet. It was an approach that had often been used in the financial world, where big banks in the City of London or Wall

Street tended to use an 'eat what you kill' mentality for traders and brokers. But Nestlé was one of the first to incorporate it so starkly into the world of consumer goods. To Idei (and the rest of the Nestlé board) it seemed to work well.

So Idei persuaded the senior Sony managers to reorganize the company on similar lines. During the 1980s, Sony had been run as a single corporate unit, subdivided into nineteen product divisions. In 1994, Sony reorganized itself into a so-called company system, which grouped those departments into eight stand-alone entities. (Consumer audio and visual; components; recording media and energy; broadcast; business and industrial systems; InfoCom; Mobile Electronics; and Semiconductors.) At the same time, the gaming, music, movie, and insurance businesses were given even more independence, run as separate satellites. This new system was not a pure 'eat what you kill' structure of the sort seen at Wall Street banks, since the salaries for Japanese staff were largely set on a company-wide basis, not dependent on the profits each department made. However, each of these 'companies' had its own top management, who would be judged on the basis of each department's P&L performance.

Initially, the reforms worked. When the top managers in Sony's new 'internal companies' realized that they were accountable for their own P&L, they reined in their costs, cut borrowing, and boosted margins. This cut Sony's debt by 25 percent between 1993 and 1997, and its profits increased sixteen times, from 15.3 billion yen to 202 billion. The share price doubled from 2,500 yen in 1994 to more than 5,000. Indeed, the reforms seemed so successful that when Idei was promoted from the position of president to co-CEO Sony (with Ohga), and then eventually sole CEO, he took them even further. In 1998 the eight companies were reorganized into ten groups. Then in 1999 the ten companies were reintegrated into three overarching companies that had twenty-five different 'sub-companies,' and in 2001 and 2003 those independent entities were reorganized, twice more. Through trial and error, Idei was determined to find the perfect silo. '[We want to] simplify the structure in order to clarify responsibilities and transfer authority so that responses to external changes would be quick,' Idei explained. '[We need to] reduce the levels of hierarchy ... [and] encourage entrepreneurial spirit in order to foster a dynamic management base for the 21st century.'[18]

But though these specialist silos made the company appear more efficient, at least in the short term, they also had a drawback. As soon as the managers of the new silos realized that they were responsible for their own balance sheets, they started trying to 'protect' their units, not just from rival companies but other departments as well. They became less willing to share experimental ideas with other departments, or even rotate the best staff between departments. Collaboration halted. So did experimental brainstorming or long-term investment that did not offer immediate returns. Nobody wanted to take risks.

Idei was aware of these problems. In his speeches to staff he exhorted them to adopt a 'networked' mentality, to pull together the different parts of the product line. Indeed, when journalists asked him why Sony kept reorganizing the company silos, he explained that he was trying to find the best system to encourage the different silos to *interact* with each other. To reinforce this point, the top leadership announced that their slogan would be 'Sony United.'[19] But rhetoric was one thing; practice quite another. As time passed, the different departments became less and less willing to interact. This, in turn, made the boundaries of the silos more rigid. Outside the walls of the electronics giant, the world of entertainment, media and electronics was changing fast: technological upheaval was blurring the different categories of software, hardware, content, and devices. This made many of the classification systems of the past outdated, if not redundant. But inside the company, the departmental walls were hardening. As a result, there was a growing contradiction between the language that Sony employees used to talk about the company, and how they actually behaved. In public, Sony liked to project an image of edgy innovation, boundary-hopping, and change. Idei and others constantly invoked the concept of 'Sony United' and the freewheeling spirit of the company founders. In their mind, they were running a company that was still based on the values that Ibuka had described in the 1940s in his first prospectus: 'Purpose of incorporation: Creating an ideal workplace, free, dynamic, joyous.'

But, as Pierre Bourdieu or any other anthropologist would have quickly pointed out, there was a big gap between rhetoric and reality. Inside the company, employees clung to the boundaries they knew. And, as time passed, those boundaries became so ingrained, in terms of how the company was physically laid out and employees organized themselves, that it seemed natural and inevitable to the staff that Sony ran itself that way. Just as it was hard for fire inspectors in New York's City Hall to imagine using data on mortgage defaults to predict fire risk, the managers working in different departments of Sony found it difficult to imagine swapping data between departments in a proactive way, even when they were all working on the same projects or problems.

By the early 1990s, it had become clear to everyone inside Sony that the glory days of the Walkman were over. For a period, the company tried to keep the product alive by offering updated Walkman gadgets with compact discs, or miniDiscs, instead of the original cassette tapes. But consumers were moving faster than Sony could update its iconic product, and toward the Internet. So Sony engineers started experimenting with different methods to distribute music using the Internet. Instead of working as a single team, however, each department started experimenting with its own ideas. The consumer electronics division developed the Memory Stick Walkman. The Vaio computing group created its own offering. Neither group collaborated. Nor did they coordinate with the salesmen working in the Sony Music Entertainment group, a division of Sony that had been created when the Japanese group acquired CBS Records, an American group, a decade before. SME was one of the biggest music companies in the world and had a rich library of content. But its officials were so terrified that the rise of digital music might undercut their revenues from the sales of records and compact discs that they refused to cooperate with other departments at all. The music department hated the idea of helping consumers download songs from the Internet, for a digital Walkman or anything else.

'Everyone said that it was great that Sony had a music label, since it could help with the next generation of music devices,' recalled Stringer. 'But it didn't work out that way at all.'

At Apple, however, the culture was radically different. Around the same time that teams at Sony starting exploring ideas about a digital Walkman, Steve Jobs, the CEO of Apple, sat down with a team of engineers to try to create his own digital music experiment. However, Jobs did not let the Apple engineers do that in separate departments. Jobs ran Apple with an autocratic style, and opposed to the idea of creating silos in the company, since he feared that these just created incentives for managers to protect existing product ideas and past successes, rather than trying to jump into the future. He believed that Apple should only ever produce a tiny collection of items, meaning that products which were becoming outdated should be killed off to make space for new ideas. 'Jobs did not organize Apple into semiautonomous divisions; he closely controlled all of his teams and pushed them to work as one cohesive and flexible company, with one profit-and-loss bottom line,' Walter Isaacson wrote in his biography of Jobs. Or as Tim Cook, Jobs's successor, later said: 'We don't have "divisions" with their own P&L. We run one P&L for the company.'[20] So when the Apple engineers pondered the future of digital music, they brainstormed a series of ideas across different product categories.

Swapping ideas across different boundaries at Apple turned out to be fruitful. Initially, the Apple engineers tried to create a gadget that was broadly similar to a Walkman but with Internet connectivity, namely a 'one-step' digital music player, which would enable users to download songs from the Internet, and then play these wherever they chose. But they quickly realized this one-step approach had a big drawback: the technology of the time demanded so much computing power to store and edit music that any portable one-step device could only hold a limited selection of songs. Worse still, if they used a proprietary technology to store music in a compressed form, this would not be compatible with most music libraries.

So the Apple engineers debated the issue and eventually decided to use an innovative two-step solution. The first step required consumers to download music from the Internet on a computer such as an Apple Mac. They could then edit their selection of songs into a playlist. Then, in the second step, consumers could transfer the music to a small portable listening device, that enabled consumers to enjoy the music lists they had assembled. The beauty of this two-step process was that a device that just enabled consumers to listen to music did not need much computing power, unlike a device that edits or downloads songs. So Apple could keep the gadget very small. As a side benefit, this two-step process also encouraged consumers to use another Apple product, the Apple Mac computer. 'The phrases [Jobs] used were 'deep collaboration' and 'concurrent engineering,' Isaacson observed. 'Instead of a development process in which a product would be passed sequentially from engineering to design to manufacturing to marketing and distribution, these various departments collaborated simultaneously.'[21]

Then the Apple engineers blurred the product lines further to deliver more innovation. The Apple engineers knew that the music companies had no incentive to help consumers download music over the Internet, because they feared that people would listen to music for free. So Jobs and his colleagues hunted for a way to combat this piracy and bring the music groups on board. Eventually they hit on the idea of creating an 'iTunes store,' a website where music companies could sell songs to consumers for a nominal fee of 99 cents. This produced far less revenue than CD or record sales. But it did at least provide music groups with some royalties, and gave them more incentive to cooperate. And to boost sales, the Apple engineers designed the platform so it could be accessed by anybody, using any technology, not just Apple products. At Sony, by contrast, digital music systems relied on proprietary technologies.

So in 2001, Apple launched its own portable digital music device, the iPod. This gadget was so tiny and elegant it could fit into a shirt pocket, and it could store such a vast array of songs that it was marketed under the tagline '1000 songs in your pocket.' It became a huge hit. Within a few months the word 'iPod' had not only become a powerful brand in its own right, but defined an entire product category, in much the same way the original Sony Walkman had done. Eventually Sony conceded defeat and withdrew its inferior, competing offerings from the market. Apple had seized the crown.

IN THE SUMMER OF 2005, as humid air enveloped Tokyo, hundreds of staff at Sony crowded into a large room in the company headquarters to watch a once unimaginable spectacle. Howard Stringer, the British man who had been in charge of Sony's operations in North America in the previous years, had just been appointed CEO, and was now addressing the company.

The appointment was another signal of the degree to which Sony's former success was turning into painful decline. By 2005, the humiliating defeat in the battle to create a digital Walkman symbolized a bigger trend. The company's profitability was slipping fast, along with its reputation for innovation. It still had some dazzling products in its stable, such as the PlayStation. But it had lost its former dominance of the television market because it had failed to anticipate the rise of flat screen TVs. Sony still made iconic cameras and computers (the latter with an elegant purple and black design). But these did not inspire the same cultish following as the Apple brand.

Unsurprisingly, investors had taken fright. In the 1990s the Sony share price soared from around 2,000 yen a share to touch a peak of 16,300 in 2000. But after the internet bubble collapsed in 2001, Sony's share price tumbled to around 5,000 yen and stayed there for several years. Other tech companies had suffered too. But the trajectory of Apple, say, was notably different: between 2000 and 2005 its share price rose five-fold. So too, at Samsung: between 2000 and 2005 its share price jumped 50 percent, as evidence emerged that the Korean upstart was challenging Sony on its prized turf, grabbing away a big stake in the television market.[22] For Sony, this was profoundly humiliating. Nobody was surprised when Idei indicated in 2004 he planned to leave the company.[23]

For many months, the Sony leaders and board members debated who should replace Idei. As so often in Japanese culture, it was unclear who was empowered to pick the next CEO: though the power technically lay with the board, decision making was collective and numerous people were able to exercise a veto. The most flamboyant and best known of the senior Sony managers was Ken Kutaragi, the creative genius who had developed the PlayStation division. However, Kutaragi was also a forceful, impatient man who had guarded his PlayStation silo so forcefully against internal rivals that he had many enemies. There were other, less flamboyant, individuals in the top management, such as Ryoji Chubachi, a slight, balding engineer and Sony lifer who ran the consumer electronics group. He did not present the face of change that the Sony directors knew investors wanted to see.

The Sony leaders in Tokyo tossed names around. Finally, as much out of a sense of desperation as anything else, the name Stringer popped into the debate. It was a peculiar twist.

Stringer had been born in Cardiff, Wales, the son of a Royal Air Force pilot. He spent his formative years in Oundle, a traditional British private boarding school, where he acquired the self-deprecating, self-effacing manner typical of the British upper class. After getting a degree in modern history at Oxford, he moved to America, searching for adventure, and became a writer at CBS Radio. That was unexpectedly interrupted when he was drafted and sent to serve in Vietnam. But once that war was over, he returned to CBS, where he worked as a television producer and journalist for two decades. He started his career in a lowly position, answering phones backstage for *The Ed Sullivan Show*, but jumped up the hierarchy until he ended up running the CBS group, and then joined Sony in 1997 to run their American media operations. That background gave him a transatlantic air: though he owned a graceful apartment on New York's Fifth Avenue, his main home was a manor house in the verdant setting of England's Cotswold Hills, and he had retained his British accent. He had never lived in Japan, did not speak Japanese, and (by Japanese standards) he had not even worked at the company for long.

'People from Sony called me up late at night from Tokyo. I can't remember exactly who it was who called, because it happened several times, the way it always does in Japan – and asked if I wanted to be CEO,' Stringer later recalled. 'I thought they were mad. Completely mad! I told them over and over again: "I am not the person you want in that job. I don't speak Japanese, I won't move to Japan." If someone told me in 2000 this might happen, I might have suggested we could set up shop on the moon.'

But the Sony elders were persistent. To some of them, the company was facing such a big crisis that Stringer's disadvantages suddenly looked like strengths. He presented a fresh face. He seemed able to charm outside investors (particularly since another foreigner, Carlos Ghosn, was already earning great acclaim by implementing a radical turnabout plan at another deeply troubled Japanese company, Nissan). The Japanese liked his British mannerisms and humor, which seemed less abrasive than those of an American. And *precisely* because he did not come from the head office, Stringer was not allied to any particular silo, or corporate tribe, within Sony. That would give him more freedom to act, or so the hope went. 'If one wishes to start a major change, a sea change, a person who stayed away from the mainstream, who is from a remote area, may be called for,' observed Chubachi, who was appointed as president of Sony to work with Stringer.[24]

But what did Stringer want to do with Sony? Could he find a way to stem its decline? As the staff assembled in the auditorium for Stringer's speech in the summer of 2005, they were distinctly nervous. At Nissan the new foreign-born CEO Ghosn had made his mark by slashing jobs, earning him the tag 'cost killer.' The Sony staff were terrified this would occur at their company. However, Stringer did not perform quite as expected. Speaking in English, with a harried translator, he started by saluting his mighty predecessors and the brilliant engineers. But then he changed tack. 'Sony is a company with too many silos!' he declared.

Silos? Japanese listeners were baffled. The American word for 'silo,' or *sairo* as the Japanese pronounced it, was unknown in Japan, since the country grew rice, not grain. Indeed, the word was so unfamiliar that, in desperation, the translator turned the phrase into *takotsubo* or 'octopus pot.' That captured Stringer's meaning perfectly, since Japanese octopus pots are narrow containers that are easy for an octopus to slide into, but almost impossible to exit. If you put your hand in the pot, it can get trapped. But the Sony staff had never heard the word *takotsubo* invoked to describe their beloved company. Was this some kind of clever British joke? Stringer pressed on. He told his staff that it was essential that the company act to remove the 'octopus pots' to create a more 'connected' company, ready for the twenty-first-century high-tech world.

*

IN THE MONTHS THAT followed, Stringer set about trying to turn his declarations about silos into action. It was a topic dear to his heart. Most of the staff who worked at Sony had never thought of the issue of silos before. They had generally grown up inside Sony, and it was the only corporate world they had ever known. To them, that the company was fragmented was unremarkable: it was a pattern so deeply ingrained that they took it for granted, just as the Kabyle Berber studied by Bourdieu had come to assume it was entirely normal to divide their houses in two. That was not unique to Sony. Most company employees assume that their working practices are normal. But at Sony the problem was made doubly worse because the Japanese staff tended to stay with the company for life.

Stringer had a different perspective. By 2005, he had already worked with Sony for almost a decade. But he was not Japanese and not an engineer. Most of his career had been spent in television journalism and entertainment. That meant he could imagine a different way of doing things. His years of working in journalism had left him convinced about the importance of keeping cultures and structures as flexible as possible. At CBS he had earned a reputation for being deft at persuading difficult Americans to work together as a team. He had produced the successful *CBS Evening News with Dan Rather*, working with a highly strung crew, and he persuaded David Letterman to leave NBC for CBS. Then, when he had joined Sony in 1997 in America, he had earned acclaim by bringing more control and order into Sony's American entertainment and media divisions.

He wanted to repeat that trick more widely. He knew it would be hard. When he was running the American operations, he had constantly been surprised by the scale of silos he had seen. Although he had a tight control over the entertainment business, he had often struggled to work out what was happening in the consumer electronics division or the secretive PlayStation unit. He knew they rarely collaborated with each other. Many of Stringer's European and American colleagues blamed this on Japanese culture, or the management style of other Sony leaders, such as Idei. 'You have a culture which is totally hierarchical, where people are just trained to sit in their box, and take orders,' commented one senior New York–based Sony executive. 'In this culture, when people are assigned into a role, they *become* that role – they became totally one-dimensional.' However, Stringer did not think the problem of silos was purely a Japanese phenomenon. Though Sony was an extreme case, dysfunctional silos had caused problems at plenty of other large American and European companies. Microsoft was one company that was renowned for silos, as was Xerox. So he hunted for examples of large companies that had managed to address the issue head-on. And as he did so, he became fixated with IBM, the gigantic American computing group.

In many ways, IBM was a thought-provoking story for Stringer. Like the Japanese giant, IBM had enjoyed stellar success in the 1970s and 1980s, dominating the business of making and selling computer mainframes. But in the early 1990s its mainframe business went into decline, the group lost its reputation for innovation, and the company became sclerotic and bloated, dragged down by rigid silos and a wave of internal bickering. In 1993, the

IBM board removed the chief executive officer and installed Lou Gerstner, who implemented radical restructuring. Previously the company had been split among separate software, hardware, and services departments; like Sony, IBM was marred by silos. But Gertsner forced the different departments to collaborate to create a more unified technology offering, and that helped to refocus the company away from the dying mainframe computer business to new areas, like software. That sparked bitter battles. But Gerstner's silo-busting reforms eventually triumphed, delivering one of the most remarkable turnabout stories in American corporate history.[25] So Stringer contacted Gerstner and asked for advice on how to revitalize Sony. 'Lou became like a mentor of sorts,' Stringer recalled. 'He kept saying: "You have to tackle the silos! You have to be bold!" So that is what I decided to do.'

Stringer set to work. He asked his staff to prepare a PowerPoint with some pictures of Midwest grain silos to show the baffled Japanese officials what a silo was. 'The silo metaphor in business is really a description of the subcultures within an organization that have become islands and don't communicate horizontally or even vertically within their own organization,' he told the Sony staff via an internal newsletter.[26] Of course, he went on to explain, the presence of silos was not *always* bad; specialization was often beneficial, if not essential, when companies became big. 'The original design of silos in the business sense of the word was to create a self-contained team [so] they can be quite positive ... and foster good qualities such as teamwork, friendliness, shared experience, and loyalty. PlayStation is an example of a very successful silo where a group of people were able to start something, create a vertically integrated business model, and flourish outside the giant bureaucracy of a big company.' But the problem with silos was that they could become dangerously introverted. 'When the team doesn't communicate with other teams ... [or] communicate up and down its own vertical hierarchy, it ceases to become transparent and is not able to take advantage of the changes in the rest of the company or in the rest of the world,' he noted. 'When people talk about silos in Western businesses, they usually mean that a company has grown too large ... [the silos are] all very guarded and protective, the management of the company simply loses touch with what's going on.'

So Stringer announced that he would shake up the company. In the autumn of 2005 he and Chubachi unveiled a big restructuring plan, which tried to slim the company down by cutting almost a tenth of Sony's 180,000 staff,[27] reducing the different business models by 20 percent,[28] and trimming the manufacturing sites from sixty-five to fifty-four.[29] The aim was to turn a company that had become dangerously sprawling – or a 'corporate octopus, with tentacles in multiple different business lines,' as *The New York Times* described it[30] – into a streamlined, focused entity. 'If a company like Apple can build its financial strength around two or three products ... we can redesign the look and feel of Sony to be as strong as we once were,'[31] Stringer explained. The plan incorporated another crucial twist: Sony would no longer treat separate units of the company as quasi-companies, but pull the different divisions into a single, integrated structure. Idei's silos were being dismantled. 'This significant structural change is designed to eliminate the corporate silos that have prevented us from focusing our vast resources on our most competitive prod-ucts,' the restructuring announcement declared, pledging this would 'foster coordinated, efficient and rapid decision making.' Or as Stringer added: 'The digital age is about communication between people and devices ... that puts a whole new emphasis in the way we design products and market them.'[32]

To reinforce this cultural change, Stringer decreed that groups of young software engineers would rotate between the different departments to disseminate new ideas and practices. Members of the 'content' teams, who were creating software, were told to work with the engineers engaged in producing hardware. Stringer convened town halls in different departments, and put teams of software engineers in the center of the room to emphasize the point that software and hardware had to be connected. He even asked junior employees to express their views at meetings – and subvert the normal Japanese hierarchy.

At first, Stringer thought that his silo-busting mission was going well. In the middle of 2006, when the group unveiled its results, these included some good news: after several years of losses, Sony was producing profits again, selling more of its sleek gadgets. Confidence inside the company was rising and some analysts and journalists were starting to hail Stringer's success in turning the company around. 'Sony's picture is looking brighter!' *The Wall Street Journal* declared.[33] Or as *Fortune* observed: 'Sony slept through the dawn of digital media. Now Sir Howard Stringer and his polyglot crew are trying to wake the company up.'[34] With an admiring tone, *Fortune* described all the 'victories' that Stringer had won: Sony had shut down production of the

Aibo robot dog, shuttered nine factories, and closed the Qualia line of boutique electronics. It had also launched a new LCD television, which had become market leader.

But the sense of progress was short-lived. In 2007, the company posted red ink again, and its reputation and share price began to slump once more. In part, that reflected bigger economic trends. In the summer of 2007, strife hit America's subprime mortgage market and then its banks. As the financial turmoil spread, the yen strengthened, making Sony's exports much less competitive. In 2008, a full-blown crisis erupted, creating a global recession. That cut demand for Sony products. Then in 2010, a terrible tsunami and earthquake hit the Fukushima district of Japan, creating havoc with Sony's supply chain. In 2011, floods in Thailand disrupted Sony's production processes again. 'I kept thinking: what else is coming?' Stringer later grimly laughed. 'Plagues of frogs? Locusts? Whirlwinds? Pestilence?'

The problems at Sony were not just due to freak weather or bad luck, though. As the months passed, Stringer realized he was dealing with entrenched resistance. In public, none of the Japanese staff ever challenged Stringer's commands. They always nodded in acquiescence whenever he spoke. But Stringer found it impossible to monitor what was happening on the ground once he had issued his commands. He did not have his own team of loyalists installed in the Sony head office in Yurakucho, since when he had been appointed as CEO most of the senior management roles were filled by long-standing Japanese Sony officials. Stringer could not do his own casual research either, since he did not speak Japanese. 'I couldn't just wander around the corridors and bump into people and chat to them, like I had done before, because I didn't speak the language,' Stringer later recalled. 'People would say yes to me, but nothing would happen. It was like the joke Clinton made about walking over a graveyard – you can walk around as leader and have 1,000 people beneath you but it's all deadly quiet and nobody ever talks back.' At IBM, Gerstner had been able to force through change because he had been obsessive about watching the details of what was being done. 'People don't do what you *ex*pect, but what you *in*spect,' Gerstner used to declare to his colleagues.[35] Indeed, the phrase was tossed around so frequently that it later became one of the guiding mantras, if not hackneyed clichés, within IBM. But Stringer found it painfully difficult, if not impossible, to inspect much at all. 'To be a really great leader you have to have a sense of what people at all levels are saying and thinking – you have to read the mood. Stringer could do that at CBS. He couldn't do that Sony,' one of Stringer's senior colleagues later observed. 'Personally I don't think he should have taken the job.'

Stringer battled on. Time and again he would deliver orders, and later discover that these commands had simply been ignored. At IBM Gerstner had been able to shift the cultural patterns by force of his will: when he outlined a new policy, he had ways to make his staff fall in line. He ferociously monitored everything, watching his staff and talking to them all the time. Stringer, however, lacked the tools – or temperament – to achieve Gerstner's results.

One of Stringer's first battles revolved around PlayStation. Until 2005, the division that produced the PlayStation console had operated out of its own building, as a self-contained silo, under the leadership of the powerful executive Kutaragi. This sense of independence had served the unit well in its early days, since it fostered an entrepreneurial spirit. But as time wore on, this detachment sparked more and more conflict with the Sony head office. So after he became CEO, Stringer announced that he wanted to pull the powerful PlayStation group into the Sony headquarters building in the Shinagawa district of Tokyo and integrate their operations into the rest of the company. Stringer hoped that PlayStation could be an inspiring model for other departments, showing how software and hardware could be combined in a flexible way, as technology overturned the traditional boundaries. 'PlayStation was one of our crown jewels – it combined different skills and functions in a really creative way. It was all about networks,' Stringer later recalled. But the powerful PlayStation department was fiercely independent. Initially they simply ignored appeals for them to move into the head office. Then the board decided they should move. But when the PlayStation team did finally move into head office, they immediately erected a glass wall around their operations. The PlayStation team claimed the wall was needed to protect proprietary secrets; however, the symbolism was clear.

Stringer faced similar resistance whenever he tried to streamline operations. Over the years, Sony had drifted into a sprawling mess of different products and business lines. It produced more than 1,000 gadgets, many of which operated on separate, proprietary technologies. 'I have 35 Sony devices at home. I have 35 battery chargers,' Rob Wiesenthal, one of Stringer's key allies at the company, told reporters. 'That's all you need to know.'[36] Stringer was determined to change this. 'I went around saying "What are we doing in the utility sector? In health care?"' Stringer recalled. 'But nothing ever got cut, or not fast. I would be in the Tokyo headquarters and we would announce 10,000 job cuts, or whatever. Then, when I returned, we would somehow always have the same number of staff.' Eventually, in a desperate attempt to shock the staff into action Stringer decided to organize a display inside the Sony headquarters of all its products. He hoped this would demonstrate how unwieldy the Sony empire had become. But when the display case was finally installed in Shinagawa building, it had the opposite effect: to the Sony employees, the sprawling display seemed to be as much a source of *pride* as shame. It was a classic chicken and egg scenario: silos had created products that employees wanted to defend at all costs – and successful products were deepening the silos.

Stringer then stopped talking about cuts and started emphasizing 'collaboration.' He reasoned that if he couldn't kill the silos, he could at least try to make them cooperate. After all, the company's motto was 'Sony United.' But getting cooperation was difficult. Shortly after he moved into the CEO slot he urged the Sony engineers to use digital technology to create a device that would let consumers read books. Sony seemed well placed to exploit this niche, since it had media, computing skills, *and* consumer electronics expertise sitting inside different parts of the Sony group. Indeed, the engineers even had some prototypes. However, when Stringer pushed the idea of a digital reader, it became clear that the managers in different departments did not want to collaborate with each other, or with book publishers, partly because they would have to share the revenues. The project ran into the sand. 'Two whole years before Amazon launched its own e-reader, I had the same idea [of creating an e-reader],' Stringer fumed. 'I asked our guys to do this, but we delayed and delayed and nothing happened. So then Amazon beat us to it.'

ON FEBRUARY 20, 2013, over a thousand journalists gathered in Manhattan's Hammerstein Ballroom to listen to the Sony executives. The mood was electric. Earlier that month Sony had announced plans to release PlayStation 4, the first time in seven years that it had updated the famous, device. The Hammerstein event was intended to showcase this leap forward. Above the stage, a gigantic wraparound screen beamed a dizzy jumble of game images down on the audience. Searchlights strafed the dark. Deafening music bounced off the walls. Slogans flashed up. 'Imagination is the one weapon in the war against reality!' 'To win we don't need to fight. WE need to play!' 'Our ordinary self becomes extraordinary. EPIC!' 'We were born different! We grew up renegade! Explore the boundaries of play!'

The watching journalists sat in the theater seats, rapt. Play-Station commanded extraordinary respect among gaming enthusiasts. Indeed, it was arguably Sony's most successful product of all, as iconic as the Walkman. And the new PS4 looked particularly impressive, with its blend of software, hardware, and content.

But as the Sony executives looked down from the stage, as they presented the new console, they might have noticed something striking. Around them the game images were flashing up and the journalists were tapping on laptops in their seats, or snapping shots with their mobile phones. But almost none of these devices in the hands of the reporters was made by Sony. Instead, the auditorium glimmered with hundreds of tiny white pinpricks of light, shining like stars from numerous Apple logos. Sony had been eclipsed by Apple, even in its moment of pride.

Stringer knew this only too well. Back in 2006, during his first year as CEO, he had initially thought he could transform the company. By 2013, he had all but given up. Some individual divisions were doing well, such as PlayStation. But in most fields the reputation of Sony kept crumbling, along with its share price. When Stringer had taken over the company in 2005, the stock was trading on the New York Stock Exchange at $38.71 a share. By 2012, it was trading at $18 a share. Apple, by contrast, had seen its share price more than double, while Samsung's share price had also more than doubled. What was particularly humiliating, though, was what had happened to the relative size of the companies, measured by market capitalization. Until 2002, Sony had always been well ahead of Samsung in the *Forbes* list of the world's largest 2,000 companies. By 2005, when Stringer took over, Sony however had slipped behind, ranking 123rd, while Samsung was the 62nd largest group. By 2012, Samsung was ranked number 12 on this list, but Sony was 477. It was one of the most startling swings even seen on the *Forbes* list.[37] Nobody was surprised when Stringer announced that he would step down as CEO.

For a while, Stringer stayed on at Sony as chairman of the board. He was replaced as CEO by Kazuo Hirai, a Sony lifer. But the decline continued. As its share price sank toward 1,000 yen a share – a level last seen in 1980 – Daniel Loeb, the American activist investor, started a campaign to break up the Japanese group, to spin off the entertainment arm.[38] The move horrified the Sony staff, as well as a generation of Americans who had grown up wearing Sony Walkmans or watching Sony films, and thinking that the brand was the ultimate symbol of 'cool.' 'Loeb is trying to manipulate the market,' George Clooney, the actor, fumed, when news of the activist bid emerged. 'I am no apologist for the studios, but these people know what they are doing.'[39] But Loeb, like many other analysts, could not see any reason to keep the disparate silos glued together. They no longer made sense at a company that had now been eclipsed not just by Apple, but Samsung too.

Just before Stringer left the company, his board gave him a striking present: a metallic case with '007' painted on the lid, like a prop from a James Bond movie. Stringer was thrilled. He had always loved the James Bond books; so much that he kept a collection of first editions in his New York apartment and took enormous pride in the fact that Sony Studios owned the rights to the 007 franchise. But the really clever aspect of the parting gift – which made Stringer chuckle with joy – was buried inside the metal box. Sony's engineers had installed a set of miniature gadgets that might have been invented by Q in a Bond movie: there was a collection of tiny plastic figures next to a boardroom table, each of which was a likeness of a real, living Sony executive, and tiny flashing dials that spoke messages when pressed. Some had farewell messages from Stringer's colleagues. Others repeated all the phrases that Stringer had used during his tenure. 'Strong yen!' the box squeaked. 'Economic crisis!' 'Lehman Brothers [shock]!' 'Earthquake!' 'Tsunami!' 'A plague of frogs!' 'Locusts!'

And then, there was one more button with a message: 'Breach silo walls!'

'Well, I guess that one didn't work!' Stringer liked to joke. He installed it next to his prized collection of James Bond books as a bittersweet memorial.

FROM TIME TO TIME, when he reflected on his time at Sony, Stringer would wonder if he could have done anything differently. He knew he had been astute at diagnosing Sony's problems. He also knew that Sony was not the only company with these woes. On the contrary, numerous other corporations were grappling with the silo curse. At Microsoft, like Sony, individual departments had been slow to collaborate, partly because the company had enjoyed so much earlier success that its employees did not see any reason to change.[40] 'It's been an issue for us,' said Satya Nadella, a long-serving Microsoft executive who was appointed CEO in 2014. 'Whenever you become good at maximizing past successes there can be a tendency to have less synergies ... and the competition does not respect internal boundaries.' Many public and quasi-public institutions are also beset by silos. A few months after he left Sony, Stringer started working as an adviser to the BBC, and discovered a similar pattern of tribal infighting. 'It feels very familiar!' Stringer joked to friends. 'There are lots of silos at the BBC too!'

But it is one thing to analyze the problem. It is quite another to actually find a solution to the silo curse. Could any company, Stringer wondered, actually build the kind of culture that would reduce the danger of silos? Could they be dismantled when they appeared? Or was it just inevitable that companies had debilitating silos, whenever an institution became large? Did those silos always become more rigid as time passed? Stringer did not know.

However, unbeknownst to him, out in California a group of officials at Facebook *did* have some ideas. And these were rather intriguing. As Sony ailed, the Facebook engineers had taken close note of Sony's fate, along with the troubles that beset so many other technology giants such as Xerox and Microsoft. Moreover, they were trying to find some answers to Stringer's questions by exploring ways to avoid succumbing to these silos. In the second half of this book I shall tell this story, by explaining how Facebook has tried (and is still trying) to be an 'anti-Sony' or 'anti-Microsoft,' as some of its senior officials like to say. But first I shall look at some other ways that silos can manifest themselves, and present dangers, starting with the ailing of a gigantic company in a completely different field and part of the world – the mighty Swiss bank UBS.

3
WHEN GNOMES GO BLIND

How Silos Conceal Risks

'It is very difficult to get a man to understand something, when his salary depends upon his not understanding it.'[1]

—Upton Sinclair

ON MARCH 9, 2007, A TEAM OF REGULATORS FROM SWITZERLAND FLEW from Bern to London for a meeting at the offices of UBS, their country's largest bank.[2] It was a fateful encounter. To a casual observer, UBS seemed a shining success story. It had produced stellar results in previous years from its offices in Zurich, London, and New York. It was also famous – or infamous – for being cautious in how it ran its business. No surprise perhaps: Switzerland is a country that makes a virtue of being quiet, if not downright dull; a place where bankers are dubbed 'gnomes' because they usually toil away in sober silence. And UBS epitomized this gnomic culture. No fewer than 3,000 people worked in the bank as risk managers,[3] charged with spotting threats to the bank's business. These half-hidden banking gnomes were considered to be so diligent that UBS was sometimes described by regulators as 'exemplary' in the industry, in terms of how it controlled risk.[4]

So, as the Swiss regulators flew to London for their meeting in March 2007, they were not worried that the bank had any big problems lurking. But there was one cloud on the wider economic horizon that they planned to discuss. Over in America, the housing market was booming, as bankers and mortgage brokers issued a flood of mortgages. UBS, like most banks, had gotten involved in that game by buying bonds and derivatives linked to those loans.[5] But though the business had produced fat profits, the Swiss regulators wanted to know whether the UBS bankers understood all the risks of this new development. Could the bank be hurt if house prices fell? Would it suffer losses if homeowners defaulted?

The answer that day was an emphatic no. For several hours, the Swiss regulators sat in the UBS office in London, an imposing skyscraper with blackened windows, near Liverpool Street. The bank's risk officers explained to the regulators that the bank was well protected against any future house price falls, since UBS had not just insured itself against losses with derivatives trades, but also placed additional bets in the market that would create profits if the housing market soured. In financial jargon, the bank had thus gone short the market – or made a bet that house prices would decline. Thus the bank was actually '*profiting* from the deteriorating market' in mortgage bonds – and not at risk at all.[6]

There did not seem to be any sign that the UBS bankers in London were lying; on the contrary, as far as the regulators were concerned, the explanations seemed credible and confident. So the regulators returned to Switzerland, and reported that UBS 'had taken the changes in the US real estate market into account and that no major risks had arisen in this area.'[7] UBS was safe.

Six months later, however, it became clear that this verdict had been disastrously wrong. On October 30, the Swiss bank presented its annual results. These showed record-high levels of revenues. But it also revealed something else: UBS had suffered a dent to its earnings totaling some 726 million Swiss francs (a sum then worth about $700 million), due to bad American mortgage investments.[8] Far from profiting from falling house prices, the bank was suffering big losses.

This reversal was embarrassing. But it got far worse. In early December, Marcel Rohner, the bank's Investment Bank chairman and patrician chief executive officer, suddenly revealed that the bank had somehow lost $10 billion – ten *billion* dollars – from bad mortgage bets.[9] He also admitted that the group had secretly accumulated $50 billion worth of U.S. subprime mortgage securities on its balance sheet, apparently without any of the top managers at UBS noticing.[10] Indeed, the losses were so vast that the bank was forced to tap Singaporean and Middle Eastern investors for an injection of funds to stay alive.[11] It was a shocking turn at a bank that 'only a year ago was considered one of the most financially sound institutions in the world,' as David Williams, a London-based stock analyst, observed.[12] Or as Marcel Rohner told investors, with some gnomic Swiss understatement: 'I understand if some of you [investors] are surprised and frustrated with this change in outlook . . . there has been serious dislocation.'[13]

The dislocations – and shocks – worsened. In February, the bank revealed another wave of mortgage losses, taking the total hit to almost $19 billion.[14] UBS tapped its shareholders for 15 billion Swiss francs of new funds, a sum equivalent to around $15 billion.[15] But even that was not enough to plug the gap: by October 2009 the damage was so bad that eventually the Swiss government itself was forced to use 6 billion Swiss francs (or $6 billion) of taxpayers' money to help it clean up its operations.[16] Swiss taxpayers and politicians were appalled – and angry. So the Swiss federal banking commission, the main regulator, demanded that UBS write a report to 'name names,' and explain who was to blame. After all, losing almost $19 billion – *nineteen billion dollars* – was not a trivial matter. Most observers assumed that someone at the bank had done something criminal and told some lies, and would go to jail.

The bank produced a neat report, on time; Switzerland is a land where bankers, voters, and politicians alike have a strong sense of duty. But this report was not what the regulators had expected. Instead of naming the individual or individuals who had created the losses, such as a rogue trader, the report argued that the entire *system* had gone wrong. Somehow a collection of supposedly boring, conservative bankers had gone mad and taken some crazy bets on the housing market, which none of the 3,000 or so risk officers inside the bank had spotted.[17]

Was this a cover-up? Were the bankers lying? Most politicians and journalists thought so, particularly since a few months later a second scandal erupted at UBS when the U.S. authorities accused the bank of helping wealthy Americans evade American

tax laws.[18] The Swiss government demanded that the UBS management try harder and write a second report on what had gone
wrong. Once again, UBS produced a precise document. But this
tome was equally baffling. On its second attempt, the bank asked
independent outsider experts to comment on the scandals. They
hoped this would give the conclusions more credibility. But these
did not offer what the politicians wanted either.

'Ever since the size of the Bank's losses – going into the
billions – and the nature of its legal violation [about U.S. tax
evasion] have become known, the public has queried the true
causes of the UBS crisis,' Tobias Straumann, an economics
history professor at Zurich University, wrote. 'It [seems] simply
inconceivable that a large international bank with a reputation
for its conservativeness, would suddenly incur such huge losses,'[19]
Straumann continued, pointing out that most observers assumed
that the 'top management at UBS [had] behaved like gamblers
at a casino, constantly taking greater risks as their profits and
their bonuses increased, until they finally lost everything and
almost landed in prison.'[20] However, the professor rejected the
idea that this was a plot. He did not think that the leaders of the
bank had taken deliberate gambles, or knowingly concocted a
plan to fool everyone else. They genuinely believed that the bank
was healthy and safe, and that it had 'first-class subprime mortgage securities' on its books. So did the auditors and regulators.
'Its image as a conservative bank was not made up to deceive
the public,' Straumann argued. 'It corresponded fully with the
picture that the bank had of itself.'[21] Or to put it another way, the
terrifying thing about UBS was not that dastardly bankers had

lied to everyone else; it was that the banking gnomes at UBS *had collectively fooled themselves*. 'This [story] is more than just an accident involving a single large bank ... [it] fits perfectly into a pattern that has repeated itself again and again in the past. In reality, the biggest losers in a financial crisis are not those who have exposed themselves to major risks with their eyes wide open, but rather the ones who believed [they had] their affairs well under control.'[22]

Why? Straumann put much of the blame on the bank's top managers. These officials were too complacent and failed to ask the right questions about what was happening at the bank. But there was another problem too: silos. What the Straumann and UBS reports also showed was that the bank, like Sony, was riddled with structural silos. Warring departments failed to cooperate with each other. Crucial pieces of information were not passed across the bank. The managers at the top of UBS were not aware of what was happening in the grass roots, because the climate was so defensive that each department hugged data to itself. Worse still, the leaders operated in such a bubble, or intellectual silo, they did not ask the right questions of their staff.

But in one respect, the story of UBS is more alarming than Sony. At the Japanese electronics group, the presence of silos had crushed innovation, and prevented it from seeing opportunities. But at UBS, the silos had prevented the bankers from seeing *risks*. In that sense, then, it is a cautionary tale, since it reveals a pattern that is endemic in so much of the rest of the financial world – and in many parts of the nonfinancial world too.

*

THE STORY OF UBS is a particularly painful one for the Swiss government since the bank is a powerful symbol of the nation; the financial equivalent of cuckoo clocks, luxury watches, or chocolate bars. Its main headquarters are found on the historic Bahnhofstrasse in the heart of Zurich, just a short stroll from the beautiful lake that carries the city's name, tucked into a vista of towering mountains. Unlike most Wall Street banks, the group does not operate out of any flashy skyscraper. Instead its building is made of dull gray granite that blends discreetly into the streetcar-lined street, outshone by nearby luxury watch stores and designer clothes shops. Even the marble in the lobby is discreet. The only eye-catching detail on the sober facade is a flash of scarlet from the UBS logo. It is the same shade as the Swiss flag.

The bank was created, in its modern form, in 1998, when Switzerland's second and third largest banks – then known as Swiss Bank Corporation and Union Bank of Switzerland – combined to create a banking behemoth.[23] (In 1998, the bank had $590 billion of assets inside the investment and corporate bank and approximately $910 billion in its asset management unit, mostly in the private bank. That made it one of the largest in the world.)[24] Its roots go deep into Swiss history. Swiss Bank Corporation and UBS themselves were cobbled together from numerous mergers of Swiss companies, along with a few famous American and British names: Phillips & Drew (the asset management business of Chase Manhattan Bank),[25] Dillon Read (another U.S. financial group),[26] and SG Warburg (the British merchant bank).

Initially, when the modern bank first emerged, UBS seemed

a stodgy, domestic entity. During the 1990s, the two banks had
tried to build up overseas operations. But Union Bank had been
badly burned by an investment in an American hedge fund,
Long-Term Capital Management, and in the aftermath of those
losses, some of the UBS managers were wary of venturing overseas too aggressively again. The two men who combined UBS
and SBC – Marcel Ospel and Mathis Cabiallavetta – had different
ideas. They could see that the global markets were becoming more
tightly entwined and other American and European banks were
grabbing new businesses, and they were determined that UBS
should follow the trend.[27] So, around the turn of the century, they
created an expansion plan that aimed to build a business not just
in Zurich, but in London and New York as well. They started in a
time-honored fashion, by making a flurry of new hires.[28] Between
2001 and 2004 they spent an estimated $700 million recruiting
a clutch of big Wall Street names such as the former Donaldson,
Lufkin & Jenrette investment banker Kenneth Moelis, Olivier
Sarkozy,[29] Ben Lorello,[30] Blair Effron,[31] and Jeff McDermott.[32] The
most notable of these, however, was John Costas, a flamboyant
former bond trader, who was appointed head of UBS's investment
banking division in 2001.[33]

Then, Costas on board, the UBS management started to look
for ways to expand their bank. Compared to most other banks,
UBS was unusually cash rich, since its private bank was one of
the biggest in the world and pulled in a vast quantity of savings
each year from ultra-wealthy clients. This financial pile potentially gave the bank a formidable arsenal. Ospel and Costas were
convinced that if they could find some way to deploy this money

in high-earning business, the bank would be able to rival – or eclipse – even the mightiest Wall Street names, such as Goldman Sachs, Morgan Stanley, or Credit Suisse. 'This is a once in a life-time opportunity,' Costas declared in 2002, predicting that UBS was about to become one of the biggest five banks in the U.S. markets. Ospel was even more ambitious. He declared that UBS could become one of the top three investment banks in the world.[34]

Ospel and other senior managers started hunting for new businesses they could enter and spoke with management consultants such as Ernst & Young, and Oliver Mercer Wyman. The advice from the consultants was clear: if UBS wanted to grow itself quickly, and challenge the mightiest Wall Street names, it had to jump into the corner of finance known as securitization, particularly the subsection linked to mortgage bonds. This sector is distinctly specialist, if not technical.[35] What it essentially does is turn loans, such as mortgages, into bonds – which are then traded between banks and other investors. These so-called securitized bonds are then often turned into new packages of securities, using derivatives too, which adds an extra layer of complexity.

Until that point, the bankers at UBS had not considered the bank to be an expert in securitization. On the contrary, the UBS bankers had focused on the parts of the financial markets that are better known to ordinary people, such as extending loans, taking customer deposits, or trading stocks, shares, and currencies. But while the UBS bankers were not market leaders in securitization, they could see that this business line was producing juicy profits for the big Wall Street banks. So Ospel and Costas drew up plans for the Swiss giant to jump into the securitization business, confident it would deliver big returns.

IN THE AUTUMN OF 2005, regulators from Switzerland traveled from Bern to New York to conduct their annual inspection of UBS's American operations. It was supposed to be a routine inspection. In previous years, the key rival to UBS in Switzerland – Credit Suisse – had developed a large footprint in America, as it had earlier acquired First Boston, an American bank. But unlike Credit Suisse First Boston, UBS was not considered to have a particularly exciting American operation: its business there seemed sober, if not dull. But when the regulators started inspecting the UBS books, they noticed something striking. A few months earlier, UBS had created a department in the New York office dedicated to trading something called 'collateralized debt obligations' or CDOs. This was a particularly specialized field in the business of securitization. Essentially, it revolved around the craft of taking bundles of different loans and bonds, and turning these into complex new financial products. One way to visualize this process is with the image of how a butcher makes sausages. Instead of simply grabbing a carcass and selling steaks, a butcher will sometimes take numerous different joints, chop them up, and mix them according to somebody's taste, and then sell it inside new casings. The process of creating CDOs echoes this, in financial terms. The banks start by amassing loans they have made to customers (companies or consumers), break these down into different pieces of lending risk, mix them up, and sell them to new customers in new cases called CDOs. Like sausages, these can be blended to different customer tastes, to contain more or less risk, and higher or lower returns.

If a casual observer had wandered into the UBS offices in 2005 and seen the desk making those CDOs, they might have thought it was a tiny, if not irrelevant, business. By that date UBS had a global workforce of 82,000 and vast departments in America that traded equities and currencies. Indeed, it had so many traders in America that it was in the process of building a cavernous trading floor out in Stamford, Connecticut, which was billed as one of the biggest such arenas for bank traders in the world. The CDO desk, by contrast, had only a few dozen employees. It was run by Jim Stehli, a veteran trader, who worked out of a UBS office in central Manhattan, near Radio City Music Hall.[36] Most people who worked in the UBS global network did not even know the CDO desk existed at all.[37]

But when the Swiss regulators looked at UBS's American books, they spotted that the tiny CDO desk was generating an extraordinary amount of activity. According to the official accounts, the bank had amassed some $16.6 billion worth of mortgage bonds, largely via that CDO desk, in the course of a mere nine months. 'UBS presented the results [to us] of an internal study summarising the overall exposure of UBS investment Bank to the US real estate market,' the Swiss regulators later explained. 'The study was very comprehensive and included both direct ($16.6bn) and indirect ($7.1bn) exposure (e.g., to construction firms).'[38]

The Swiss regulators tried to find out why this seemingly tiny CDO desk was generating so much activity. Was this business really safe? Was the CDO desk under control? The risk managers in New York insisted it was, and cited two reasons for that. The first was that the CDO desk was only supposed to handle assets that were very safe, or securities that had been given a AAA tag from credit rating agencies. Second, the bank was only holding these CDOs in a temporary manner, so was not really exposed much risk.

The reason lay in how the bankers visualized the CDO business; or explained it to outsiders and themselves. Before the 1970s, when a bank such as UBS conducted its business, it tended to make loans or buy assets and then hang on to these. In financial terms, these assets stayed on the bank's books. However, since the 1970s, as the securitization business took hold, banks have tended to sell a large part of their loans to other investors, to spread their risks. The CDO business took this to a new level. According to the theory, what banks such as UBS were doing was acquiring loans (or 'originating,' in financial jargon) and repackaging them into new cases, to be sold to other, outside investors. Thus if the bank held loans or CDOs on its book, via that New York desk, it only expected to keep them for one to four months. Indeed, at UBS (like most banks) the desk was called a 'warehouse,' to distinguish it from other parts of the bank that were buying assets for investment reasons. 'We are in the moving business, not storage business,' Robert Wolf, president of UBS Investment Bank, liked to say.[39] Or as the Swiss regulators observed in a report that they wrote in late 2005: 'The bank has always presented itself . . . as an organisation that consistently followed an "originate to distribute" approach. . . . Under this approach the exposure arising from securitisations is only held on the bank's own books for a short time and then immediately passed on to others.'

Taken together, that meant there was no reason for the regulators to worry about the CDO warehouse. Or so the UBS bankers argued. The $16.6 billion of mortgage assets sitting on the bank's books were unlikely to ever default, since most of them had a AAA tag. They had received that designation partly because the assets inside the CDO were thought to be 'uncorrelated' in banking jargon, meaning that even if one of two households defaulted on their mortgages, that was unlikely to cause widespread defaults – or so the theory went. However, many of these instruments were thought to be even *safer* than normal AAA securities, because they were a subset of CDO called 'super senior' tranches. They had that label because the structure of the CDO implied that in the unlikely event that lots of mortgages did go into default and reduce the value of those super senior CDOs, it would be other investors, not anyone holding super senior tranches, that would take the hit.

In reality, if an anthropologist had peered into those books, he or she might have spotted some problems with these assumptions. For one thing, the loans that lay deep inside the CDOs were not actually ultra-safe at all. Many of these had been extended to the risky mortgage borrowers known as subprime creditors. When the banks assembled those loans into CDOs, they used complex financial techniques that appeared to transfer the risk of default to other investors. As a result, the credit rating agencies had given the CDO securities a AAA stamp. Many of these were deemed to be super senior, which were supposed to be even safer than normal

AAA assets. But very few people outside the rating agencies or specialist CDO desks had any idea how the banks seemed to work this alchemy. Nobody knew whether those AAA CDOs were really safe.

There was a second oddity. Whenever people such as Wolf talked about the CDO business, they described it as a 'moving' business. It was all about selling CDOs to other investors. But in reality, the bankers did not have much incentive to sell all the CDOs. When the bankers created these products, they typically created several parts, called 'tranches' (after the French word for slice). Outside investors were eager to buy the CDO tranches that appeared to pay high returns. However, they had little appetite for buying the safest chunk, or the super senior tranches, since these produced extremely low returns. So the super senior tranches tended to end up unsold on the bank's books, like the unwanted bones from a butcher's carcass. At first the bankers were worried about this. But then the traders working on the CDO desk spotted something important. When the CDOs were stored on the bank's books, they produced a small return, which the traders could book as a 'profit.' This return was very low, in percentage terms, worth just 0.1 percent a year or so. But 0.1 percent of billions of dollars was enough to provide an attractive revenue stream for the CDO desk. Since UBS, like other banks, operated with an 'eat what you kill' pay structure, which paid bankers a bonus according to profits produced by their team, that gave the CDO desk a strong incentive to hold as many CDOs as they could. At other banks, there might have been a ceiling on this activity, because it was expensive to borrow money to buy loans. But the UBS bankers did not have any problems accessing cheap cash, since the private bank supplied them with as much money as required, at a price that seemed almost free. Indeed, the incentive to expand was so strong that by early 2006 Stehli's team was not just holding onto the super senior CDOs that it was creating. It was also buying additional super senior CDOs from other banks.[40] There was a sharp gap between rhetoric and reality of CDOs.

From time to time, some of the bankers inside UBS would crack jokes about these contradictions. The traders on the CDO desk knew that they were exploiting some of the peculiarities of the system. Because the business was supposed to be a client activity, UBS did not feel the need to post big reserves against the assets sitting in this warehouse. Those assets were earning reasonable returns. However, the traders had no incentive to point this discrepancy out to their bosses, or the regulators. And to most of the bankers and regulators, the oddities in this pattern were not immediately clear, partly due to a sense of tunnel vision. Like the Kabyle village that Pierre Bourdieu studied in Algeria, twenty-first-century investment banks operated with a deeply entrenched classification system. AAA assets were considered completely different from BBB assets. Bank activities that served clients were viewed differently from 'proprietary businesses,' or those where the bank took calculated gambles with its own funds. The latter was considered very risky. The former, known as client business, was not. In reality, these categories often blurred. Client businesses could be dangerous. AAA assets might not be ultra-safe. But once activities and items were defined into particular mental categories, financiers would not usually reclassify them. And what made this classification system even more rigid and powerful was that accountants and risk managers used it to measure and manage banks' assets. So did regulators, When the Swiss financial supervisors decided how much reserve capital a bank needed to hold against the danger of losses, they did this by first dividing the bank's assets into different categories.

On one level, the bankers knew this was odd; the classification system contained numerous contradictions. But generally the classification system in Western banks, like that in the Kabyle village, existed at 'the borders of conscious and unconscious thought,' as Bourdieu observed. Or as anthropologist Karen Ho, who studied Wall Street banks in the late 1990s, suggests, the bankers were behaving in accordance with patterns of learned behavior that seemed natural to them because of their habitus.[41] In the Wall Street habitus it seems natural to treat 'client' and 'proprietary' businesses separately. It also seems natural for the individual teams of traders to do everything to maximize their profits. That is how they get paid. Nobody had much incentive to challenge the contradictions in the status quo, or the classification system. A silo mentality ruled. After all, as Bourdieu observed: 'The most powerful forms of ideological effect are those which need no more than a complicitous silence.'

So, after looking into the bank's books, the regulators issued their verdict. 'Securitisation was not deemed to be a key risk due to the apparently purely client orientated nature of the business,' the Swiss regulators stated.[42] 'These [$16.6 billion] figures were not seen as a major concern by either the bank or the supervisory authorities.'

*

BY THE SPRING OF 2007, some two years after UBS created its CDO desk, the senior managers in the bank's granite headquarters building in Zurich were getting worried about their company. That was not because anybody was paying much attention to the CDO warehouse in New York. On the contrary, most of the senior officials who worked at the elegant Bahnhofstrasse office still had only the scantest idea what the CDO desk was doing. But the UBS leaders knew that whenever a financial system enjoys a period of heady expansion, banks – and bankers – tend to do stupid things. And by the spring of 2007, global markets seemed to be in the grip of a wild party. There was so much money swirling around the system that the cost of borrowing money had collapsed, and financiers were competing with each other to invest in all manner of risky ventures. Loans to subprime mortgage borrowers, or American households with a bad credit score, were booming. So were loans to finance leveraged buyouts, venture capital, and other risky corporate ventures.

This pattern made the UBS bankers very nervous, particularly given that they liked to think of themselves as a risk-averse, prudent group. They were keenly aware that back in 1998 Union Bank had suffered embarrassing losses from its ill-judged investments in the Long-Term Captial Management hedge fund. The UBS managers were determined to avoid making similar mistakes. So the top managers held a series of meetings to discuss the risks facing the bank, to rein these in before they caused any damage.

They identified two main problems. One was the state of the bank's corporate lending book, and its loans to potentially risky companies. A decade earlier, some of UBS's rivals, such as Credit

Suisse, had suffered big losses from the collapse of the Internet bubble, since that had caused a host of technology companies to default on their loans.[43] As it happened, UBS itself had not been hit too badly during that particular episode. But the headquarters of Credit Suisse sat a few yards away on Zurich's Bahnhofstrasse, in another sober gray building, and the UBS bankers were determined not to suffer the same fate. So in early 2007, the bank asked Ernst & Young to conduct an audit of all of UBS's risky corporate loans.[44] The results of the exercise were fairly reassuring: after looking at the corporate loans that UBS held on its books, Ernst & Young declared that the Swiss bank had managed its risks prudently. The bank had stayed out of most of the potentially dangerous leveraged buyouts and private equity loans in 2006, and where it was involved in making risky bets, it had charged a high fee that helped to compensate it for the danger.[45] 'We had a conservative stance toward leveraged finance,' Phil Lofts, a UBS banker who was running the credit risk section (the part of the bank that oversaw risky corporate loans), later recalled. 'We were [only] in one or two deals that ran into trouble, like LyondellBasell [a deal to fund a chemical company merger].'

The second source of concern lay with a hedge fund that UBS was running, called Dillon Read Capital Management. This had been created back in 2005, when some of the Wall Street traders that Costas and Ospel had hired at the start of their expansion campaign had become fed up with the conservative style of the bank and threatened to leave. To stop this, Costas persuaded the UBS management to create a dedicated hedge fund, and then gave up his job as head of UBS Investment Bank to run this unit.[46]

DRCM was free to take risky trades, but it was ring-fenced from the rest of the bank. This was initially done to ensure that DRCM could attract funds from outside investors without violating any regulations. However, ring-fencing the hedge fund had another benefit: many of the more conservative Swiss bankers hated the idea of using UBS money to take big proprietary bets, and wanted to keep the hedge fund at a distance. They liked to think of themselves as a sober, risk-averse bank.

During 2006, DRCM expanded and its proprietary bets appeared to perform well.[47] But by early 2007, DRCM was producing losses, partly because the hedge fund traders had misjudged the direction of the U.S. housing market.[48] By the spring, the losses were estimated to be heading towards $300 million. The UBS managers were horrified. The losses confirmed all their worst fears about the dangers of proprietary trading.

The UBS bankers conducted an audit of the hedge fund's portfolio, and forced the fund to sell some of its assets. But these were so illiquid that when the fund tried to sell $100 million of specialized housing bonds, this created a $50 million loss in just one day.[49] Bitter fights erupted between Costas and UBS management in the Zurich headquarters. The top managers knew it would be embarrassing to shut the fund down so quickly after creating it. Costas was a formidable name. But the UBS board could not stand the idea of suffering these losses. So in May 2007, after months of wrangling, the bank announced that it would close down DRCM.[50] It was such a humiliating retreat that in the following month Peter Wuffli, the chairman of the board, was forced to resign. But the closure also underscored a crucial message that UBS wanted to project to the outside world (and itself): it considered itself risk-averse.

Yet, even as the UBS board fretted about Costas's hedge fund, and conducted endless surveys of its corporate loans, there was one issue that it did *not* debate: the mortgage-linked CDOs that were sitting in the CDO warehouse. By the spring of 2007, it was widely known that America's long housing boom was coming to an end. House prices were no longer rising as quickly as before, and even falling in some states. There were reports of mounting subprime defaults. At some banks, this news had prompted the top management to clamp down on businesses that dealt with U.S. mortgage bonds. Just down the Bahnhofstrasse in Zurich, Credit Suisse was cutting its exposure to the market. Brady Dougan, the CEO of Credit Suisse Investment Bank, was a seasoned bond trader[51] who had lived through violent swings of the credit cycle on Wall Street before, and he could sense that the financial climate was changing.

At UBS, however, the top managers did not feel any need to act. That was partly because the men running the investment bank had less experience of bond markets. The man who replaced Costas as head of UBS Investment Bank, Huw Jenkins, had risen through the ranks of the equity department.[52] But the other reason that the UBS leadership were more relaxed than Credit Suisse was that they did not think the bank was running any risk from its exposure to U.S. mortgage products at all.

Back in 2005, when the bank had first started creating CDOs, its own internal risk managers had conducted a brief debate about how they should classify these new instruments in the bank's accounts. Should they be placed in the category of 'mortgages,' which were considered moderately risky? Or should they be simply treated as AAA assets, since they were considered ultra-safe? It was not an easy issue to resolve, since nobody had created a AAA bond with risky subprime mortgage loans before. The UBS risk managers were thus like botanists in a jungle, confronted with a new plant that did not fit into the existing taxonomies. But in the end, they simply chose to focus on the AAA tag, and placed these instruments in that bucket, in the accounts. That meant that the bank did not need to post a big reserve against possible losses if it held these assets on its books. But it also meant that the banks' own risk managers tended to ignore the CDOs. When they tallied up all the assets that the bank held in internal reports to the board, the risk managers and auditors generally did not even split the CDOs into a separate category in the accounts, but simply lumped them together with other AAA assets, such as treasuries. Due to this system of classification, the assets in the CDO warehouse in New York had vanished in plain sight.

This did not mean that the bankers entirely ignored mortgage risk. From time to time, regulators would visit the different teams in New York and London, and ask them about the bank's exposure to the American housing market. The senior managers from UBS headquarters did the same. But the team that worked in London did not have much information about what was happening in New York, and vice versa; each team only knew about its own books.

In London, for example, one team of UBS traders was trading mortgage bonds, and during the course of 2006 and early

2007 they placed big trading bets that would produce profits as American house prices fell. So when the regulators from Switzerland visited the London offices, the UBS risk officer told them that the bank was 'short' housing risk. But the CDO operation in New York was 'long' the market, because the warehouse was creating CDOs. The bank also had exposure to mortgage bonds as a result of trades it had made with a category of insurance companies known as 'monolines.'[53] The New York long exposures were dramatically bigger than the short positions that the London team held. But nobody normally tallied these positions up, or presented them to the UBS board that way. 'There were many formal reports [in the bank] which sought to present a portfolio view of UBS's risks, including reports that sought to capture real estate securities and loan exposure,' UBS later admitted in a report that it wrote for shareholders.[54] 'However, there was no comprehensive view available ... due to incomplete data capture.' What was true on a micro level was not correct on a macro level.

Inside UBS, there were plenty of people who could have spotted that discrepancy – if they had chosen to do so. The traders who were handling mortgage bonds in London, for example, could have asked hard questions about what was happening in the CDO warehouse. The financiers in New York who were running the CDO warehouse could have told the investment bankers in London to take a look at the swelling size of their books. But none of the teams had an incentive to share much information with each other. The CDO traders in New York did not want anybody in London meddling with their profit streams. The traders in

London did not have much incentive to speculate in public about what might be happening in New York, since that was unlikely to help them get paid. As Upton Sinclair the novelist once observed, 'It is difficult to get a man to understand something, when his salary depends upon his not understanding it!'[55] In theory, UBS liked to say that all these departments were joined together on a single matrix. In practice, though, the operations looked more akin to a collection of competing tribes.

The risk officers were also fragmented. In theory, the bank had 3,000 risk officers who were supposed to monitor in a holistic way what the bankers were doing,. But these risk officers worked in three different departments that tracked different types of risk (credit risk, market risk, and operational risk[56]). These teams did not talk to each other very much. Nor did they swap information. That made a mockery of the idea of risk management, since the risk department was supposed to look at the dangers facing the entire bank. However, the bankers rarely noticed this; like every other part of the classification system, it was simply taken for granted. Generally, the bankers at UBS did not have any incentive to question it.

In the spring of 2007, when the Swiss regulators went to London to conduct their usual examination, they asked the UBS risk managers to describe the bank's exposure to the U.S. housing market. The risk officers talked about the shorts that the London team had taken out. They also spoke about some of the positions held by the Costas hedge fund. However, they did not mention the New York positions at all. 'The super senior CDO positions . . . were not included in the risk reports,'[57] the regulators later observed, adding that the 'Chief Risk Officer of the Investment Bank was not [even] aware of the existence' of the super senior CDO warehouse.

The regulators did not see any reason to query the picture presented by the chief risk officer, who seemed genuinely convinced that UBS was short housing market risk. So the regulators passed this message back to the UBS management, who were relieved that they had been given a clean bill of health.[58] 'If [those CDOs] had been included, the internal calculations would not have shown any short exposure at that time ... [but] this incorrect assessment resulting from the incomplete data was also passed on to the [UBS] Corporate Center [in Zurich],' the regulators noted. 'From this point on the bank's management placed its trust in the supposed short positions and shifted its attention to other, seemingly bigger risks.'

As the spring wore on, the managers in the granite building on Bahnhofstrasse kept fretting endlessly about the dangers of risky corporate loans. But they barely talked about mortgages at all. 'The Group Senior Management was alert to general issues concerning the deteriorating US housing market [but] they did not demand a holistic presentation of UBS's exposure to securities referencing US real estate assets,' the UBS shareholder report later admitted. '[This] was in contrast with the attention that Group Senior Management gave, for instance, to leveraged finance transactions which were subject to extensive debate.'[59] It was a situation akin to the operators of a nuclear plant fretting endlessly about how to control the dangers arising from ultra-complex fission processes, while ignoring deadly cracks in the concrete walls of the building that were expanding under their very nose, hidden in plain sight.

ON AUGUST 6, 2007, the UBS edifice started to crack.[60] By then, the party in the global financial markets had turned sour. In the early summer of that year it had emerged that a fatal problem was besetting the business of securitization. This had boomed between 2002 and 2007, as bankers repackaged mortgage loans and corporate debt and sold these to new investors. But when the U.S. housing market started to deteriorate, some mortgage borrowers began to default, creating a contagious sense of fear. To return to the analogy of the butcher again, the financial markets faced the equivalent of a food poisoning scare: as investors realized that some bad mortgage loans (or rotten meat) might be sitting in the financial sausages that bankers had been selling into the market, they became worried about the health of complex products such as CDOs. Nobody could quite identify where those losses were likely to be sitting, because the packages of remixed loans were so complex. But as fear mounted, investors played safe and stopped buying all mortgage assets. Prices plunged and the markets froze.

Initially, the UBS directors did not think that this panic would hurt their bank. After all, it was *corporate* loans, not mortgage loans, that UBS managers were worried about. 'The board of directors and group executive board were convinced, up until the end of July 2007, that their investments in the subprime market were secure,'[61] as Straumann, the Swiss professor who was asked to write a report on the UBS, debacle later observed. 'All risk reports, as well as the internal and external audits, had arrived at the conclusion that UBS would be able to deal with declining [U.S.] real estate prices without any difficulty.' But when the board gathered for its regular meeting in Zurich in early August, they received a shock. They were told that though the traders in London had gone short the U.S. housing market, the bank had a CDO warehouse in New York that was holding more than $20 billion super senior CDOs.[62] The board members were stunned. 'Most of us had no idea what "super senior" meant – we had never heard this word before,' one of the UBS directors confessed.[63] Or as the regulators noted in a report: 'Many senior managers claimed that they only found out about the super senior CDOs when the crisis broke in August 2007.'[64]

Initially, the board members did not panic. After all, they reasoned, those bonds were called 'super senior' because they were super safe. It was client business, not the type of proprietary activity that had caused such havoc at the hedge fund. 'People were probably more worried about the leveraged loans,' Lofts observed. So after the UBS board finished its meeting in early August it issued a bland warning to shareholders that indicated there might be some modest future losses from the mortgage markets – and asked the top managers to investigate further.

What this report revealed, however, was alarming: mortgage borrowers were defaulting on their debts on a large scale and scared investors were dumping bonds linked to those mortgages. That had caused the price of the super senior CDO tranches to plunge by 30 percent or more. That was alarming in itself. But what was doubly worrying was that UBS bankers had never made any preparations for this type of scenario. The problem, once again, lay with the classification system, and the UBS bankers' failure to question it. Back in 2005, when the UBS bankers started buying those super senior instruments on a large scale, they had classified them as 'marketable' instruments (or products traded in the markets) rather than 'credit' or 'banking book' assets (loans). The distinction sounded complex and theoretical. However, it had a practical implication: when instruments were classified as marketable, banks were not required to take a large reserve of capital onto its book. Thus UBS had never posted big reserves of capital against the risk that the CDOs might lose value. The models that the bankers use to measure the risks of these instruments suggested these should never lose more than 2 percent of their value. Thus UBS was only equipped to deal with losses up to that level. Now the market price of these CDOs had tumbled 30 percent, blowing a hole in the bank's accounts.

As the losses mounted, the UBS chief risk officer for the bank was unceremoniously fired. A new man, Joseph Scoby, who hailed from the asset management business, put in charge.[65] He promptly set about changing the entire classification system. For the first time, CDOs were ripped out of the 'safe' category in the bank's accounts. Instead of being lumped together with treasuries and other AAA assets, they were moved into an accounting category of their own. Then the risk managers tallied up the different pieces of the bank's exposure to mortgages for the first time. The picture shocked them. 'We would sit in these meetings, and go: "Whaaaat the fuck?"' one risk officer from that period later explained. 'People just could not believe it.' Almost overnight, the bankers realized that they had completely misunderstood the world: the 'risky' hedge funds had actually been less dangerous than the 'safe' client business. The entire classification system had been upside down. 'It suddenly hit me that we'd been worrying about that $300 million that [the hedge fund] dropped – but we had ignored ten times that in the CDO book!' another senior banker observed.

Frantically, the UBS board scrambled to repair the damage. But the losses on the mortgage CDOs kept swelling as the price of the bonds dropped. First, the bank admitted to $10 billion in losses. Then, this swelled to $18.7 billion.[66] By the spring of 2009 the bank had revealed a loss of more than $30 billion.[67] As the pain spread the anger of politicians, regulators – and Swiss voters – intensified. From time to time, the UBS managers tried to point out that they were certainly not the only bankers suffering from these losses. Banks such as Citigroup and Merrill Lynch announced similar devastating write-offs.[68] So did other institutions, ranging from insurance giant AIG to Allied Bank in Ireland. As the scandals spread, the same themes kept reemerging over and over again: almost anywhere you looked, banks, insurance companies, and asset managers had failed to spot the risks building up in separate desks and departments, because different silos of gigantic institutions did not communicate with each other and nobody at the top could see the entire picture. 'All of these leadership flaws are virtually a hallmark of large banks,' Straumann observed in his report, noting that 'Citigroup was compelled to undertake write-downs in even greater amounts' than UBS.[69] But that UBS was in a widening club was not much comfort. Or not when the reputation of the bank lay in tatters. Nobody was surprised when UBS announced in the middle of 2009 that Ospel would resign. By then many of the other senior managers from the bank were gone too.[70]

IN THE MONTHS AFTER the crisis, the new leaders at UBS tried to repair the damage. The bad mortgage assets were scooped off the bank's books and placed in a special vehicle at the behest of the Swiss government. The idea was that this ring-fencing would create more transparency and make it easier to remove the rotten assets. The section of the bank where the risk managers worked – or the 'risk controllers' department,' as it came to be called – was overhauled, and its fragmented divisions combined, supposedly into a seamless whole. 'We have changed the reporting lines completely – risk controllers don't report to the business heads anymore,' Lofts explained. 'We brought market risk and credit risk control together in the business divisions for the first time. They don't just sit in silos anymore, but are joined, and not just at the top of the bank.'

The information technology systems were overhauled to make it easier for top managers to see all the trading positions held by the bank. 'The recording of positions, their valuation, and the assessment of their risks and the effect on the profits and loss account are now regulated on a group-wide basis,' the bank explained. 'Each business unit must be able to explain its balance sheet ... on standardized measurements.'[71] Independent directors were brought into the board in a bid to combat the dangers of groupthink. 'Now we have a risk committee comprised of all nonexecutives, and none of these had previously worked for the firm,' explained Lofts, who was appointed as chief risk officer for the entire bank after the crisis hit.[72]

Different branches of the bank tried to introduce ways to think and act in a more holistic and lateral manner. Alex Friedman, chief investment officer, started holding brainstorming sessions with staff from different parts of the bank, encouraging people to toss around ideas in a free-form manner. In Switzerland, the retail bank started cooperating with the private bank in order to swap customers and ideas. Traditionally, these two units had been run as competing fiefdoms; now everyone was being encouraged to collaborate. 'We manage the business in a more integrated way now,' explained Christian Wiesendanger, head of UBS Wealth Management in Switzerland.[73] 'We look at how we can leverage across business groups and we are now trying to talk about the company.' In New York, initiatives were launched to force different desks to collaborate in different asset classes and take a holistic view. The new mantra was that UBS would aim to be a flexible, joined-up bank. Rigid boundaries were to be torn down.

The UBS managers insisted that these reforms were changing the culture. In places it was true. But reform was, at best, patchy. In September 2011, a year after the bank had repeatedly declared that it would never again let itself suffer poor risk controls, it admitted that it had lost over $2 billion due to unauthorized trades carried out by Kweku Adoboli, a junior member of the synthetic equities trading team in London. Adoboli traded an instrument known as exchange traded funds, or ETFs.[74] Like the mortgage CDO world, the business of trading ETFs was a corner of finance that was supposed to be slow-moving and safe. But, as with CDOs, the ETF world carried subtle risks. Nobody outside the department had spotted the problems until it was too late, since the ETF department sat in a tiny silo.

The UBS management tried to brush the incident off as an idiosyncratic mistake. They unveiled more reforms to the bank's risk control system, senior managers resigned, and the remaining officials pledged to make the bank even more transparent and better run. But shareholders in UBS were wearily cynical. 'The lesson from the banking crisis is that the management of all the banks that collapsed, or would have collapsed but for taxpayer funding, were not up to the job,' observed Tony Shearer, the former chief executive of Singer and Friedlander, a small British-Icelandic bank that failed during the 2008 crisis when the Icelandic parent company went bankrupt.[75] 'Management just does not appreciate that the task [of running banks] is bigger than they are capable of handling [and] institutional shareholders are too often part of those same "too big" financial institutions to address the issue,' he added, lamenting that 'financial institutions are too big, diverse, complex and geographically spread for any group of management.' The silo problem, in other words, seemed like the Hydra from Greek legends, or the famous snake monsters with multiple heads. From time to time the bank would slay its silos. But just when people hoped the problem had died away, it reared its head again. Fragmentation was an ever-present threat, and not just at UBS, but at almost every other big financial institution, too.

But thankfully, this is not the entire tale. There is another, more encouraging aspect to this saga, which this book will explore in later pages. The story of the Great Financial Crisis shows that silos were (and are) debilitating for banks. But there is another side of this coin: although silos create losers at the institutions that are plagued with tunnel vision, they can also create opportunities for rivals. After all, it is a long-standing adage of finance that whenever somebody loses money in the markets, somebody else is usually making it at their expense. The stunning losses that UBS and others suffered on CDOs were gains for somebody else. Silos spell disaster for people who are afflicted by them. They can also create opportunity for others.

In chapter 8, I shall turn to this aspect of this story, by telling the tale of how one hedge fund has deliberately exploited the silos that exist in finance and at big banks such as UBS. But first, we shall turn to another story, which illustrates another set of distortions in the financial markets, but one found in the public sector, not private companies: namely the tale of how economists at places such as the U.S. Federal Reserve and the Bank of England misread the financial system before the great crisis of 2008.

4

RUSSIAN DOLLS

How Silos Create Tunnel Vision

'An expert knows all the answers – if you ask the right questions.'

—Claude Lévi-Strauss

THE QUEEN OF ENGLAND WAS STANDING IN A HALL AT THE LONDON SCHOOL of Economics looking a little perplexed. The date was November 4, 2008, and the queen had arrived at the LSE, one of the premier universities in the world, to open a new building. Cheering crowds of tourists, students, and children lined the narrow streets, waving Union Jacks, as she arrived wearing suitably formal attire: a speckled cream suit, large matching hat with a cream bow, discreet pearls, and black gloves.

The event was supposed to be a celebration of academic achievement and genius. But the timing was poignant. Two months earlier the brutal financial crisis had erupted in London and many other parts of the West, which had caused a string of banks to collapse, the markets to freeze up, and the Western world to slide into a deep precession. The impact had damaged the fortunes of wealthy families (such as the queen). But it had had even more devastating consequences for the less well off: unemployment was spiraling upward, and thousands of families in America and the U.K. were being tossed out of their houses.

These dramatic events had left hordes of economists and pundits scurrying to provide analysis. The London School of Economics was no exception. Its economists were deemed to be among the most brilliant in the world, and the university has close connections with the British government, as well as ministries all over the world. Mervyn King, one LSE luminary, was governor of the Bank of England, an institution that sat just a couple of miles east. The dean of LSE, Howard Davies, had been the top U.K. regulator. Charles Goodhart, another LSE professor, also had a top role at the bank. All of these brilliant minds had strong views about how the financial system and economy was supposed to work; or sometimes *not* work. So, as the queen toured the building, Luis Garicano, yet another highly regarded economist, presented her with some charts that purported to show what was going on in finance.

The queen peered at the brightly colored lines. 'It's awful!' she declared, in her clipped, upper-class vowels. It was a startling break with the usual protocol: the royal family was famous for avoiding any comment on sensitive political matters.

'Why did nobody see the crisis coming?' she asked. 'If [the problems] were so big, why did nobody see it?'[1]

Smoothly, Garicano tried to present an answer: the real issue, he argued, was *not* that economists and financiers were ill-intentioned or stupid; it was rather that they had been looking in the wrong places, at the wrong time. A dramatic shift had occurred in the financial system due to innovations such as securitization. But though lots of people had understood separate pieces of the picture, nobody had been able to take an overview, and see that a crisis was about to hit. 'People were doing what they were paid to do, but nobody could see the whole picture, or join it up.'

The queen clutched her black handbag; she did not seem to find the explanation entirely convincing. No wonder: her subjects were baffled too, along with much of the West. To noneconomists it seemed almost impossible that a collection of people who were supposed to have some of the smartest brains on the planet, and be involved in running governments, could have been so foolish. It was hard to believe they could have all turned blind, or stupid, overnight. It seemed easier to presume that bankers had somehow 'tricked' the regulators by hiding their activities in a fraudulent way.

But in truth, Garicano's 'explanation' was more telling than perhaps even he realized. For the story of the credit crisis shows that even experts (or, perhaps, *especially* experts) can collectively become very blind when they organize their surroundings into excessively rigid silos. Chapter Two of this book narrated the story of Sony to demonstrate how fragmented structures inside institutions can sometimes cause people to miss opportunities for innovation. Chapter Three related the tale of UBS to show that silos inside institutions can also make people blind to risks. This chapter provides another twist on this silo issue by telling the story of what happened to economists at places such as the Bank or England and the London School of Economics (or the U.S. Federal Reserve and Harvard University) before the 2008 crisis. Silos do not just arise inside institutions. They can also affect entire social groups. Networks of experts can become captured by silos, in the sense of displaying blinkered thinking and tribal behavior, even if they work in different institutions and countries. This is not a problem that is unique to the economic profession, any more than silos are an issue that is just found in banks. However, the story of the economics tribe is distinctly revealing, not least because it shows how skilled experts can become so confident in their own ideas that they end up missing dangers hidden in plain sight. Like the villagers in Bourdieu's dancehall, economists were so busy watching the 'dancers' (or the pieces of the economic picture that everyone was expected to watch), that they ignored the 'nondancers' (or the parts of the picture shrouded in social silence). 'Why did the crisis happen? It was partly about epistemology, the knowledge systems that we used,' Paul Tucker, the deputy governor of the Bank of England, later observed. Or as Charles Goodhart observed: '[The credit crisis] isn't really just a story about the structure of the Bank, or the Federal Reserve or any other organisation, but about the mental map we used – in academia, in policymaking, everywhere.

'Ideas matter and economists were all using the same ideas.' They were sitting in the same mental silo.

*

THE TALE OF PAUL Tucker's own journey through the tribal world of economic policy illustrates the problem of silos well. If a casual observer had met Tucker, the Bank's deputy governor, in the autumn of 2008, or just as the queen was touring the LSE, they might have thought he epitomized the modern economist-cum-policymaker. A mid-sized man, with a round, ruddy face, he exudes an avuncular air and speaks with crisp, polished vowels. Friends sometimes quipped that he sounded like a cerebral Winnie-the-Pooh. But he also exuded gravitas and whenever he spoke about the economy his words commanded respect in financial markets.

Tucker never set out to be an economist. Born in 1958 to a middle-class family, he grew up in England and went to Cambridge to study mathematics and philosophy. He vaguely liked the idea of public service. So in 1979 he applied for a job at the Bank of England, and though he lacked an economics degree he was accepted. 'In those days nobody thought that everyone had to have a PhD in economics to work at a central bank,' he explained. 'We had people who had double firsts in greats [Greek and Latin], history, and things like that.'

That reflected a particular vision of economics at that time. The root of the word 'economics' comes from two Greek words: the noun *oikos*, meaning 'house,' and the verb *nemein*, meaning 'to manage.'[2] Originally *oikonomia* was considered separate from markets and trading. It referred to 'the imposition of order on the practical affairs of a household,' or putting one's 'house in order,'[3] as the anthropologists Chris Hann and Keith Hart point out. Echoes of that original sense have appeared in subsequent decades: the nineteenth-century English novelist Jane Austen writes about her female characters being 'skilled at economics,' meaning clever at handling servants, while cookery and sewing classes in twentieth century American and British schools were sometimes called 'home economics.' This vision of 'economics' being akin to 'stewardship' has also influenced the development of the Bank of England.

During the first two centuries of the Bank's existence, it was taken for granted that money, society, and politics were entwined. Not only did the Bank create money at the behest of the government, but it also issued government debt, oversaw finance, and protected the interests of the City. Thus when young graduate recruits joined the Bank in the middle decades of the twentieth century, they were expected to be flexible about their jobs – and get a holistic view of how money moved around the economy. When Tucker joined the Bank he was initially placed in the financial monitoring section, where he tracked what was happening in the banking system and inside the commercial banks. Later he was sent to the macroeconomic research department, where he worked on monetary strategy using formal economic forecasting models (after teaching himself economics from lots of books he read on his vacations and weekends).[4] Then he changed again, moving to Hong Kong, where he kept an eye on the securities markets in Asia. 'By the late 1980s there was a clear sense that the Bank needed to upgrade its economics capability if we were to be a front-rank economic policymaker. But [we looked at] lots of signals, not just the economic data,' Tucker explained.

However, as Tucker ascended the Bank's hierarchy in the 1990s, he started to notice a subtle shift in how *oikonomia*, or economics, was perceived – and practiced. Back in the eighteenth and nineteenth centuries, when men such as Adam Smith, Thomas Malthus, David Ricardo, and John Stuart Mill pioneered the idea of studying the economy, it was considered normal to look at underlying economic forces alongside political and cultural analysis. But by the late nineteenth century, economics was becoming a distinct discipline of its own, separated from the other social sciences. And as the twentieth century wore on, this separation grew deeper. In the middle of the twentieth century economists such as Robert Lucas, of the University of Chicago, developed a theory of economics that assumed humans were always driven by rational expectations that could be accurately modeled. It lead to an assumption that economies were driven by uniform forces or laws of motion that could be equated to the universal laws of physics. Then economists started to use increasingly complex quantitative mathematical models to identify and make sense of economic trends. 'In economics, you get kudos from the subtlety and complexity of the mathematical approach as any ability to actually meet empirical tests,' points out LSE's Goodhart. 'The mathematical model is everything.'

The obsession with mathematics did not just affect academic economics; it spread into finance too. Just before Lucas was developing his vision of economies based on 'rational expectations,' Harry Markowitz, another economist, created the so-called capital asset pricing model, which tried to measure the risk of assets (and thus their supposed price) with statistics. This approach used a set of models that had been created by Kenneth Arrow and Gerard Debreu and became very influential. '[The Arrow-Debreu] mathematics was seized on as a road map towards the utopia of complete and efficient markets,' as Bill Janeway, an American venture capitalist and economist, observes.[5]

From time to time, social scientists poked fun at this obsession with numbers. So did some maverick economists. In 1973, for example, an unusually freethinking economist named Axel Leijonhufvud at the University of California, Los Angeles, wrote a droll essay called 'Life Among the Econ' in which he teased his colleagues over their obsession with mathematical models, describing these in the same terms that a Victorian-era anthropologist might employ to talk about a primitive tribe. 'The extreme clannishness, if not xenophobia, among the Econ [tribe] makes life among them difficult, if not dangerous, for an outsider,' he wrote.[6] 'For such a primitive people their social structure is quite complex. ... The status of the adult male is determined by his skill at making the "modl" [i.e., mathematical model] of his "field."'

Indeed, economists were so obsessed with their 'ornate, ceremonial modls,' Leijonhufvud joked, that it was almost impossible for an academic to become a tenured professor at a university unless they could show competence with these tools. Economists who were less interested in mathematics, and consorted with nonmathematical 'tribes,' such as political scientists or sociologists, tended to have low status. Quantiative economists sat at the top of the tribal hierarchy. 'The fact that the

Econ are (a) highly status-motivated, (b) that status is only to be achieved by making "modls," and (c) that most of these "modls" seem to be of little or no practical use, probably accounts for the backwardness and abject cultural poverty of the tribe,' he continued.[7]

Leijonhufvud's comments created mirth in social science departments. But mainstream economists ignored them. The discipline was not used to thinking of itself as a 'tribe,' or reflecting on its own cultural patterns. That was partly because economists were downplaying social analysis in their own work. But another factor – as the anthropologist Bourdieu often liked to point out – was that the 'Econ tribe' was becoming so powerful that it had no incentive to question the status quo. By the middle of the twentieth century, governments, companies, and banks were increasingly hiring economists to work out what was happening to the economy and predict what might happen next. Most ordinary onlookers had little idea how economists actually made these seemingly impressive predictions. The complex mathematical models they used were as mysterious to nonexperts as the Latin that priests spoke in the Catholic Church in Europe during its Middle Ages. But to outsiders, these models seemed powerful and the economists almost priestlike. University economics departments, such as that of the London School of Economics, began to look like seminaries.

And as the twentieth century wore on, this sense of an economic priesthood became more intense. In the 1970s men such as Tucker had been able to join the Bank with 'just' a degree in philosophy and math. By the end of the twentieth century it was assumed that a BA or PhD in economics was an essential qualification for working at a Western central bank or finance ministry. '[Former Bank governor] Eddie George and I wanted to recruit more economists because we needed people who could match the [British] Treasury in terms of economic analysis,' King later explained. 'We realized we had to have people who understood how things worked and were not scared of analysis.' The same pattern was at work at the Federal Reserve and U.S. Treasury. In the middle decades of the twentieth century, the American central bank had sometimes recruited officials who had law degrees, science degrees (or sometimes no degree at all). By the end of the century, however, its junior recruits invariably had degrees in economics, if not doctorates, and its leaders were expected to be equally well qualified. Alan Greenspan was typical of the new breed. When he was appointed chairman of the Federal Reserve in 1987, he arrived with a PhD in economics.[8] It had been acquired fairly late in his career, and it did not carry quite the same intellectual prestige as some of the doctorates of his successors. But Greenspan clearly felt that having a PhD in economics was an important – if not essential – tool to gain credibility. And in subsequent years Greenspan was at pains to highlight his passion for economic models. Indeed, he loved creating economic models so much that even after he arrived at the Fed he continued to construct his own private models in his spare time. He liked to describe it as his 'hobby.'[9]

*

IN 2002, TUCKER WAS promoted to run the market surveillance division of the Bank of England, or the piece of the Bank's bureaucracy that oversaw how the financial system operated. On paper, it seemed a big honor since running the markets team had traditionally been a high-status job. 'Eddie George used to grab the best economists and put them into the markets team, because everyone thought it was so important,' King recalled. 'Before 1992 ... the Bank's entrée into monetary policy was through "markets," although Eddie realized the importance of economic analysis.' Indeed, the promotion was so symbolic that it left Bank staff speculating that Tucker could end up becoming governor of the entire Bank one day; beneath his bluff, jolly exterior, he was an ambitious man.

However, as Tucker settled into his new, high-ceilinged office at the Bank, there was one big catch to his promotion. By the early twenty-first century, the status of the market surveillance department had declined. In 1997, a new British government came to power, and decided to overhaul how the central bank was run. The Bank was given formal independence for setting monetary policy and became a much more specialist organisation.[10] Most notably, the task of selling government debt was handed to a different government agency, called the Debt Management Office, and the job of supervising individual banks was handed to yet another body, known as the Financial Services Authority. That left the Bank with just a vague mandate to maintain 'financial stability.'

There was a second, more subtle issue. Economists were becoming less interested in money, and by default, in financial markets. In some respects, this shift might sound odd; after all, most noneconomists assume that money is at the heart of any modern economy, and the task of analyzing it central to what economists do. But in the second half of the twentieth century, as more economists started to imagine the economy as a 'system' governed by universal laws – or the vision of rational expectations that Lucas developed – a shift occurred in terms of how economists viewed money. Instead of regarding it as an interesting topic in its own right, it became a mere transmission device. The only reason that money was considered to be interesting was that it emitted price signals about supply and demand, comparable to the electrical wires on a circuit board. And insofar as economists studied money, they did so to understand what was happening with *other* interesting parts of the 'real' economy (such as consumer demand or productivity). This shift could be seen on the bookshelves of the Bank or LSE. Back in the middle of the twentieth century, when men such as Tucker had joined the Bank, new recruits studied books such as *Money, Interest and Prices* by Don Patinkin. Another popular text was a book that the LSE professor Charles Goodhart himself had written called *Money, Information, and Uncertainty.* However, by the start of the twenty-first century, the iconic text for new graduates was a tome called *Interest and Prices* by Michael Woodford. The word 'money' had vanished from the titles. 'There wasn't a manifesto claiming that we must push money out of the models, but it was almost instinctive – money had become passive, like a veil. More or less everyone assumed that all the forces of the economy are elsewhere, on the real side of the economy, and money just responds,' Tucker said. Or as Adair Turner, the man who later ran the Financial Services Authority, echoed: 'In the 1970s and 1980s you had a big change. Economics became much more mathematical – everything had to be put in a model, and it became hard to put credit or money into those models. Banking courses were removed from under-graduate economics courses.'

The man appointed as Bank governor in 2003, a year after Tucker's promotion, reflected this trend. A seemingly mild-mannered man with an impish sense of humor and owlish glasses, Mervyn King was a renowned economics professor at the LSE,[11] before he was appointed into a part-time role as an adviser in 1990. He then became chief economist before he was appointed governor. It was a move greeted with delight inside the City of London. King commanded great academic respect, and was determined to make the Bank independent and 'professional.' But though King was interested in monetary policy and macro-economics, he was perceived to be less interested in how money worked. He knew the contours of financial history and had written academic papers about stock market contagion. He had even established a group at the LSE when he was a professor to analyze finance. 'One of the things I did [in the 1990s] was force all of our recruits to do courses on financial history, and then I set up a dining society to talk about financial history,' he related. But he did not have much passion for studying the minutiae of modern markets. 'Mervyn was a macro [economics] man,' his colleague Goodhart recalled. That stance partly reflected expe-diency: King believed that the Bank's primary responsibility was to keep inflation low. But his views also reflected an intellectual bent: most economists believed that the grubby machinations of bankers sat in a different mental box from high-status economics. 'There was this strong sense in the Federal Reserve that economics and finance were two quite different things,' Charles Calomiris, a professor at Columbia Business School, observed. 'The people looking at markets sat in an entirely different department from the macroeconomic researchers.' A similar split was found at universities. 'Pure' economic analysis tended to take place in dedicated economics departments, while finance was studied in business schools. The media reflected this divide and reinforced it. (On my own newspaper, the *Financial Times*, the economics department sat in a different section from the markets team. And as I have described elsewhere, a similar pattern was seen at *The Wall Street Journal*, Bloomberg, and Reuters, and almost every other large news group.12) 'Almost everywhere you looked across the economic policy world, many of the people studying markets just felt like second-class citizens compared to people looking at economics,' Tucker observed. 'Some correction had been needed from decades in which markets were at the center of things, but it overshot.'

This schism frustrated Tucker. So, in 2002, after he was promoted inside the Bank to the run the markets team, he started to hunt for ways to put his department on the map. Twice a year the 120-strong market surveillance team wrote a comprehensive report on the financial system, known as the *Financial Stability Report,* which tried to understand how banks and other financial entities were performing. It also wrote more regular quarterly reports. Traditionally this research had focused on banks or stock markets, since these were the most visible and regulated institutions in the system. However, Tucker and his colleagues decided that they wanted to widen the lens, not least because the FSA, not the Bank, was now in charge of regulating the banks on a day-to-day basis. The FSA staff there did not want the Bank to step on its turf. So Tucker encouraged his team to start poking into the pieces of the financial system that lay *outside* the banks, or the areas the FSA did not control.

This research revealed something striking. Traditionally, when central banks and regulators had monitored the financial world, they had focused on regulated banks, since these appeared to be the most important parts of the system. Then, in the latter part of the twentieth century, regulators (and journalists) had started paying more attention to entities outside the banking world, such as hedge funds. This focus intensified after the Long-Term Capital Management hedge fund in New York almost collapsed in 1998.[13] But as the Bank staff widened their lens away from the banks after 2002, they spotted something important: although hedge funds tended to spark headlines, they were *not* the only beasts in the hinterland of finance that lay outside the regulated banks. A whole host of new entities and products were also emerging that carried strange names unfamiliar to people outside finance. Some of these new products were CDOs (the type of financial structures that I described in the last chapter). Others were 'conduits' or 'structured investment vehicles' (SIVs), which were essentially investment vehicles that could buy securities such as CDOs.

Those entities did not fit into the usual classification system that central bankers and regulators had previously used to classify the world. They were not like traditional banks; they did not take deposits or make loans. Instead the people running these vehicles raised money by selling short-term bonds to investors, and invested that cash in long-term securities, often bonds backed by American housing loans. But these entities were *not* hedge funds either. Hedge funds were best known for raising money from private individuals and wealthy institutions to invest in risky assets. But SIVs and conduits tried to look as dull as possible, buying instruments that were supposed to be ultra-safe, such as AAA-rated CDOs.

From time to time, Bank officials would debate what these shifts in finance might mean. Over in America, officials such as Greenspan tended to assume that the new innovations were good. They showed, he argued, that bankers were creating more efficient and innovative ways to move money around the economy. Over in Europe, some observers took a different view. In Basel, Switzerland, two leading economists at the Bank for International Settlements, Claudio Borio and William White, warned that the innovations might be dangerous, since nobody knew where they were spreading credit risk. Some of Tucker's colleagues, such as economist Andy Haldane, expressed unease about excessive levels of borrowing. But inside the Bank of England, most officials were either unaware of what was happening or reluctant to speak out in public. They assumed that it was the job of regulators – such as the Financial Services Authority – and not the economists to watch the new financial trends, since it was the FSA that had the authority to keep banks under control. Moreover, as King sometimes pointed out to his colleagues, the Bank did not have the policy tools to curb any potential bubble. The only thing it was formally allowed to do in relation to the banks was issue the financial stability reports, or tell the Financial Services Authority about its concerns, in private. 'Even if we had spoken up [about what we saw], we couldn't have done anything since we just did not have the powers,' King recounted. He was not somebody who liked to break bureaucratic rules or try to redefine the Bank's mandate. Instead he preferred to focus his attention on what he thought was his primary mandate: worrying about the 'real' economy.

IN LATE DECEMBER 2006, some four years after he had been promoted to run the markets surveillance team, Tucker traveled to the City of London headquarters of the Honourable Artillery Company, created by Henry VIII in 1537. He had been asked to give a speech to a collection of British grandees about the outlook for the economy. It was a routine task. However, Tucker was feeling baffled.[14] To most observers, the West seemed to be experiencing an economic golden age. Indeed, conditions seemed so upbeat that economists had christened the first decade of the twenty-first century the era of 'Great Moderation' or 'Great Stability.' 'The characteristics of the Great Stability, as some economists call it, are by now familiar. Essentially low inflation on average . . . and much lower volatility in both output growth and inflation,'[15] Tucker declared, as he stood in the historic wood-paneled hall. 'Private sector demand growth has been reasonably robust and looks . . . to continue to be robust for a little while at least. World growth weighted for its significance to UK trade has remained solid. . . . Business investment appears to be recovering. And consumption . . . looks most likely to grow close to its average rate.' Translated out of central bank jargon, that meant that if you imagined that the economy was like an airplane, it was heading in the right direction, with most of the dials on the pilot's instrument board signaling that all was well. Everyone could relax.

But there was one other economic statistic, or dial on that instrument board, that made Tucker uneasy. This was the statistical series called 'broad money,' or M4, which showed how much cash and credit was floating around the economy. Classic economic theory suggests that when economies are expanding fast, broad money in the economy grows in tandem with the price of goods, or inflation. Conversely, when growth is slowing, the pace of broad money expansion slows too, which often reduces inflation. Indeed, that relationship has been so well defined that in the middle of the twentieth century, central bankers often decided whether to raise interest rates on the basis of what the broad money data showed.

But in December 2006, this long-standing relationship had broken down. The British inflation rate was low, running at around 2 percent, and the growth rate seemed healthy but not excessive. The M4 data dial on the instrument board of the economic airplane, however, was spinning out of control. 'UK broad money is up around 15 per cent on a year and more than 25 per cent since the beginning of 2005,' Tucker declared.[16]

Did this mismatch matter? A few months earlier, Tucker had

asked some of his staff to carry out some detective work, to work out why M4 was expanding so fast. His team had told him that the main reason was a rapid increase in the amount of borrowing and lending by a group of entities labeled 'Other Financial Corporations' in the statistics. This OFC bucket was essentially the 'miscellaneous' box, where statisticians put anything that did not fit into the normal classification system. These were entities that were defined by what they were *not* – i.e., not banks, brokers, insurance companies, or the other entities that statisticians knew well.

Tucker asked his staff to dig into that miscellaneous OFC box. They uncovered a *second* miscellaneous category of unidentified entities inside the OFC box called 'Other Financial Intermediaries.' That was where statisticians placed the misfits of the misfits, or things that sat even further out of the classification system. The data on these entities was sketchy. But Tucker's colleagues guessed that the entities in this box were mostly the CDOs, SIVs, conduits, or the strange new beasts in the jungle that Tucker's team had first spotted back in 2002. 'Over the past year, the largest contributions to OFC money growth have, in fact, come from . . . what the statisticians label "Other Financial Intermediaries" (contributing a whopping seventeen percentage points),'[17] Tucker explained to the crowd in the Honourable Artillery Company hall. 'Collectively, [OFIs] . . . have been growing at an annual rate of over forty per cent for the past two years.'[18]

Did that have any significance for the economy as a whole? It seemed impossible to tell, since the people doing macroeconomic analysis had not tried to link the trends in the core economics statistics to what was happening in this murky OFC world. 'It is extremely difficult to judge the macroeconomic significance of what the growth of broad money – or OFC money – might mean' Tucker lamented. 'There is relatively little research on the macro-economic significance of OFC money.'[19] The area was a blank space on the map; or like the nondancers in Bourdieu's village hall. The economists were looking at what they presumed that they were supposed to watch, namely models of 'real' economy statistics. But they did not look at the bits of the economy that sat outside that world, or try to connect the different realms. Indeed, the split between finance and economics was so deeply ingrained that many economists barely noticed it at all. They spent hours questioning the finer details of their mathematical equations. However, they rarely pondered the classification system they used. Or noticed the boundaries this imposed.

'Did anyone try to link what was happening in CDO land to the macroeconomy? With hindsight, the answer is not enough,' King said. 'But the question is what follows from that? It was not because people were not studying CDOs. ... [But] there were too many people focused on detail and there was so much paper produced that it was impossible to see the woods for the trees.' Indeed, when King later tried to work out what had gone wrong, he tended to think that the Bank had too *much* intelligence sitting inside its walls, not too little. However, those brilliant minds were simply not focusing on the right thing. Men such as King knew about the existence of all the new financial innovations. Indeed, soon after Tucker's speech King referred to them in a talk to an audience at the Mansion House, another venerable City of London institution. But men such as King did not spend much (if any) time pondering what the appearance of these strange financial beasts might mean for monetary policy. 'Most public sector institutions suffer from the problem of an excess of bright young people and too few experienced people with the ability and perspective to see what detail matters and what does not,' he lamented. 'Our biggest problem with analysis was the difficulty in persuading young people to see the big picture and their managers to draw out the big picture.' Including, some of his colleagues might have added, the top managers at the central banks, such as King himself.

FOUR MONTHS LATER, IN April 2007, Tucker gave another public speech. This time the venue was a conference for hedge funds at a smart London hotel organized by Merrill Lynch, the Wall Street bank, for hedge funds. The mood was exuberant. 'World growth has been robust ... headline inflation across the industrialised world has remained contained. ... In short, the world has enjoyed a further period of monetary and financial stability,' Tucker told the crowd in the conference room. 'Banks and dealers have posted fairly remarkable profits. Returns of the fund sector – and so probably for most of you here today – have been healthy.'[20] Translated out of central bank jargon, that meant that times were good. Those men (and a few women) attending the Merrill conference were getting richer.

But, once again, Tucker felt unease. To his eyes, the dials on the economic instrument board did not seem to be moving in the normal way. The numbers on inflation and growth still looked healthy. But broad money kept rising. So did the price of assets such as houses and shares. In an effort to curb these increases, central banks such as the Bank of England and the Fed had repeatedly raised interest rates to make it more expensive to borrow money. But this monetary policy tightening had not stopped the party. Money kept swirling around the economy at a pace that did not entirely make sense. Or not if you looked at the normal economic models.

Tucker suspected that the reason for this discrepancy lay in the entities outside the banks. Somehow all those CDOs, SIVs, and conduits were pushing money around the financial system in a manner that policymakers and economists did not understand. But it was one thing to have a hunch. It was much harder to actually prove that something was going wrong when there was so little data. In any case, King had made it very clear to his colleagues that he did not want Bank staff ringing too many alarm bells; that was the FSA responsibility.

So Tucker decided that the best thing to do was simply to point out that this strange new hinterland of hard-to-define entities existed – and let investors draw their own conclusions. He hoped that more public debate and scrutiny might keep these innovations under control. 'The key intermediaries [in finance] are no longer just banks, securities dealers, insurance companies, mutual funds and pension funds,' he told the Merrill Lynch audience. 'They include hedge funds of course, but also Collateralised Debt Obligations, specialist Monoline Financial Guarantors, Credit Derivative Product Companies, Structured

Investment Vehicles, Commercial Paper conduits, Leverage Buyout Funds – and on and on. … SIVs may hold monoline-wrapped AAA-tranches of CDOs, which may hold tranches of other CDOs … and hold LBO debt of all types as well as asset-backed securities bundling together household loans.'[21]

Tucker knew that this sounded like gobbledygook to most listeners. Indeed, one reason it was easy to ignore this shadowy world was *precisely* because this language sounded so alien. In a world where technology keeps becoming more complex, we all tend to turn our eyes away from specialist jargon we do not understand. Professional experts wield power precisely because they wrap their craft in language that is labeled as the preserve of 'geeks.' It is hard to start a public policy debate if there are no widely accessible words to explain the ideas being conveyed, and when it came to nonbank finance, it seemed that there were no good phrases available at all.

So, as he stood in the hall at the Merrill conference, Tucker tried to offer his audience some mental labels to cut through the jargon. Instead of calling these new financial innovations by strange acronyms such as SIVs or CDOs – or OFIs of OFCs – why not use a catchier label? Might, he suggested, 'vehicular finance' work? After all, money was being moved via financial 'vehicles.' Or could a phrase like 'Russian doll finance' express what was going on? These new entities were so tightly entwined, they nestled together like Russian dolls.[22] Then Tucker presented a chart to the audience of how he thought these financial entities worked. He hoped that a picture could communicate what words did not capture. 'This may or may not help,' he joked.

It did not work. The phrase 'vehicular finance' was difficult to say and evoked images of cars, not high finance. 'Russian doll finance' sounded as if it was linked to shadowy oligarchs. When journalists later wrote reports about Tucker's speech to the Merrill conference, almost all of them ignored the part of his speech talking about modern finance. Instead, they just focused on some bland comments in the other parts of his speech that touched on issues that journalists (and economists) *did* recognize: the state of the British housing market, inflation trends, interest rates. These, after all, were the issues that were at the center of economists' and journalists' mental map. A newspaper headline about 'OFIs of OFCs' did not make sense; it sat too far off the mainstream mental map. OFIs were an area of social silence.[23]

FOUR MONTHS LATER, THE cognitive and linguistic breakthrough that Tucker had sought occurred. However, this step did not take place inside the Bank, but 4,000 miles to the west. Each August since 1978, the Federal Reserve Bank of Kansas City has organized a high-profile gathering of academic economists, central bankers, journalists, and government officials in Jackson Hole, the Rocky Mountain ski resort.[24] These high-altitude debates are often dull and academic. However, in August 2007, the annual gathering took place against an alarming backdrop: around the world, financial markets were freezing up.

The first signs of this crisis had emerged at the start of the summer, when the price of bonds linked to mortgages in America had tumbled. Initially, most observers thought that this development was simply a temporary wobble. After all, they reasoned, by the summer of 2007 the global economy had just enjoyed a long boom, which had pushed house prices higher. It seemed natural – if not inevitable – that some correction would take place. Over at the Federal Reserve, Ben Bernanke, another economics professor, who had replaced Alan Greenspan as the new chairman, declared the turmoil would soon be over, and create no more than $25 billion in losses on mortgage bonds, a tiny fraction of the overall U.S. economy.[25] The Bank of England's Mervyn King expressed similar thoughts. There did not seem reason to panic.

But as the summer wore on, the sense of anxiety steadily worsened. Around the world, a host of different investment groups were refusing to trade with each other. Market confidence in the banks was crumbling. The price of assets such as mortgage bonds was collapsing. This scale of panic was baffling to the economists gathered in Jackson Hole in August. After all, the data suggested that the underlying – 'real' – economies in Europe and the United States were healthy. Statistics about the state of the banking sector seemed reassuring too.

But on the second day of the Jackson Hole conference, an asset manager from California called Paul McCulley made an electrifying comment.[26] He was something of a maverick in the economics world. Though he worked for PIMCO, the giant bond fund, he sported a long gray ponytail.[27] He was trained as an economist, and familiar with abstract models. But he also loved talking with traders, to see what was happening in the darkest weeds of the global financial system, and the seemingly dull 'plumbing' mechanisms that moved money around the world. That perspective meant McCulley knew all about the financial vehicles that had caught the eye of Tucker. He did not like them: he feared that the design of these new innovations was fundamentally unstable, and had repeatedly told his colleagues in PIMCO's office in Orange County in California (and anyone else who might listen) to avoid cutting deals with SIVs, conduits, and so on. Somehow, as he debated the issues with his colleagues in the PIMCO office, McCulley started using the term 'shadow bank' to describe these strange beasts. 'I don't know where the word "shadow bank" came from, I might have heard it from an academic or something,' he later recalled. 'But we just started using it because it seemed convenient.'

As he stood on the conference podium in Jackson Hole with central bankers and economists, McCulley reached – almost unthinkingly – for his favorite phrase to tell the central bankers and other economists what was happening in the global markets. 'The real issue going on right now is a run on [the] shadow banking system,' he announced, likening the pattern to an old-fashioned run on banks. And if this run continued, the impact could be very dangerous, he added, precisely because almost nobody had paid any attention to this sector before.[28] 'It is the shadow banking system which is about $1.3 trillion in assets which is [the issue] at hand.'[29] The comment had an electrifying effect. Until then, most economists and policymakers had never pondered what lay outside the 'known' world of the banks or hedge funds. But McCulley had suddenly given a *name* to this world. Central bankers now had a phrase they could use in speeches. Journalists had catchy words to insert their headlines. Economists had a title to put into their charts or use in their columns and blogs.[30] Better still, McCulley had also offered a framework to understand why the markets were freezing up. The technical details of this run were complex. But the fundamental point was that investors who had been funding these shadow banks were panicking, since they had realized that these entities had quietly acquired a large volume of mortgage-backed securities.[31] Without funding, these vehicles were starting to collapse.

If the shadow banks had been tiny in size, this panic might have had no wider impact. But the problem, McCulley explained, was that the shadow banks were entwined with numerous parts of the financial system, in ways that policymakers had not spotted. They were like the tree roots in a forest, concealed from the gaze of a casual observer, but vast in scale, a network that tied the entire ecosystem together. More importantly, they were pumping credit into the economy in a way that had affected numerous different asset prices, causing parts of the economy and financial system to overheat. These entities alone had not created the credit that was inflating the bubble; that emanated from the savings glut in places such as China and other elements of imbalance in the world. But these entities had recycled money around the economy with such a speed and scale that few observers had understood that the system was overloaded with debt (or 'leverage,' to use the term that economists prefer) in a dangerous way. It was a classic cycle of boom and bust, of the sort that economists like Hyman Minsky had often warned about during the middle of the twentieth century. But in the case of this twenty-first-century bubble and bust, few observers had realized the scale and dangers of the excess leverage until it was too late, largely because they were ignoring the shadow banks. Now, with a name, they finally had a way to reframe the scourge that was creating such turmoil

IN THE MONTHS AFTER the Jackson Hole meeting, the credit crisis deepened, and policymakers recast their vision of the world. At the New York Federal Reserve, a team of researchers set about trying to create a map of the new shadow banking world to better understand it. This task was long and arduous, since data on the sector was patchy. But the team painstakingly tried to work out how the financial flows interacted with each other at the new frontiers of finance. 'We got all the information we could, from lots of different sources, hunting for clues and more clues – and tried to put everything together,' explained Zoltan Pozsar, a young Hungarian-born researcher who headed the Fed project.

After many months, this exploration produced a map of sorts. By then, Zoltan's team at the New York Fed had realized that the world they had uncovered was so vast and complex that the only way to plot it all out in a diagram was to create a poster that measured several feet wide. The diagram was far too big for most people to hang on their walls, even in the cavernous, high-ceilinged offices of a central bank. But in a sense, that illustrated the crucial point: the shadow bank sector was so big that nobody could afford to ignore it. Anybody who glimpsed that vast 'shadow bank poster' had to change their mental image of finance. Instead of assuming that the banks were the center of the financial system and shadow banks a mere footnote, it was clear that the shadow banks were at the center of the system too. Entities such as money market funds, say, were key pillars of this shadowy financial world. Looking at that map created a cognitive shift a little similar to the one that had occurred back in the sixteenth century, when the mathematician Nicolaus Copernicus showed in his diagrams that the earth revolved around the sun, not the other way around.

Zoltan's team gave a copy of the shadow banking poster to Tucker. It was too large to hang on any of his office walls; in any case, it would have looked odd against the backdrop of marble floors, subtle pastel paint, ornate ceiling moldings, and heavy oil paintings that decorated the historic corridors of Britain's central bank. But he put a rolled-up copy of the map in the corner of his office, and sometimes pointed it out to visitors. 'It's there for spiritual comfort!' he joked, by way of explanation, tinged with a sense of regret. 'If we had understood the shadow banking sector better before 2007, the bubble might never have become so bad.'

In subsequent months Tucker and other regulators pushed for more and more analysis of this shadowy world. So the Financial Stability Board in Basel, a joint committee of central bankers and supervisors, set about trying to measure the size of the shadow banking world. Initially, when Paul McCulley had popularized the phrase, he had suggested the shadow banking world might be $1.3 trillion in size, using a narrow definition of the term. However, the FSB decided to take a much broader definition, which captured not just conduits and SIVs, but hedge funds,

mutual funds, and a host of other vehicles. On that basis, the
sector was sixty times larger than McCulley's initial estimate,
running at about $67 trillion in 2011, the FSB declared. That
was half the size of the official banking sector in the world –
and four times larger than the size of the American economy.
Some financiers disputed this, and complained that the FSB's
definition of shadow banking was too broad. The FSB subsequently recalculated the figures, using a narrower definition,
and concluded that the real size of the sector was nearer to $27
trillion, not $67 trillion. But what nobody disputed was that
regulators and economists needed to pay attention to this world,
and rethink their mental image of finance. 'For far too long, the
global regulatory community has ignored the shadow banking
world,' declared Mark Carney, the man who had headed the
Bank of Canada during the crisis and later chaired the Financial
Stability Board (but then moved to the Bank of England).[32] 'That
needs to change.'

IN THE SUMMER OF 2009, almost a year after the queen had visited
the London School of Economics, the Royal Academy – one
of the most prestigious academic clubs in Britain – organized
a conference of economists. The attendees included a host
of senior figures from the economic priesthood, such as Jim
O'Neill, chief economist at Goldman Sachs, Tim Besley, a
member of the Bank of England's monetary policy committee,
and Nick Macpherson, a top official at the U.K. Treasury. Tucker
indirectly contributed to the discussion too. For several hours,
the group debated the question that the queen had posed in

2008: why had nobody seen the 'awful' crisis coming? Then the economists decided to write a formal letter of explanation to the Palace. This ran to three pages and set out in exhaustive detail all the reasons why the economists thought that they had missed seeing the problems. But the fundamental message was simple. The single biggest reason why policymakers had become blind was that the entire system was fragmented. Macro economists had looked at economic statistics, but ignored the finer details of finance. Banking regulators had watched individual banks, but had not looked at the nonbanks. Some financiers working in the private sector banks had been experts on how the shadow banks worked, but they did not speak to the senior economists at central banks. Meanwhile, the people who were actually borrowing money in the 'real' economy, such as homeowners, or companies, had no idea how the bigger financial ecosystem operated. Just as the institution of UBS had been fragmented, with the traders in London having little understanding of what New York was doing, so too the different policymakers had failed to swap crucial information, or look outside the narrow sectors that they were trained to explore. Economists had stayed inside their narrow field, and had felt no need to venture out of that box, since the economy seemed fine. As a result, they had missed spotting the most crucial point of all, namely that the system was overloaded with leverage, or debt.

'There was a psychology of denial,' the letter declared, arguing that because 'low interest rates made borrowing cheap, the "feelgood factor" masked how out of kilter the world economy had become beneath the surface. ... Everyone seemed to be doing their own job properly on its own merit. And according to standard measures of success, they were often doing it well. The failure was to see how collectively this added up to a series of interconnected imbalances over which no single authority had jurisdiction.' Or as the letter concluded: 'Your Majesty, the failure to foresee the timing, extent and severity of the crisis and to head it off, while it had many causes, was principally a failure of the collective imagination of many bright people, both in this country and internationally, to understand the risks to the system as a whole.'[33]

What the queen thought about the letter is not known. She never wrote a reply. But in the months that followed, the policy-making community on both sides of the Atlantic scurried to show that they had learned at least some of the lessons. A host of initiatives were launched to train economists to take a much wider view of their discipline. George Soros, the billionaire philanthropist and hedge fund manager, backed a New York–based group called the Institute for New Economic Thinking to promote a more holistic approach toward the study of economics. Adair Turner, the former head of the main British regulatory agency, was named as its second chairman. 'We know there needs to be a complete rethink of how we talk about economics and train economists,' Turner explained. Universities launched programs to connect the study of finance to macroeconomics. There was an upsurge of interest among economics students in courses on behavioral finance, a discipline that seeks to blend economics with psychology. Even some of the most renowned and senior members of the economist community declared that it was time to rethink the way that economics was done, and stop relying on models and a narrow vision of numbers. 'The whole period [of the credit crisis] upset my view of how the world worked,' admitted Alan Greenspan.

'The models failed at a time when we needed them most.'[34]

Policymakers also tried to promote more joined-up thinking by implementing structural reform. In London, the British government announced that it would reverse the moves made back in 1997 to separate the task of running monetary policy and financial regulation. Instead, it wanted to combine these different functions, once again, into a single institution. So the Financial Services Authority was closed as an independent agency and its responsibilities handed to two new entities (known as the Financial Conduct Authority and Prudential Regulation Authority).The FCA operated under the oversight of the Bank and it was hoped that by restructuring the institutions in this way policy makers would be forced to think about micro-level financial issues alongside macro-economic goals, instead of keeping these in separate mental and bureaucratic buckets.[35] A new 'financial policy committee' was created to match the 'monetary policy committee' that advised the Bank. The Bank quietly changed its recruitment policies: instead of just taking its staff from the economics departments of universities, it started to hire a few noneconomists too. 'We know we need to get more diversity of thought,' explained Mark Carney, the man who was appointed to run the Bank of England in late 2013, replacing King. Then, in early 2014, Carney went even further and unleashed a wholesale restructuring of the Bank. The old departments were broken

down, and the institution remodeled into a 'one bank' structure.[36]
Haldane, the man who had been running the financial stability
group, was moved to run the economics team. The idea was to
force economic and financial analysis to coexist as a whole, at
every level of the Bank.[37]

Similar initiatives got under way on the other side of the
Atlantic, albeit not quite as radical as in London. In 2010, the
U.S. created the Financial Stability Oversight Council to coordinate how all the different American regulators operated.[38] A
new Treasury division known as the Office of Financial Research
was established to monitor financial data in a holistic manner.
To illustrate the mission, Richard Berner, an economist who was
appointed to run the OFR, stuck a poster on his wall with a slash
of red, like a traffic signal, that declared that silos were banned.[39]
'We are a silo free zone!' he liked to say. 'We know that silos were
a big problem before. But now we want to change!' It was the
mantra of the post-crisis world.

But would this dizzy list of reforms be enough to stop policymakers being as blind again? It was a question that Paul
Tucker often asked himself. For him, the years after the crisis
were bittersweet. In 2013, he was promoted to the post of deputy
governor of the Bank of England and was perceived as the leading candidate to replace King when he retired in early 2014. But
in late 2013, George Osborne, the Chancellor of the Exchequer,
passed over Tucker and picked Carney instead. It was a bitter
blow for Tucker, who had devoted his entire career to the Bank.
However, it was also a sign of the degree to which the Bank's
leadership – along with the rest of the policymaking world and

economics community – was perceived to have failed. Inside the City of London, Tucker was thought to have done a better job than many of his colleagues in spotting what was going wrong. But the leadership of the Bank was so tarnished that Osborne presumably felt under pressure to seek a new face.[40]

From time to time, Tucker wondered what might have happened if he and others had spoken out more forcefully about his concerns. Might the Bank have been able to prick the bubble at an early stage? Could a few early, clear warnings have forced Greenspan or King to ponder what was going on, with their staff then forced to look beyond the macroeconomic statistics and their beloved models? Should they have peered closer at the grass roots of finance? If they had done that, would they have understood how much leverage, or debt, was in the system? Nobody could know. But what Tucker did know was that it would take more than a bureaucratic reshuffle or rhetorical declarations to fix the problem of silos. 'It's an issue of phenomenology, of epistemology,' he declared, using the ancient Greek word for a body of knowledge. He had first pondered epistemology – or what counts as knowledge – many years before, when he had studied philosophy after a degree in mathematics at Cambridge University. In the intervening decades he had moved away from those fields, burying himself in orthodox economics instead. The crisis, though, made him realize afresh the value of a liberal education.

'Breaking down silos isn't about series of actions but an attitude of mind – it's about having curiosity and a generosity of spirit [to listen to others],' he explained. 'In the past we had underlap because things fell between the cracks of what the regulators looked at. Today we have overlap, because we want to prevent silos. And because different subjects are connected overlap is inconvenient for bureaucrats. But underlap is dangerous for society.'

That meant, Tucker concluded, that the real test would come in the future. 'When things are working well, no one wants to know about silos. In fact overlap too easily becomes a turf war. Silos become an institutional equilibrium – people only notice silos when there are problems.' Or to put it another way, the really crucial time that a group of experts needs to start a debate about how they classify the world is *not* when there is a crisis. Instead it is at the moment of success.

Could anybody, at the Bank or anywhere else, change that blindness? Tucker often asked himself that. He did not have any easy answers. But in the second half of the book I will now turn to this crucial question, looking at how some individuals and institutions have tried to avoid falling into the traps suffered by institutions such as UBS and Sony, or the wider economics profession. These narratives are not finished success stories. The stories include victories and failures. But what links them all is that individuals have recognised the dangers of silos and tried to respond in creative ways. Thus they offer lessons that we can all learn from. We shall look at how Facebook has tried to be an anti-Sony by introducing measures to stop its specialist teams from becoming too defensive and inward-looking. We explore how a hedge fund called BlueMountain Capital has tried to avoid falling into the type of silo mentality that has beset banks such as UBS and Citigroup, and actively exploit the weaknesses of big banks. We also look at how one team of professional experts, doctors at the Cleveland Clinic hospital in Ohio, have introduced measures to force themselves to question their classification systems, to become more innovative and freethinking. That tale sits a long way from the Bank of England. However, if the economics profession had employed some of the tactics used by the Cleveland Clinic doctors, the policymakers might have understood the financial system better before 2008.

However, this account starts not with an institution but an individual: a geeky tech entrepreneur who decided to leave a comfortable job at the OpenTable Internet start-up and engage in a silo-busting mission of his own, working with the police in some of the toughest, most blood-spattered streets of Chicago.

PART TWO

SILO BUSTERS

5

GUN-TOTING GEEKS

How Individuals Can Silo-Bust Their Lives

> 'You can't connect the dots looking forward. You can only connect them looking backwards. So you have to trust that the dots will somehow connect in your future.'
>
> —Steve Jobs[1]

BRETT GOLDSTEIN SAT IN HIS SEAT AT THE BACK OF AN AIRPLANE THAT WAS taxiing across the tarmac on Chicago Midway Airport. He felt a frisson of fear. It should have been an unremarkable day. Goldstein, twenty-six, had spent the previous two years running operations for OpenTable, one of the last of the Internet start-ups of 1999, which helped people book tables online at their favorite restaurants. As jobs went, it was a good fit at the time, the type of role that any young professional might dream of. Goldstein spent a great deal of time on planes, since the website was keen to expand its global footprint.

But as Goldstein sat on the tarmac that day, September 11, 2001, he sensed that his cozy world was unraveling. Around him, cell phones and pagers were starting to buzz. A voice came over the intercom and told everyone to leave the plane. Baffled, Goldstein walked with a stream of passengers back into an unusually silent airport terminal, and saw crowds of people frozen around television screens. 'It was a funny dynamic because usually at an airport everyone is going in opposite directions. But that day they were not,' he later recalled. Instead, they huddled, silently watching as a plane smashed into the World Trade Center. Confused and panic-stricken, he tried to call his wife at home in Chicago, and his colleagues scattered around the world, but the cell phones no longer worked. Eventually, he located a pay phone. 'I was able to call 1-800-OpenTable, which was our call center number, and start checking all my employees, because we had a very large traveling staff,' he later recalled. 'And I was able to get a message to my wife, and I was saying "I don't know what to do here."'

Goldstein stumbled into a car, and asked it to head to the outskirts of Chicago where he lived. He heard the car radio declare that the World Trade Center had collapsed, a plane had crashed, thousands were dead. 'It was a long car ride home,' Goldstein recalled. And then, as he sat listening to the radio, something inside him snapped. Until that moment, Goldstein had assumed his life was going well. But suddenly he felt dissatisfied. 'Listening to NPR, and watching CNN, I realized that there were a lot of people doing really important things that day,' he explained. 'So I asked myself: do I want my whole life story to be about building a large Internet network which allowed people to go out to dinner? I was helping the portion of the population that could afford to go out to nice restaurants, to go out better. It was a really good idea and I think we were doing it pretty well – but it dawned on me that I needed to do something that *mattered*.'

It was not the first time that Goldstein had contemplated service; he had been a volunteer emergency medical technician in college and briefly contemplated medical school. But what could he do now? For the next few months, Goldstein went back to work as he and the rest of the country rebounded from the tragedy. OpenTable was expanding at a ferocious speed, and the travel and work kept him busy. But in his rare, quiet moments he kept tossing around ideas about what else he might do. He initially assumed the best way to give back would be to make a donation to charity, or do some community volunteering. That, after all, was the normal route that most people would take. 'There was a local TV piece in 2002 or 2003 that talked about the Public Health Department needing volunteers to do winter checks on the elderly and homeless, and I'm like "that would be great, that would be reasonable."' But it still left him dissatisfied. He had an urge that he could not quite articulate to make a substantial change. Then one weekend, as he flicked through the newspapers, he saw a piece about a new campaign to recruit white-collar professionals for police counterterrorism work in New York.[2] Goldstein was intrigued. He did not want to move to New York from his home near Chicago. But could he replicate that idea with the Chicago police?

When he floated the idea to his friends and family, most of

them were bemused. Chicago is known for being one of the most violent cities in America. The FBI has dubbed it the 'murder capital' of the United States, with the number of deaths per capita in some Chicago neighborhoods sometimes as high as those in a war zone.[3] The city's police force is (in)famous for being a rough, tough tribe too, which has been embroiled in scandals. They have long, proud traditions and do not take kindly to outsiders. Goldstein had grown up in a quiet suburb of Boston and attended 'one of those private boarding school things' as he sometimes joked. He was thin and so shy that he got nervous when he had to make public presentations to his OpenTable colleagues. He had never touched a gun. Indeed, the nearest he had ever come to a patrol car was watching Hollywood movies. 'My parents freaked out. No one understood why someone who had helped to grow OpenTable would want to be in the police. People were like "fine, if you want to go and do public service, great – but get an academic job or a job with RAND."'

The one person who was supportive, however, was Goldstein's wife, Sarah. So he decided to persevere. He did some research and discovered that it could take five long years to actually join the Chicago Police Department. So he quietly registered to take the written examination, and shortly afterward went along to the cavernous UIC sports pavilion to take the test for the police, along with thousands of other hopefuls. He duly passed and was given a number in the application process. Then he waited.

When they got his application, the police officers were almost as baffled as Goldstein's parents. 'There was a background check and a woman came over to interview me and my wife, Sarah,'

Goldstein recalled. 'She gave me this look, which said: "You're *sure* you really want to be the police?"' But Goldstein insisted he wanted to join. At the back of his mind he had a fledgling idea: If he managed to be accepted onto the police force, could he put some of his professional experience to good use there? Could he find a way to serve, or even improve the system? He had little idea exactly *how* he might do that. But against the odds, and without quite realizing it, Goldstein was about to embark on an adventure that would not just change his life – but also illustrate a point about silos. Or, how we might fight them.

In the first half of the book, I explained how humans tend to organize the world around them into mental, social, and organizational boxes, which can often turn into specialist silos. When these are rigid, they often cause people to behave in foolish or damaging ways; silos can make people blind to opportunity and dangerously unaware of risks. However, in the second half of the book I want to look not at the problem of silos – but some potential solutions to problems created by this silo effect. Some of these responses involve big strategies to change the culture of institutions or structure of groups. But before looking at institutions, it pays to think about individuals. After all, institutions are just gigantic collections of people and one of the most basic steps that we can make to fight the risks of silos starts *not* with a leadership committee or organizational chart or grand strategy plan, but inside our heads.

Think back to the tale in Chapter One about the anthropologist Pierre Bourdieu. He used the experience of immersing himself in a different culture to get a new perspective on life.

Plunging into another world not only enabled him to understand a different society, but also to look afresh at his own. That carries a wider lesson, namely that when we become insider-outsiders, like Bourdieu, and dare to jump across borders, we can escape from the prison of the classification systems that we inherit. This can break down tunnel vision and give us a powerful new insight on the cultural patterns that shape us, including those patterns that we usually barely notice. However, this point does not apply solely to anthropologists. Anybody who is willing to jump out of their silo and break down some boundaries in their own lives in unexpected ways can gain a new vision. Sometimes this produces immediate benefits, in the sense of inspiring innovations. Sometimes it takes years before the advantages appear. Take Steve Jobs. When he was at university, at Reed College in Portland, Oregon, he dropped out of his formal studies. However, he continued to hang around the campus and dipped into creative classes, including a course on Japanese calligraphy. At the time, it seemed to lack immediate benefit. But years later, when he was creating his designs for Apple computers, Jobs realized that he had created his winning designs by blending his training in information technology with the seemingly unconnected skills he had learned with Japanese brushstrokes. 'If I had never dropped in on that single calligraphy course in college, the Mac would never have had multiple typefaces or proportionally spaced font,' Jobs told students at Stanford University.

'You can't connect the dots looking forward; you can only connect them looking backwards,' Jobs concluded, urging his students to take risks and 'trust that that the dots will somehow connect in your future.' Or to put it another way, breaking down silos can spark innovation in unexpected ways. If people are willing to take risks by crossing boundaries in their own personal lives, this can deliver unexpected benefits. Even – or especially – in the case of a geeky tech entrepreneur who suddenly decides that he wants to join the Chicago police.

THOUGH HE DID NOT know it, Goldstein's decision to jump out of his safe world of OpenTable into the police came at an opportune time. In decades past, the Chicago Police Department has been renowned as being one of the largest and most tradition-infused forces in the country. Many of its 13,000 members have spent their entire lives working for the force, and their parents, grand-parents, or even great-grandparents have often been policemen too. Unsurprisingly, the city's police chiefs have almost always hailed from the ranks of this tight-knit tribe. The force is noto-riously slow to trust anybody who is not one of their own, and many members of the Chicago police tribe are particularly sus-picious of people from outside the area.[4]

But in the early years of the twenty-first century, or just as Goldstein was wondering what to do with his life, the Chicago police force underwent a bout of upheaval following significant incidents of brutality and corruption in the police force, which managed to stand out in a city whose history was littered with tales of corruption, violence, and other wrongdoing. In 2007, the superintendent of the police, Phil Cline, resigned. And in a bid to provide a fresh face, the city leaders decided to recruit the first outsider seen for fifty years into the role of police superintendent: Jody Weis.[5]

Weis was appointed into his \$310,000-a-year position on February 1, 2008. He looked like an archetypal policeman; indeed, he might have starred in a Hollywood cop movie, since he was broad-shouldered, with a chiseled face and wide-set eyes. But he had spent his twenty-two-year career with the FBI, not police, based in places such as eastern Pennsylvania. Many local police officers thought that made him unsuited to the job. 'The Fraternal Order of Police, the powerful Chicago Police union, hated Weis before he got in the door,' Locke Bowman, the director of the Roderick MacArthur Justice Center, later observed. 'The last thing the FOP has ever wanted is any outsider – it doesn't matter who – meddling in police business.'[6] But Weis preferred to think of this as an advantage. 'Coming from the outside I didn't really have any particular ties to the police department or really the city [and] I think that allowed me to take a very objective look at the department,' Weis observed. 'I recognize that the Chicago Police Department is a very historic and proud organization, so I certainly wasn't going to make it, you know, very FBI-centric. But I thought there were some best practices we could apply from the FBI.'

In particular, Weis had some distinctly different ideas about how the police should be run. During most of his career at the FBI, Weis had worked in a world marked by extensive silos. Just as the different departments of a company such as Sony or UBS tended to hug data to themselves, so too the different sections of the police, FBI, or CIA tended to hoard information, out of a mixture of defensiveness, suspicion, or tribal rivalry. This created informational logjams, sometimes with disastrous results. One well-known example of this arose in the American intelligence services in the run-up to the 2001 attacks on the World Trade Center: several different parts of the American intelligence forces had received signals that al Qaeda was planning some attack, but did not take a coordinated approach to fighting the threat because different pieces of information were held in different corners of the bureaucracy. Nobody was able, or willing, to connect the different signals to get an overview.[7] However, the problems with silos that were seen in the CIA before 2001 were repeated multiple times across other parts of the intelligence and security worlds, including the FBI. 'When I was a young [FBI agent] one of my friends used to say: 'You know what? If we wrote all of our intelligence paper on toilet paper, at least it would be of some value,' Weis observed. 'We would have hundreds and hundreds of hours of taped conversations between a bad guy and one of our undercover agents, or a bad guy and one of our sources, and the tapes would sit in a box. Nobody would make use of it.'

From time to time, police chiefs had tried to break down this fragmented bureaucratic culture. In New York, Police Commissioner Bill Bratton developed an innovative form of policing while he was running the NYPD in the 1990s, which tried to combine proactive community measures with crime fighting. This was called the 'broken windows' approach to policing, since Bratton was convinced that policing could not be effective unless tough enforcement was carried out alongside initiatives to make communities stable and united; if the windows in the street were broken, this signaled that nobody had much sense of shared responsibility to the community, making it harder to fight crime. Bratton believed that a community needed to feel a sense of pride in itself to become safe. If policemen wanted to reduce crime, the argument went, they needed to care about fixing broken glass windows as much as simply making arrests. That required collaboration. It was essential to take a joined-up approach, Bratton argued.

But Weis thought there was another way to combat crime: use better types of information flows. 'When I was in the FBI, we realized that we had to change the way we do business after 9/11,' he explained. This meant that the different agencies which had traditionally operated as suspicious rivals needed to collaborate, to pool their data, contacts, and tips. During the time that he was running the FBI in Philadelphia, Weis had overseen a project to create an interactive live computer system that enabled the different agencies, such as the FBI, CIA, and police, to talk to each other about criminal and terrorist threats. 'We took all our sources of information, plotted it on a map so we could show where we had coverage. And if there was no source coverage then we would try to target and develop sources, so that if something happened like a shooting we could go to our sources and say "You know, [somebody] just got shot, we need to find out who did it, so start working the streets,"' Weis recounted. 'We would get all the outstanding warrants, all the sex offenders, various census data, and we could lay more and more data sets across the maps. So if there was a child abduction, and we knew it happened in this location, say, we could immediately see if there were a lot of registered sex offenders in that area.'

To anyone outside the world of security operations, this data-sharing might have seemed like an blindingly obvious step. And in some parts of the security apparatus, other officials were trying to develop versions of this idea. Most famously, Bill Bratton, for example, in the 1990s had pioneered a policy known as compstat, which tried to take a much more rigorous approach to tracking crime statistics.

But many of the long-serving police officers and FBI agents hated the idea of this holistic approach to managing security risks. They did not like the idea of changing their long-established practices or losing control of 'their' data. 'Even ten years after 9/11 some of my closest friends [in the FBI] were still saying that we shouldn't do all this terrorism and intelligence stuff,' Weis admitted.' But he was convinced the security forces in America had to change how they operated: the world around them was becoming so interconnected and fluid, nobody could afford to stick in just one professional box. The FBI and CIA needed to break down their silos. So did the police, particularly in forces that were very large, like Chicago's.

IN THE MIDDLE OF a sweltering August in 2006, at the age of thirty-one, almost three long years after submitting his application, Goldstein reported for training at the Chicago Police Academy, a squat gray building on the city's West Side. He was filled with idealistic dreams of making the world a better place. The reality of being a police recruit, though, was a shock. On the first day, he was put into a pack of other new recruits and marched into a cafeteria. 'They are barking orders at you,' he recalled. 'You are broken into what they call "home rooms" and you're marching single file, with this quasi-military organization and they are talking about uniforms. Stuff I know nothing about. You have all this gear you are supposed to get, shorts, T-shirts, shoes that have no logos! *No logos!*' Goldstein had never given much thought to whether sneakers had logos or not. In the trendy tech start-up world where he had worked there were no official rules about what anybody wore. However, sneakers were widespread and somehow it seemed that shoes always had logos. In the CPD auditorium, though, Goldstein realized he was standing in a world with different cultural rhythms; his idea about what was normal no longer worked. Suddenly he was forced to notice assumptions he had never pondered before.

It was a brutal immersion. After marching in file, Goldstein's unit was ordered to conduct a time-honored maneuver known as a 'lean and rest,' a procedure where recruits were frozen still in a push-up, motionless, for long periods of time, while they were inspected. Goldstein could not see what the point of the ritual was; to him, the exercise seemed utterly useless. But the police considered the lean and rest a crucial part of the training; it was just there, part of the bonding experience. 'That first week of August was exceptionally hot and there wasn't any AC. So you are in your lean and rest, sweat dripping from your head and creating a pool under you. But you know if you break your position you're going to get yelled at. And, then, just when you think you're done, then you have calisthenics, which is jumping jacks, push-ups, and it just goes on and on. Then they take you on a run, and you are doing this exercise on this uphill driveway thing where you are lifting one of your classmates and carrying them up.'

That night, Goldstein hobbled home, dazed and aching. He threw himself into an iced bath and gobbled down 800 mg of ibuprofen. 'I just thought to myself: "So I quit my job for *this*? What have I done?"' But, the next day he returned, clutching ibuprofen, and went through the routine again. Then again, and again. He was older than almost all of the other recruits, and had far more academic qualifications. The course work seemed childishly easy. But it was the physical training that he struggled with. So he pushed himself to do endless runs and spent hours frozen, motionless, in a lean and rest, trying not to ask, 'Why?' Then he was given a gun. He set about shooting at a target, with the same analytical intensity he had applied to all other areas of his life. 'I actually found I was good at that,' he later recalled, with surprise. 'I shot fourth out of the hundred people in my class.'

The next phase of his training was even more brutal. Goldstein graduated from his class as Valedictorian, an honor which gave him the right to choose what part of Chicago he wished to work in. The range of options was very wide. Many parts of Chicago are safe and quiet, particularly around the wealthy suburbs. But Goldstein reckoned he needed to be near the action to learn the job. So he shunned the suburbs and asked to join a patrol in the 11th District, an area tucked into the West Side. This was one of the most violent, gang-ridden districts of Chicago. 'I didn't grow up in an urban environment, I grew up in the suburbs. So my first day on the West Side was – oh my God. There is drug

dealing, there's violence, there's shooting, there's everything.' He
tried to bond with the other officers. But they were suspicious of
a recruit who was obviously wealthier and better educated than
most cadets. Eventually, during one lunch hour, Rod Gardner,
assigned as Goldstein's training officer, furtively pulled him aside
in the gym in the basement of the police headquarters in the 11th
District.

'You know everyone thinks you're a Fed [plant], right?'
Gardner said.

'Huh?' Goldstein replied. Chicago had a long history of corruption and plants, but it had never occurred to him that he might
become entangled in that.

'Yeah, everybody thinks you're undercover FBI,' Gardner told
him. 'You learn exceptionally fast, you never ask questions about
paperwork, you're quiet, you're older, and you're professional.
Everybody thinks you're undercover FBI.'

Goldstein was startled. However, he took it in stride. And as
the months passed, and Goldstein continued to patrol his beat
with the other police officers, he could sense that the experience
was slowly changing him. Some days, he sometimes wondered
if his whole adventure was as pointless as the lean and rest. On
others, he realized that he was learning about a new world. A
few years earlier, he had assumed that violence and poverty were
something that happened to other people. To him, being normal
was living in a calm, safe environment where children went to
school and entrepreneurs made money by designing brilliant
apps or websites. Normal was a place where everyone wore ath-
letic shoes with logos. But viewed from a squadron police car in

Chicago's West Side, Goldstein could see that his former life was not the rule, but the exception; most people die not live like that. He had gained a bigger vision. His assumptions were changing too.

Almost exactly three years after he had first turned up for training, in the summer of 2009, an incident happened that highlighted this sense of change. By then, he had spent innumerable hours with his police officers on patrol, moving around the streets of the 11th District. He no longer felt that they considered him a spy; he was adapting in that world. But he still wondered whether he would ever be a 'proper' policeman; did he have the right instincts to react properly in a fight? Then one day, on a July day, Goldstein was in his family car with his pregnant wife and one-year-old son, on the way to get an ice cream when he saw a gang member pull out a gun and start shooting at the car in front of him. Shots were fired, and Goldstein realized that the gunman had just killed someone. Three years earlier, Goldstein would have fled the scene to protect his family, and then have called the police. But instead he slammed on his brakes, grabbed his gun, leaped out of the car, and ran toward the gunman, chasing him down the street and into an alley, where he managed to disarm him and conduct an arrest. 'People say that time slows down during these things. Not for me. Everything just happened exceptionally fast. I went into an alley with someone who was armed and had just killed someone and I didn't get shot,' he recalled. 'Everything was training, because certainly if I had to think about it, what is the right choice in a situation like that? My pregnant wife is in the car, and the dude is shooting, so what do you do? It was instinct.'

After the incident, he tracked down the family of the murder victim and discovered that he was a nineteen-year-old called Jeff Maldonado Jr., an aspiring black rap musician. The killer, Marcelino Sauseda, appeared have fired his gun as revenge for an earlier gangland fight. However, Maldonado's family insisted that their son was not involved in gangs. He was attending community college and was simply caught in the crossfire while hitching a lift in an acquaintance's van.[8]

Goldstein subsequently received multiple awards for bravery.[9] But he knew he had been lucky to have survived. He would never look at crime statistics in quite the same way again. Suddenly murder felt very personal.

BY THE MIDDLE OF 2009, Jody Weis, the new head of the Chicago police, was feeling frustrated. He had arrived in Chicago determined not just to clean up the image of the Chicago police – but also, above all, to cut the city's sky-high murder rate. But he faced a fearsome battle. In 2008, the first year of Weis's command, the murder rate went up. 'More people have been murdered in Chicago this year than in New York – even though New York's population is three times greater,' the New York *Daily News* observed in shock in late 2008 after relatives of Jennifer Hudson, a well-known Oscar-winning actress and singer, was murdered on the city's South Side.[10] Weis blamed this soaring violence on the demise of the 'special operations section' or SOS, which had been disbanded when it was mired in the scandals that preceded his arrival in Chicago. The SOS was designed to provide rapid response mobile teams of police experts that could rush to any place that violence erupted, and it had been lauded for its effectiveness in tackling crime. Unfortunately, a number of its then members had engaged in criminal activity themselves. Now, as 2009 got under way, he quietly reinstated the unit back onto the streets, under a new name, Mobile Strike Force.[11] Weis thought that this policy was the only effective way to quell the worst gang fights. 'If there is a gang shooting, you know there's then going to be retaliation – and with Special Forces we had hundreds of officers that we could saturate an area and stop retaliation and keep everything calm.' The murder rate then fell slightly in 2009. By most measures, though, the death toll remained shockingly high. 'When Chicago is compared to its big-city brethren, Chicago's per capita murder rate is double that of Los Angeles and more than double that of New York City,' an editorial in the Chicago *Sun-Times* declared.[12] 'Violent crime is clustered most intensely on Chicago's West and South Sides, terrorizing law-abiding citizens.' Indeed, the killings were so bad that from time to time local politicians would ask whether Chicago needed to deploy the National Guard onto the streets.[13] Meanwhile Weis himself repeatedly faced questions about whether the city was spinning out of control. He insisted it was not. But with every month that passed, fresh stories broke about gangland killings, and the political impact of these was magnified as a blizzard of gory pictures and videos was disseminated across the Internet. '[This murder rate] is unacceptable in an American City, and it is totally unacceptable in a city as great as Chicago,' Weis declared, deploring parallels with a war zone. 'We are not "Ch-iraq."'[14]

As the political pressure mounted, Weis cast around for new

ideas. And in the summer of 2009, Weis's chief of staff – former U.S. marine Michael Masters – tossed out a novel thought. Masters had briefly met Brett Goldstein in the mayor's office when the recruits graduated from the Police Academy, and Goldstein had revealed to Masters that he was hoping to connect his dream of using his tech background to change how law enforcement used data. So maybe, Masters suggested, it would pay to ask Goldstein to develop some computer models to work out what was causing the murder rate to rise. Weis summoned Goldstein to hear his ideas. 'We sat down, we chatted,' Weis recalled. 'Brett is a little unusual personality, kind of a dry sense of humor, a little awkward, like your typical nerd.' Goldstein explained to Weis how he had once used advanced computer modeling techniques and sophisticated mathematics to help the OpenTable Internet site to connect customers to restaurants. That project had required a lot of tracking, modeling, and analysis and it did not seem obviously connected to the task of combating gangland murders. But maybe, Goldstein suggested, he could transpose the computer analytics he learned at OpenTable and the University of California to the police. If algorithms could work out which restaurants were hot, and match these to customers, maybe they could also track crime patterns.

The Chicago police had never done anything quite like that before. At the start of the twenty-first century, they had tried to create more transparency about crime patterns by copying some elements of New York's compstat platform (the statistical tracking system).[15] But this did not have a big impact on the force. The police were used to chasing criminals with guns, not computers.

However, Weis had seen what computer analytics could do at the FBI in Philadelphia. So he ordered Goldstein to move from the 11th District into a small, windowless office on the third floor of police headquarters. Goldstein installed a couple of old computers, collected all the crime data that he could, and started crunching the numbers with the help of some fellow technology experts at Carnegie Mellon University. As he had once done with restaurant orders, he was looking for patterns and connections in the data, in the hope these might predict future trends. Was there a rhythm to gangland shootings? A particular place and time when murders tended to occur? Then he plotted the death reports onto a big computer screen, alongside other data on violence, and then looked for other factors that might be correlated to these tensions. There was a folk belief inside the police that crime increased during a full moon or when the summers were hot, or when the winds were stiffly blowing in the city. So Goldstein compared data on past murders against the lunar cycle and temperature records, and then against the wind. This analysis showed little correlation between the moon and the murder rate. Nor was there much evidence that murders increased in heat or wind per se. But when the temperature moved by more than 15 degrees – say from 65 to 80 – in a short period there was a big jump in crime. Conversely, when it became extremely hot, say above 90 degrees, crime fell.

The factor that was most important in determining the murder rate, by far, was the movement of gangs. Across the urban landscape of Chicago, an estimated seventy-five gangs operated in different neighborhoods, who were estimated to have almost

70,000 members.[16] That made them very powerful. However, the territory controlled by particular gangs often shifted. One group might control a particular block for a few months, but then the boundaries would shift as the drug trade or other criminal activities developed. Traditionally, the police had never tried to monitor these geographical patterns in a systematic way. Insofar as the police working in different districts communicated with each other directly (which they usually did not), they just swapped stories over the patrol car radios about which gangs were operating where. If they ever needed to collaborate with colleagues in any formal way, this communication could take a long time. 'Historically, the Chicago police was so siloed,' Weis observed, 'you had towers of information going up and down [the bureaucracy]. If I needed help from [someone] I needed to go up my full chain of command with paper and then work down [another] chain of command with paper.'

But Goldstein started to collect all the reports that he could find about gang movements and put them on a centralized database, using a technique known as geospatial and temporal reporting. 'What this showed was that we were suffering a lot of gang conflicts moving from the 7th to the 8th District – you could see the migration of the gangs and this conflict,' Weis observed. 'Brett color-coded it on the chart and it almost looked like amoeba interacting. You had gangs fighting for a particular area to sell narcotics. We could get the information that day, and then see the interaction zone getting bigger and bigger.' Then Goldstein plotted his amoeba chart of gang movements against the reports of murders. Unsurprisingly, this showed a high level of correlation. Indeed, the rhythm was so closely connected that if you factored in other items such as temperature swings, the chart seemed to have predictive powers. Or to put it another way, even if you knew nothing else about what was happening on the actual streets, just watching the pattern of gang movements on a computer screen and other on-the-ground reports about violence could give you a good clue about which streets and city blocks were likely to see the biggest wave of deaths in the coming days, or even hours. The maps, in other words, did not just predict in a general sense what might occur, but gave real-time, immediate signals. 'While it's fine to say "this is a bad block" we wanted to start being able to say "this is going to be a bad block *tonight*,"' Goldstein said. Or as Chief of Staff Masters explained: 'Rather than look at data which was seven days old and base deployments of police off that pattern, we wanted to look for patterns in the data itself [and make predictions]. If you look at weather, the weatherman doesn't just look at what happened last week and say "Okay we will have you wear a raincoat on Tuesday because it rained last Tuesday."'

By the start of 2010, Weis was ready to launch an experiment. He told Goldstein to start running his 'weather maps' – or murder maps – and, based on these forecasts, issue warnings to the police officers about where crime was likely to explode next. The idea was that if Goldstein knew where violence could erupt, the Mobile Strike Force units could scramble to respond with their teams, in tandem with the regular police. To make this system work, Goldstein had to be in touch with the ordinary police patrols, like his own teammates from the 11th district. So they introduced a system of twice-daily calls. However, Goldstein insisted that this communication was a two-way interaction. He needed to collect all the live data that he could about conditions on the ground. So each day he issued his forecasts and called the patrol officers to pepper them with questions. Were particular gangs fighting over drugs? Was there an incident over a girlfriend? He pored over arrest logs. Then he plugged that data into his algorithms to predict where violence could erupt next. Until then this information had been scattered between different districts. But Goldstein was keen to centralize the information flows and remove the bureaucratic splits that had plagued the force in the past. So he passed his information out to the regular patrol officers and the Mobile Strike Units. 'Brett would roll the numbers,' Weis explained. 'Then he would [contact the police officers and] say things like: "Hey, be very careful, because in this area [the gangs] are fighting and shooting, they are trying to reestablish their turf."'

When the police in the patrol cars heard about the new system, many were suspicious. Within a couple of months, Weis had promoted Goldstein to the high rank of commander, an honor usually only given after decades of service on the streets. Goldstein tried to curb the jealousy by dressing in civilian clothes and using the title 'director' not 'commander.' But the resentment festered. Angry officers started to refer to his experiment in scathing terms as the 'crystal ball unit.' 'The jealousies were amazing,' Weis recounted. 'You have got folks who have been three, four, five generations of policing and their grandfathers never had computers. So they don't like the idea of change at all. Some guys embraced it. But a lot of them looked at it and thought this is total

BS.' Weis and Goldstein tried to shrug the criticism off. After all, as Masters kept pointing out to them, when the idea of officers carrying police radios first cropped up in places such as Chicago in the 1960s, many policemen had loathed it, fearing it would be used against them as a surveillance tool. Within a couple of years, that resistance had melted away to the point where radios were considered so normal they were rarely discussed at all. 'Whenever you are going to do something new in a large organization there is invariably going to be institutional resistance,' Weis explained. 'This was the same [as with police radios] – it called for a change in the way that people were thinking.'

By the end of 2010, Goldstein, Masters, and Weis were elated. Not only did their data maps give good signals about where murders were likely to occur in a general sense in the medium term – but they could even, on occasion, predict short-term developments. 'There was one day we ran the target [areas for likely murders], and a minute after I sent the target list, I got a shooting notification. It was the weirdest thing, since it happened exactly in one of our targets,' Goldstein recalled. 'Our machine had written up the targets [of likely places for a shooting] and someone was shot at 60 seconds later!'[17] Better still, it seemed as if the murder rate was falling. At the start of 2011 the city announced the latest murder statistics and these showed that in 2010 the murder rate for the year was 5 percent below 2009, its lowest level since the 1960s. 'Chicago's murder rate hasn't been that low since Lyndon B. Johnson was president,' two local community workers declared with delight.[18] In early 2011 it fell even faster. Traditionally in Chicago, the most intense bout of killing occurs in the summer months, when gangs are on the streets. But in the summer of 2011, the murder rate tumbled to its lowest level since the 1960s. Indeed, when Goldstein extrapolated the statistical trends forward, it looked as if Chicago would record fewer than 400 homicides in the entire year. 'It's sad that we would view that [400 figure] as a sign of being successful, but it was a milestone,' Weis observed.

Weis and Goldstein did not know how much of that shift was down to the use of their murder maps. But the anecdotal evidence seemed to be overwhelming. By sending the special units to the places identified as locations where homicides were about to occur, it seemed that the police were actually preventing some of the killing. 'The point where I knew that we had been successful was that I got a call from the SAC [Special Agent in Charge] of the FBI,' Weis recalled, speaking with the type of police jargon that is incomprehensible to anyone outside the police tribe. 'This said: "We are picking up on our Title-3s [the listening wires the FBI uses] stuff where the bad guys are saying "there's this whole new unit in town. They don't play, they are serious, they are real police, stay away from the 44 hundred units [the Mobile Strike Force]"! I took that as a real compliment. It told me that [our program] was successful. We had the right officers and Brett had them in the right location.'

ON JUNE 21, 2014, Brett Goldstein turned forty. It was a symbolic moment for him. Back on the day when the World Trade Center had collapsed, and Goldstein had decided to break out from his cozy world as a corporate employee, he had tried to imagine what his life would be like when he turned forty. At the time, it seemed almost unimaginably distant. 'I was twenty-something at the time and I just thought I don't want to turn forty and just be a person who chased money,' he explained. But now that the moment was upon him, he wondered, had he achieved what he had hoped? The answer was mixed. By 2014, Goldstein had long since left his police project.

In 2011, Rahm Emanuel became mayor of Chicago and soon after Jody Weis announced he would step down. The move left Goldstein and other reformers dismayed.[19] By then Weis had become deeply unpopular in the Chicago police and morale was low. Many police had never forgiven Weis for being an outsider who pioneered radical ideas. The final straw came when Weis became caught up in a long-running scandal over a former Chicago police commander known as Jon Burge, who had been accused of letting his police officers torture suspects to get criminal confessions back in the 1970s and 1980s. Burge left the force in the 1990s, amid controversy, but was subsequently sentenced to four years of prison. Normally that would imply he would lose his pension. But in early 2011 the police pension board voted, after an acrimonious debate, to let Burge keep his pension. Weis publicly criticized the decision, and police loyalists were incensed. In the eyes of many officers, Weis had betrayed the tribal allegiances of the Chicago police.[20]

Shortly after Weis left, Emanuel asked Goldstein to move across from the police to City Hall, with a view to replicating what he had done with crime in the heart of the Chicago government as chief data officer, or CDO. Goldstein was wary. He had become worn down by the in-fighting and was thinking of joining another start-up in the private sector. Part of him hankered to return to his 'T-shirt and jeans' life, as he liked to say. But he was flattered by Emanuel's offer and intrigued, since no city had ever before created the position of CDO. So he jumped another boundary to City Hall, hoping to start more experiments. Like most American cities, Chicago's government was sitting on a vast ream of data about its citizens. But – again, like most government entities – the data was held in numerous different silos. The same problems that plagued Michael Bloomberg's City Hall were replicated in Chicago. So Goldstein started trying to combine all this information into a single database, by pulling in local volunteers from the Chicago start-up scene, where he had once worked during his days at OpenTable. He christened them the 'nerd herd.' Their style of working was radically different from what City Hall was used to, or indeed any government bureaucracy. The nerd herd wore T-shirts. They ate donuts around their laptops. They drew diagrams on the office whiteboards. And when they ran out of space on the board, they scribbled pieces of computer code or mathematical equations with markers on the windows of City Hall. 'The mayor would walk by and give me a look to say: "What the hell is going on here?"' Goldstein recalled. But slowly some projects emerged. After one 'hackathon' (all-night brainstorming session) organized in conjunction with Google, a local web developer named Scott Robbin created an interactive map that could show the public what had happened to any car that had been towed by the traffic police. 'What people want to know in that situation is "Where is it [my car]?" "Where can I find it," right?' explained Danielle

DuMerer, the City Hall official who oversaw the project. 'When we first released it we were updating the dataset every twenty-four hours, but later we were able to start updating that dataset every fifteen minutes. Obviously if your car has been towed you want to know right now where it is, not the next day.' Then the nerd herd created an interactive map to show Chicago residents what was happening with street sweeping. Eventually, Goldstein decided to pull together all the different data series into one giant interactive map, to show residents what was happening in the city. It also showed government officials potential security threats.

The new interactive platform, known as WindyGrid, went live during the NATO summit of 2012, which was held in Chicago. It was a nerve-racking moment, particularly since the city's networks were repeatedly attacked by the hacker group Anonymous. But the system survived and took root. Then Goldstein and DuMerer looked for ways to use the interactive platform to create collaboration with other branches of government. Back in 2011, just before Goldstein left the Chicago Police, his former colleague Michael Masters moved to a new post running the Department of Homeland Security and Emergency Management in Cook Country, Illinois, a large region that includes Chicago city. In previous decades, coordination between the mayor's office and country level government officials had been patchy, at best: the different bureaucracies often competed as much as they collaborated. However, Goldstein and Masters set about trying to break down these barriers by using the data maps to swap information. In the summer of 2013, for example, Chicago hosted a food vendor fair, with 45,000 people in attendance. Just before the fair started, Masters's Homeland Security team learned that a very violent storm was about to hit. In previous decades, it would have been hard to organize a quick response, since the county government did not usually communicate well with city officials, let alone the federal weather services. But in this case, the data systems had become so coordinated that the evacuation took place unusually smoothly. 'We're breaking down these silos and recognizing that weather crosses our boundaries so information has to as well,' Masters explained. 'Problems don't stop at political borders. Nor do floodwaters or pandemic flu.'

But though Goldstein was excited by what his group had done with WindyGrid, it was his police murder map that made him particularly proud. In truth, the revolution he had tried to start at the Chicago Police Department did not evolve as he had hoped. After Goldstein and Weis left the department in 2011, the predictive analytics program was partly wound down. To a certain extent, the project was a casualty of political infighting and budget cuts. But what made the experiment doubly vulnerable was an issue that has long haunted Chicago's political scene: race. The people running the CPD were overwhelmingly white. But Goldstein's charts tended to predict that murders would happen in African American or Latino districts. Goldstein and Weis vehemently denied that this pattern was driven by any racial agenda whatsoever; their map simply reflected the homicides that were actually occurring and used this data to issue statistical predictions of where murders might occur next. But in a city such as Chicago, race was a very sensitive issue, even – or especially – when viewed through the prism of numbers.

Tragically, almost as soon as the program was dismantled, the murder rate rose. Weis was deeply disappointed. 'At the end of August [just before the units were closed], there were forty-one homicides below the previous year for 2011. The end of the summer is normally the worst time of the year for homicide counts, but that year they were just crazy low. But in the last four months of the year, when they eliminated those specialized units and Brett's program, they lost all that traction,' Weis later fumed. 'It's kind of confusing to me that the mayor would ask Brett to basically do the role that he did for the police department for the city of Chicago and yet somehow allow the police department to ignore it. It's very sad.'

But Goldstein himself tried to be philosophical. After all, he reasoned, what he had essentially done with his murder maps was plant a seed. It had not sprouted in the way he had hoped in Chicago. But in the years after he left the CPD he could see signs that this seed of an idea was growing in more fertile soil elsewhere. Soon after they left their posts, Goldstein and Weis began to receive requests from other police forces to explain how their experiment had worked. Then, ironically, just as the CPD was shuttering the program, other forces started to pursue similar experiments. Over on the West Coast, the Los Angeles Police Department created a predictive analytics capability similar to the one that Goldstein had built. The police in Memphis, Tennessee, did the same, and quickly became a leader in the field. Then when riots broke out in London in 2012, the police there started using the same types of techniques that Goldstein had pioneered in Chicago to respond to British gangs. By 2014,

Goldstein and Weis were being asked to share their ideas with police departments all over the world.

When Goldstein had decided back in 2001 to change his career he had dreamed of changing the world. But now, at the age of forty, he had come to realize that you do not need to start a revolution to make a difference. Just shifting the dial a few inches matters too. The experiment in Chicago might not have transformed the police, but it had showed what could be achieved if somebody was willing to take a gamble and jump out of their cozy mental box. 'I am not looking to solve the big problems in life. I'm completely fine with solving lots of small problems. It's small things that can make places better,' Goldstein said.

It was a message he hoped to keep spreading. By 2014, he had moved on once again in his career, and left City Hall to return to the private sector. But in his spare time, he worked as a fellow in urban science at the University of Chicago, where he taught classes on how to help governments use data more effectively.[21] He hoped it would help to convince some of the young computer scientists to jump across boundaries and silos. Most of the young tech geeks he saw dreamed of being the next Mark Zuckerberg, working in glamorous freewheeling start-ups. To them, the idea of working for government of any sort is anathema. But Goldstein hoped he might broaden their minds. 'We need to get more technology people into government,' he observed. 'So I try to tell the students to think of doing something different.'

To mark his fortieth birthday milestone, his wife contacted colleagues and friends and asked them to send a birthday email greeting. To her surprise, fifty-nine of his former colleagues sent affectionate messages. Some came from City Hall and the Chicago Police Headquarters. Others were sent by his tech friends at OpenTable. But there was also a message from Rod Gardner, his former training officer in the 11th District, the man who had once cornered him in the police gym.

'It said: "I always thought that you were an [FBI] plant. LOL!"' Goldstein recalled. He liked to think it was a compliment. But it was also a small testament to how surprising life can sometimes be. Particularly when you are willing to jump out of your normal box.

6
(RE)WRITING SOCIAL CODE

How to Keep Silos Fluid

'We want to be the anti-Sony, the anti-Microsoft — we look at companies like that and see what we don't want to become.'

—Senior Facebook executive

JOCELYN GOLDFEIN SAT AT HER DESK IN A SCRUFFY, OPEN-PLAN OFFICE AT the Palo Alto headquarters of Facebook, and felt a flush of shame wash over her. She stared with horror at her computer. A voice in her head asked: *How could I be so stupid?*

Five weeks earlier in the summer of 2010, Goldfein, thirty-nine, had joined the fast-growing social media giant, hoping to build a new chapter in her career. The move had seemed wildly exciting. A no-nonsense woman with sleek brown hair and cheerful, dimpled face, Goldfein was a rare creature by Silicon Valley standards: a female computer scientist from the hallowed ranks of Stanford University who held a top management role.

Before joining Facebook, she had worked for seven years at VMware, a group that made cloud computing technology. She started as a computer engineer who loved to write code; she was particularly passionate about 'triaging bugs,' as she liked to say (computer jargon for fixing glitches in code). 'At VMware, I built a name for myself by being like this monstrous triager of bugs! I, like, triaged one thousand bugs in my first month at VMware!' she later recounted. But by the time she left VWware in 2010, she had been promoted to general manager of engineering, a role that put her in charge of hundreds of engineers.[1] That made her a prime catch for a fast-growing company such as Facebook. And though Goldfein did not initially have much interest in the social media group, since she hated working for big, bureaucratic companies, she was converted to the Facebook dream after she met its founder, Mark Zuckerberg.[2] 'There was no question after I met him that Mark was by far the most impressive founder of all the founders I met. It's sort of a trite thing to say, in hindsight, that's like, *"duh."* But he was amazing.'

So in July 2010, she turned up at Facebook's trendy 'warehouse' style offices in Palo Alto. But then events took an unusual twist: instead of being thrown into a management job, she was told to join an 'onboarding' induction course known as 'Bootcamp,' a six-week training program for new recruits.[3] This request was unusual, particularly given that she had already been deputy head of engineering of a vast company. But everybody joining Facebook got hazed together, no matter their age and rank; it was a company rule that all new entrants should experience a joint introduction process, like recruits joining an army – or Goldstein joining the Chicago police.

So the new recruits were all pulled together into a room and asked to start working on some beginner projects, sitting side by side at a desk. Goldfein was treated just like the rookies, and given a humdrum task: triaging five bugs in the system. She was thrilled; fixing bugs was her speciality. Like most computer engineers, she had loved solving problems ever since she was a child, a trait she first learned from her grandmother in Northern California. 'This woman did logic puzzles for fun; she would solve Rubik's Cubes as a hobby,' Goldfein said. 'She taught me to do those when I was a kid and it was sort of an epiphany when I got to programming. It's sort of the same thing.'[4] But as she started battling with her bugs, Goldfein noticed something odd: three out of the five bugs she was supposed to be fixing did not seem to pose any problem after all.[5] *Is it a trick?* She suspected so. But then she realized that there was a simpler explanation: Facebook was such a fast-growing company that its computer scientists were rewriting codes at a furious pace. Any bugs attached to the old systems kept disappearing from view since those pieces of code were just not being used anymore.

Did that matter? Most computer engineers might say no. In Silicon Valley people prefer to build new products for the future, not clean up boring problems from the past. But Goldfein had a tidy, precise mind that liked to keep her world neat.[6] 'Bugs don't sound like a very sexy thing, but if you are determined to ship high-quality software, one of the things you need is information about what is the state of the software,' she explained. 'A bug database can be a faithful representation of the state of the world ... [but only] if you are really scrupulous about your bug hygiene.'

So as she sat at her desk, she decided to improve Facebook's hygiene by creating a program that would track old bugs, send emails to anybody who had ever worked on the code, and then kill the obsolete bugs. 'At Facebook things move so fast that if something has been untouched for three months, it is a pretty good sign that it is irrelevant. So [this system] would trigger an email to everybody copied on the bug and then if another three months went by and nobody responded ... it would just auto-close it.'

She christened her program the 'Task Reaper' and she set about testing her creation on a small scale. But then disaster struck. As she typed code on the computer, she accidentally pressed the copy and paste keys on her keyboard and implanted her embryonic code into the entire live Facebook system. Within seconds, the pilot Task Reaper had identified 14,000 dead bugs in the system and dispatched hundreds of thousands of emails to all the associated Facebook staff. The volume was overwhelming. The company's email system crashed, freezing the Facebook network, and locking all the staff out of their messages.[7] Furious howls erupted across the office. Goldfein was horrified. Crashing the office computers was an appalling mistake for a rookie employee to make. She assumed there would be unpleasant repercussions. 'I was brand-new, nobody knew me from Adam – and there was a pretty strong reaction,' she explained. 'Our sales team couldn't interact with customers, engineers couldn't do code reviews. The email [was] kind of the lifeblood of the company.'

But then she encountered another surprise: when other Facebook staff rushed over to find out what had happened, they seemed more interested in asking *why* she had created her Task Reaper program than in punishing her for her mistake or complaining that she had trespassed into the territory of two existing departments, the 'exchange' team and the 'bug tools' team. 'There was no one saying: "How dare you?"' she recounted. 'The people I expected to be most mad at me actually just sort of rolled up their sleeves, waded in, and started fixing the problem.'

This reaction was different from anything Goldfein had experienced. At other big companies, different teams tended to guard their turf from outsiders – and each other – and there was so much competition between different teams that they did not welcome incursions. Indeed, it was because she had seen so much tribal infighting at other big technology companies that she had initially been so wary of joining Facebook. She hated large bureaucracies – and silos.

But as she looked around at Facebook, she realized that the social media giant seemed different from what she had seen before. It was not just that the company's work practices seemed somewhat unstructured, like the graffiti used to decorate its walls.[8] It also seemed less plagued by the internal rivalries and rigidities seen at its rivals. The silos and bureaucratic structures that had undermined Sony did not seem to exist inside Facebook, or not as far as Goldfein could see.

Was that just a happy accident? At the time, Goldfein did not know. But the answer is crucial to the bigger themes of this book. In the first half, I described how silos can sometimes have a pernicious impact on institutions and social groups, making people blind to risks *and* opportunities. The tale of Sony that I described in Chapter Two was a classic example of how silos can sometimes crush innovation. There its once creative engineers ended up becoming embroiled in endless turf wars – and unwilling or unable to cooperate. However, this tale was not unique to Sony, or Japanese culture; destructive silos exist in many large institutions, even – or especially – those which have been successful in the past. Microsoft, General Motors, and UBS are just some examples.

But what is perhaps even more interesting than the question of why some individuals and institutions are damaged by silos is why some groups do *not* suffer from this curse to the same degree. Why do some companies, people, or entities avoid the type of turf warfare and tunnel vision that beset Sony and UBS? What can we do to avoid those problems? In the last chapter, I suggested one micro-level reason: people who are willing to take risks and jump out of their narrow specialist world are often able to remake boundaries in interesting ways. Traveling in a mental sense, if not in a physical sense, can set people free from silos; if nothing else because it enables them to imagine a different way of living, thinking, and classifying the world.

But while the story of how individual people can combat silos is interesting, it is only part of the issue. The other big question is whether institutions can find ways to silo-bust on a bigger scale. Can the type of journey that Brett Goldstein embarked on in Chicago be replicated on an institutional level? In this respect, the story of Facebook offers ideas that could be applied in many institutions. The company has sparked a revolution in how we all communicate and interact with each other across the world. Facebook has helped people to remodel their ties and identities in all types of communities and friendship groups. But what is less well known is that the group has also tried an experiment in social engineering *inside* the company too, by influencing how its employees interact. In particular, Facebook officials have spent many hours worrying and thinking about their employees' cognitive maps, social structures, and group dynamics. That has prompted them to implement deliberate experiments to stop silos developing inside the company and prevent Facebook from suffering from the fate of a company such as Sony.

These experiments are still at an early stage. The company is barely a decade old. But though the initiative is still developing, it throws up some fascinating lessons. The engineers who have developed these silo-busting experiments in Facebook have done so by borrowing ideas from the world of social science about the ways that humans interact – and then tried to apply them in a practical sense to their company. Most importantly, they have deliberately tried to do what anthropologists constantly do, but most companies do not: think about how their employees define the world, classify their surroundings, and navigate boundaries. Pierre Bourdieu would have felt at home.

*

IT IS NOT SURPRISING that Facebook has launched so many internal social experiments. After all, since its inception the secret of its success has been to marry quantitative computing skills with soft analysis about humans' social ties and then turn this into a hard-nosed business plan. The company's leaders are fascinated by both computing *and* social code. They know that blending these two can produce a corporate gold mine.

The origins of the company are legendary. Back in late 2003, Mark Zuckerberg, then a Harvard sophomore studying psychology, first dreamed up the idea of creating a 'Facemash' – later called 'The Facebook' – website to connect students to each other.[9] Zuckerberg hit on this idea even though he was not a wildly social creature himself. He spent most of his time immersed in computers and computing code. Yet despite his outsider, geek status, or perhaps because of it, he also had an innate instinct for what made humans tick, and how to play on their insecurities and need for interaction. His venture started small. In the winter of 2003 Zuckerberg began talking to some of his fellow students about building a website that would list all of the Harvard students next to their photographs. Then, in February 2004, Zuckerberg and Eduardo Saverin, a junior, launched The Facebook.[10] They built the site at a breathless pace, expanding it to other colleges. Then Zuckerberg dropped out of college and moved west to Palo Alto, where he rented a small, scruffy house with fellow computing enthusiasts. The site exploded. By September that year, Facebook had developed one of its first defining features: the 'Wall,' which enabled members to write titbits of information and comments on profile pages. It expanded to cover not just colleges, but high schools and corporate entities.[11] Then Sean Parker, the legendary entrepreneur, raised finance from investors such as Peter Thiel and the venture capital group Accel Partners.[12] As Facebook grew, it introduced a series of iconic features: 'News Feed' (which collects in one place feeds about friends); 'Platform' (a system to let outside programmers develop tools for sharing photos, taking quizzes, and playing games); 'Chat' (a tool to enable users to talk to each other), and 'Like' (a feature that registers approval about posts). Its popularity swelled and more milestones were passed. In the autumn of 2007 Facebook sold a 1.6 percent stake to Microsoft for $240 million and created an advertising partnership. The following year, it hired Sheryl Sandberg, the glamorous and savvy Washington insider and former Google executive, as chief operating officer. In June 2009, the company notched up another big achievement: it became the most popular social media site in the world, eclipsing MySpace.

But what was striking about Facebook's rapid growth was not simply its vast number of users; the other startling issue was how the site reshaped patterns of social interaction. As Facebook took off, groups of people who had never been connected could link up online, swapping stories, news, and ideas. Long-lost friends were reunited, memorials staged, birth announcements posted, and jobs advertised. Facebook enabled people to 'cluster' together in groups online, mimicking the way they interacted in the real world. People could collide with new people and ideas online. But they could also huddle with familiar friends. Social media created both the potential for people to open up their social world and to restrict it into self-defined groups, or cyber tribes.

Most Facebook users never gave any thought to the under-lying structural patterns that were created by this 'clustering' and 'collision' dynamic. They just wanted to connect with 'friends.' But Zuckerberg and his fellow computer scientists at Facebook took a more analytical view. When they looked at the complex ties that created friends in the real world and cyberspace they did not just see a warm, undefined lump of emotion. Instead, they saw patterns behind these emotional links. And while disciplines like anthropology, psychology, or sociology have analyzed social interactions with soft, non-quantitative techniques, the Facebook engineers were part of a fast expanding breed of data scientists who assumed they could study social interactions with mathematics, not just ideas. To them, human connections were akin to the electronic compo-nents of a computer screen or mathematical model: something that could be mapped. 'We are not anthropologists. Most of us are trained as computer scientists. But we are really interested in how people interact, how systems work, how people commu-nicate,' Jocelyn Goldfein observed. 'Because of our computing training, we tend to think of human organization problems as graph problems – we look at systems, nodes, and connections. And when you look at the world like that, it can get some really interesting results.'

IN THE SUMMER OF 2008, Facebook quietly passed a little milestone. Its leaders realized that the company was expanding so fast that it employed more than 150 computer engineers.[13] Outside Facebook nobody knew – or cared – that the company had passed this 150 number. After all, whenever Silicon Valley start-ups are success-ful, they explode in size. When Goldfein was working at VMware before joining Facebook, the staff there swelled from a few hun-dred to 10,000 in just seven years. Rapid growth is considered a badge of honor.

But when the top Facebook managers realized they had broken the 150 threshold they became uneasy. The reason lay with the concept known as 'Dunbar's number' – the theory developed by British evolutionary psychologist–cum–anthropologist Robin Dunbar. Back in the 1990s, Dunbar conducted research on pri-mates and concluded that the size of a functioning social group was closely related to the size of a human, monkey, or ape brain.[14] If a brain was small, the size of a monkey's or ape's, say, the creature could only cope with a limited number of meaningful social relations (a few dozen). But if a brain was bigger, as for a human's, a wider circle of relationships could be formed. Humans did this, Dunbar argued, via 'social grooming,' conventions that enabled people to be closely bonded. Just as primates created ties by physically grooming each other's skin by picking out nits, humans bonded with laughter, music, gossip, dance, and all other ritualistic day-to-day interactions that develop when people work or live together.

The optimal size for a social group among humans was about 150, Dunbar suggested, since the human brain had the capacity to maintain that many close ties via social grooming, but not more. When groups became larger than that, they could not be held together just by face-to-face bonds and social grooming, but only with coercion or bureaucracy. Thus, bands of hunter-gatherers, Roman army units, neolithic villages, or Hutterite settlements all tended to be smaller than 150. When they grew larger than that, they typically split. In the modern world, groups that are less than 150 in size tend to be more effective than bigger units, he argued, and humans seemed to instinctively know this. Modern college fraternities tend to be smaller than this. Most companies' departments are below this threshold. And when Dunbar examined how British people exchanged Christmas cards in the early 1990s (which he considered to be a good definition of a friendship circle in British culture back then, before the advent of platforms such as Facebook), he discovered that the average number of people reached by the cards that somebody dispatched to different households was 153.[15] 'This [150] limit is a direct function of relative neocortex size, and this in turn limits group size,' as Dunbar wrote. 'The limit imposed by neocortical processing capacity is simply on the number of individuals with whom a stable inter-personal relationship can be maintained.'[16]

Not everyone in the academic community agreed with Dunbar. After he published his groundbreaking research, other anthropologists, neurologists, and biologists tried their own tests and some concluded that the optimal size of a social group could be twice this size. But Zuckerberg and the other founders of Facebook were fascinated by Dunbar's number, and they eventually asked Dunbar to provide some consulting advice. Initially, their interest was commercially focused. As they designed their site the Facebook engineers wanted to know how many friends a Facebook user was likely to have so they could build their systems accordingly. However, as the Facebook engineers talked to Dunbar, they realized that his findings not only had implications for how Facebook should build the website for *external* users. The findings could also affect how employees interacted with each other *inside* the company. Back in the early days when Zuckerberg had first created his company, the employees had worked as a single group. Some of them lived together, they worked in close quarters, knew each other well, and had joint rituals, such as ordering food from a local Chinese takeout. However, as the company swelled in size, it was harder to maintain this sense of group identity.

Facebook was not the only company to face that challenge. It afflicted every other successful technology start-up. And the history of Silicon Valley suggested that for many companies the problems posed by a rapid expansion in size were deadly. After all, the technology world is littered with tales of companies that have started life as small, freewheeling entities, which then enjoyed great success but later turned into gigantic bureaucracies, riddled with infighting and silos. Sony was one case. Xerox another. The example that particularly worried some Facebook engineers, however, was Microsoft. Although the Seattle-based group had started off as a dynamic and creative entity, by the turn of the century it was plagued with silos. This fragmentation was not as extreme as at Sony, but nevertheless undermined Microsoft's ability to compete.

So was there any way to avoid that fate? The Facebook engineers were determined to try. 'We want to be the anti-Sony, the anti-Microsoft – we look at companies like that and see what we don't want to become,' one senior manager later recalled. They started tossing ideas around about how to combat the problem. In the summer of 2008, one of the early Facebook founders, Andrew Bosworth, a burly, baldheaded, tattooed, engineer, floated a novel idea.[17] Bosworth was known as 'Boz' to his colleagues. (The Facebook engineers loved to give each other nicknames; it was part of the process of social grooming.) In previous months, Boz had been trying to create a training program for new recruits. His goal was to ensure that when computing engineers joined Facebook they knew the same set of computer codes as all the other employees, and were assigned to a team that used their skills most effectively. So he created an introductory course that showed them the company and taught them crucial coding knowledge. But Boz then realized that the course could do more than impart technical knowledge. It could also be a tool of social engineering. After all, if you put all the new recruits through a common training experience in small groups, you could create a mechanism for some social grooming and bonding. And while these groups of trainees would not stay together as a unit, since they were destined to be scattered across the company, the joint experience could create lasting ties between them, and the type of social intimacy that fostered nicknames.

That summer Facebook declared that all of its new employees – no matter how junior or senior – would undergo a six-week induction process when they joined. Boz was named 'Bootcamp Drill Sergeant.' 'The primary goal of Bootcamp is to get people up to speed on all parts of our code base while promoting good habits that we believe will pay dividends in the long term, such as fearlessly fixing bugs as we come across them, rather than leaving them for future engineers,' Boz explained in a written message to the staff, posted on Facebook. 'A small number of rotating senior engineers serve as mentors and meet with the new engineers regularly to coach them on how to be more effective at Facebook. The mentors review all the bootcampers' code and even hold office hours to answer any basic questions that engineers might otherwise be too timid to ask. Senior engineers from across the engineering team also give a bunch of tech talks on a broad range of the technologies we use from MySQL and Memcached to CSS and JavaScript.'[18] A crucial part of that training process, Boz added, would be a rotation program to show the new recruits the entire company. 'Instead of assigning engineers to teams arbitrarily based on a small amount of interaction during interviews, bootcampers choose the team they will join at the end of their six weeks.'

However, the new recruits were not just being asked to just learn technologies such as MySQL. 'Bootcampers tend to form bonds with their classmates who joined near the same time and those bonds persist even after each has joined different teams,' Boz explained. Or to put it another way, the Facebook managers were trying to use Bootcamp to do not one, but *two*, things. First, they were organizing the company into discrete project teams, dedicated groups to perform tasks. This was essential because the process of writing code requires intense collaboration on specific projects or processes. A company such as Facebook needs silos, in the sense of needing specialist departments and teams, simply to get its work done. Project groups were needed for focus and accountability. But the second aim of Bootcamp was to overlay those project teams with a *second* set of informal social ties not defined by the formal department boundaries. This, it was hoped, would prevent the project teams from hardening into rigid, inward-looking groups, and ensure that employees felt a sense of affiliation with the entire company, not just their tiny group. 'Bootcamp [can foster] cross team communication and prevent the silos that so commonly spring up in growing engineering organizations,' Boz said. Facebook was both creating the preconditions for silos and instilling systems to break down those silos.

IN THE AUTUMN OF 2010, Jocelyn Goldfein graduated from her own Bootcamp[19] and took charge of a small team of engineers working on a project known as 'News Feed.' This was a tool on the social media platform that had first been launched back in 2006, which essentially enabled a Facebook user to see 'news' – or posts – from friends, grouped into a chronological sequence.[20] By 2010, the tool was wildly popular with many Facebook users and there did not appear to be any commercial imperative to update it. However, it was a core mantra of Facebook, like other technology groups such as Apple, that to survive the company had to constantly remake its most successful products. 'If we don't disrupt ourselves, someone else will disrupt us,' Goldfein observed.[21] So Goldfein's team dove into the challenge of improving News Feed. It was a complex computing problem. To make News Feed work well, Facebook needed an algorithm that would automatically select the most important details of all the news (or feeds) that a Facebook user was receiving from their friends, and present them in an easy-to-read manner. Initially, Facebook had done this task by just listing all the news that a user had received, in crude chronological order, on their computer screen. That worked well in the early days when the site was small and Facebook users did not receive many posts or messages. But by 2010 the site had exploded so dramatically in size that users were drowning in news. Posts that were very important, or a 'MLE' (Major Life Event) in Facebook parlance, could get drowned out by trivia. News about a death might be given the same weight as a picture of a kitten, and then almost disappear from view if there were hundreds of kitty snaps.

So Goldfein's team set about hunting for ways to create a more sensitive algorithm to rank information. It was intensive work, requiring hours at the keyboard, pushing the boundaries of coding. Or as a newspaper in India observed: 'It wouldn't be an exaggeration to say the task [of rewriting News Feed] is at the frontiers of computer science, since it uses artificial intelligence derived from the huge amounts of data FB has on user behaviour.' First, the team experimented with writing pieces of code that would group news according to clusters of topics that appeared among users. Then they tried treating the News Feed as if it were a newspaper, placing MLEs at the top of any feed. But nothing worked well. 'We could do a variation [of a code] in a week or two, but a theme [for the site] would take five weeks and there were three major themes in the course of four or five months,' Goldfein explained. Then the team tried another method called the 'boulder prototype.' This algorithm picked out the biggest stories and assigned them 'boulder status,' around which other related stories appeared as 'pebbles.' This system worked better. 'If you log on after a week, you get all the important stories since you last logged in,' Goldfein said, '[but] if you hang out on FB, you'll see changed feeds. It has the magic element because you see the best stories first, but it feels less deterministic, which is something users like.'[22]

As the months passed, and the News Feed team spent hours at their keyboards, tossing ideas around, they became increasingly close. Indeed, to Goldfein the experience was so intense that she often felt as if she was working on a start-up. That was deliberate: Zuckerberg and the other Facebook managers wanted to give the separate coding groups as much freedom as possible to brainstorm, experiment, and develop ideas on their own, in a fast-moving and entrepreneurial way. They reckoned that the sense of independence was crucial to enable the company to develop quickly. But even as the team bonded as a quasi-start-up around a project, the Facebook managers also kept trying to pull them back into the wider group. Each week, Goldfein would meet with the other senior engineers to explain her progress. 'Mark [Zuckerberg] was the hub around which we moved – we would meet once a week with him and explain what we were doing,' she observed.[23] The Facebook staff often met up with the other members of their Bootcamp groups. Under the guise of conducting social events, they were being encouraged to swap ideas and news. 'Facebook started doing the Bootcamps to solve a really different problem, which was giving people greater freedom of choice about where they wanted to work later,' Goldfein explained. 'But this has serendipitously been huge for silo busting. The power of knowing at least one person in each silo is crucial for making the company work.'[24]

Goldfein also shuffled her own team. To do this she used a second Facebook ritual: the 'Hackamonth.' This practice had developed out of the Bootcamp idea. 'Hackamonth is basically the second part of Bootcamp. It's effectively a rotation program,' Michael Schroepfer, the chief engineer of Facebook, explained. A small wiry man, he was normally known as 'Schrep' inside the company.

'If you have been working on the same thing for 12–18 months we then tap you on a shoulder and say get to work on something else for a few months! Most people end up choosing something pretty far away from what they are doing.'[25] As with the Bootcamp idea, the Hackamonth ritual had arisen partly by accident and partly by experimentation. Schrep and Boz had started it with the aim of keeping the engineers motivated by their jobs. Technology companies in Silicon Valley were growing so fast that when engineers got bored, they were liable to be poached by rivals. 'When people actively choose to do something, they are going to do better work,' Schrep explained. 'Passion is a force multiplier – and that offsets everything else.'[26] However, once Hackamonth started, it became clear that this ritual could break down silos too. Moving people around prevented the different teams from hardening into inward-looking units. So the Facebook managers expanded the scheme. Facebook was born out of a culture that liked to constantly experiment with small steps and then chase after whatever worked, in an iterative way, irrespective of whether that was in the field of management practices, such as Hackamonth, or computer code. 'About 50 percent of the people who go on Hackamonth switch teams and half return to the original team. But either way we think we win,' said Schrep.

The Hackamonth system had some big drawbacks. It was time-consuming to find places to put the engineers who wanted to move, and fill the gaps in their original teams when they left. Inevitably there was some duplication and overlap, if not waste. 'All of these processes are painful and inefficient. Sometimes you have two or three people away from a team, one on Hackamonth, one on parental leave, or whatever. It would be much easier to just put one person into each team and tell them to stay there,' Schrep admitted.[27] But he concluded it was a small price to pay to meet the goal of keeping the organization fluid and connected; it was crucial to have a bit of slack, or inefficiency, to breed creativity and give people time to stay connected.

So, a few months after she had embarked on the News Feed project, Goldfein rotated one of her key engineers into another group. This second team was working on a separate project linked to the Timeline feature. At first it seemed like a loss for News Feed, since the battle to develop the boulder prototype was at a delicate stage. But then she realized that the rotation had produced a benefit too: the different project teams started swapping ideas. 'Timeline owed a lot of its code to News Feed and we hoped that having [the News Feed engineer move teams] would give us closer lines of communication,' Goldfein said. 'And it turned out to be very valuable ... on a day-to-day basis nobody in the company has time to understand what everyone else in the different project teams are doing. But the key thing is to get this rich surface of community and information sharing, in whatever way you can.'

IN DECEMBER 2011, EIGHTEEN months after she had joined Facebook, Goldfein and the other staff moved from the office in Palo Alto into a brand-new campus building in a nearby district, Menlo Park[28] By then the Facebook staff had risen above 2,000;[29] breaching the Dunbar principle multiple times. However, as the ranks swelled, the social experiments grew apace. The Facebook managers were determined to use whatever social tool they could imagine *both* to create dedicated, specialist project groups *and* to prevent those little teams from ossifying into competitive silos. Architecture was one weapon in this fight. The new Facebook campus was based at a site previously been owned by Sun Microsystems, and its logo still sat on the back of the entrance address sign. Sun was yet another tech giant that had once flourished in Silicon Valley in earlier decades, initially as a freewheeling start-up, but later turned into a stodgy behemoth, plagued by silos. When Sun had owned the site, whose official address was 1601 Willow Road, its employees had been tucked into dozens of different buildings, which were subdivided into numerous small offices and cubicles. 'It felt like a cattle pen!' laughed Schrep, who had worked there. 'You didn't have much contact with anyone at all.' However, when Facebook bought the site, Zuckerberg decided to christen it 'One Hacker Way' and the address sign was painted over in blue and the image of a giant white thumb pointing upward was added on top, the 'Like' symbol on the Facebook platform. Builders ripped out most of the internal dividing walls in the old Sun buildings and added whiteboards, bare pipe work, and graffiti walls. Insofar as there were meeting rooms, these were surrounded by walls made of glass, so that anyone could peer into anyone else's room. Even Zuckerberg worked in the open plan space, visible to all. So did Sheryl Sandberg, the high-profile chief operating officer. Zuckerberg had a 'private' office too. However, this was lined with glass and placed in the center of the campus, next to a walkway along which all the employees constantly strolled. A sign saying 'Do not feed the animals!' was fastened to the window. 'We call it Mark's goldfish bowl!' quipped Schrep. 'Everyone can see him.'

Then Schrep went further. He asked the architects to connect the higher floors of the separate buildings with walkways. These stretched high in the air above the Facebook walkways, painted in the same bright orange-red as San Francisco's famous Golden Gate Bridge. Doors were installed at the end of these walkways that opened automatically when anyone passed; they were modeled on supermarket doors. Schrep's goal was to ensure that the engineers never need to pause when they rambled around the building. 'There is all this research out there which shows that if you can keep people moving and colliding with each other, you get much more interaction,' he explained. The space between the buildings was turned into attractive 'rambling' zones, to encourage employees to hang out together in the balmy California weather. In the center of the campus an open meeting spot was created, known as 'Hacker Square.' A couple of times a year Zuckerberg held 'all-hands' meetings in this open space. He also held town halls (or 'Q&A' sessions, as Facebook preferred to call them) every Friday afternoon in a vast cafeteria. Sometimes employees would throw unexpected questions at Zuckerberg. Other times the events seemed more formulaic. But either way, the symbolism was clear: the Facebook managers were determined to present the company to the employees as a single, open mass, where everyone could – and should – collide with everyone else, in a free-wheeling, irreverent way.

Hacker Square was also used to stage another of the experiments in social engineering, the hackathons. Every six weeks or so, several hundred engineers would congregate in the square around a piece of yellow machinery that had once been part of a crane, before later retiring to a large meeting room with bright orange walls plastered with inspirational posters.[30] There they would spend all night working in small teams on coding problems; the idea was that the engineers would test out ideas together, or 'hack,' to use the slang that computing experts loved to toss around. Being pushed together in a small space and asked to work intensively overnight was one way to unleash the creative juices.

These Hackathons were not unique to Facebook. On the contrary, they are a well-worn ritual across the technology world. At the City Hall in Chicago, Brett Goldstein arranged hackathons with his nerd herd, to develop programs the city could use.

But at Facebook the hackathons had an unusual twist. These events had initially simply occurred whenever some engineers clustered together with their friends and teammates around a laptop. Thus in the early days of Facebook, Zuckerberg had spent all night brainstorming ideas with the other founding members of the company in the house he shared with the engineers. But as time passed the Facebook managers insisted that the groups who coalesced in a hackathon night had to cluster together with people from *different* teams from their normal projects and work on something outside their day job. Sometimes engineers congregated together into short-term mini-teams because they had made contact in the days leading up to an event, or because they were all interested in a specific problem. On other occasions engineers decided to work with each other almost by chance. Either way, hackathons – like Bootcamp and Hackamonth – were intended to break down the normal departmental boundaries. They were another tool to ensure that while Facebook had dedicated project teams, these could not ossify into inward-looking silos.

Soon after joining Facebook, Goldfein used a hackathon to write some computing code that could add the category of in-laws and step relations to the Facebook platform. This project was not connected to her News Feed job at all. But it was a project dear to her heart. 'I am really close to my husband's mother, but didn't want to call her just an in-law, but when I started looking at the Facebook site after I joined I saw that although we had "family" as a group on the site, we couldn't do in-laws. But that seemed wrong, so I used a hackathon to think about it.' Or as Pedram

Keyani, an Indian-born computer engineer who organized many of the hackathons, explained: 'The whole point of hackathons is that they shake up the hierarchy. We break down the silos, at least for a period, and get a communal spirit.'

ANOTHER TOOL THAT THE Facebook managers used to fight silos was the Facebook platform itself. Right from the earliest days of the company, the Facebook managers realized that one of the advantages of Facebook was that it enabled communication to occur in a horizontal way, instead of via a rigid hierarchy. When somebody made a post, everyone could access that piece of information. This was a contrast to the usual communication pattern of many big companies via email, where information tended to get passed up, or down, hierarchies, creating potential bottlenecks and logjams.

As time passed, the managers spotted that there was a second advantage of the Facebook platform: it provided a way for the staff to build deeper connections with each other, on multiple different levels. The Facebook managers believed that this was another important weapon in the war against silos. 'One technique we teach managers here is that we insist that people use names – *real* names – to talk about each other,' Schrep said. 'If we ever catch anyone using a depersonalized moniker then you interrupt them and stop them. We never let people refer to anyone else as, say, "those idiots in team six" or "'those stupid marketing guys," since it is one sign of dehumanizing a group. When you don't know who people are and depersonalize groups, then you get into problems.'

The Facebook platform could help that goal of humanizing

staff, the managers hoped. So the top managers were urged to create their own Facebook posts and share ideas, messages, and details about their lives with their colleagues. Some people hated that. 'I am a pretty shy, introverted person naturally,' Goldfein admitted. 'Before I joined Facebook I didn't post very much at all. I was pretty inhibited.' But soon after she arrived, she bowed to the pressure and started posting to her colleagues. Her opening post was reserved: *'What's the worse bug you've seen caught in a code review? Can you recommend a better OSX-based IRC client than adium?'*[31] Then Goldfein started to open up. *'Hi there, subscribers!'* she declared on her fifth post. *'I work in Facebook engineering on core features of the site, like news feed, photos, and search. In my previous life, I ran engineering for VMware's desktop products. I'm passionate about getting more women into engineering careers and the challenges of scaling software engineering organizations. I have kids instead of hobbies. Science fiction and Glee are my guilty pleasures.'*[32] As the weeks passed, she started revealing more details about her private life. *'I'm kind of fascinated by the variances in my commute at different weird times of day. Anyone know of an app for tracking this? Preferably one w/ facebook integration?'*[33] She posted her favorite recipe for madeleines on her Facebook page. She talked about a cause dear to her heart: the gender imbalance in the computing world. *'In the 1970s, boys outnumbered girls 13:1 for perfect scores on the math SAT. Today, the ratio is 3:1 and falling. (And average score is identical.) Is there anyone left who seriously thinks differences in math performance are biological? If so, I have a science lesson for you on how fast evolution works.'*[34] She championed media outlets trying to buck gender stereotypes. '*So* Brave *is the first Disney princess movie I've ever seen in which mom is neither gone nor evil. And, it appears to be pulling down the big bucks.* Crossing my fingers in case the world might be changing for the better.'[35] When she traveled to Washington on a lobbying campaign, she revealed details of that too. '*It was particularly cool to meet Cady Coleman, a colonel and NASA astronaut. My ambition to be an astronaut when I grew up did not survive high school, but I definitely think NASA, Sally Ride, and Christa McAuliffe helped fuel my interest in math and science from early on.*'[36]

Sometimes Goldfein felt nervous about revealing so much. But as time passed, she realized that it was the personal that helped her connect. 'Every time I share a little more outside my comfort zone it feels so rewarding. I end up making new connections in the company, and it's become like a positive feedback loop.' She was not the only one. During 2012, the reticent Zuckerberg started to post details of his wedding, his backyard, and his daily life, albeit with a corporate spin. '*The Facebook foxes that live on our campus are pretty amazing,*' he mused to staff in one post.[37] Or: '*I updated my grilling app, iGrill, today and it now has Facebook integration that lets you see what other people are grilling right now around the world. Awesome! I'm making a Fred's steak!*'[38] Sandberg posted information about the company and used the site to promote her book, called *Lean In,* that urged women to take more responsibility for their careers. Schrep used the platform to share tips with other engineers on how to work effectively. '*Focus. Focus, Focus. Facebook engineers are used to*

hearing me say the word focus A LOT. De swiss cheese your sched-
ule! Abide by no-meeting Wednesday. Mind your health as this is
a marathon not a sprint: exercise and good sleep make you more
productive.'[39] Then he revealed that his secret tips for success were
'*1) Eliminate all visual distractions on my screen and focus on one*
app at a time. FocusMask works great for this. 2) Set up intervals
for focused time, breaks, and interrupt driven time. Using a simple
timer during focus intervals helps me not accidentally wander. 3)
Large over-ear headphones which block out sound and tell others to
not interrupt me now. Music without lyrics – Mogwai or classical
depending on mood. What works for you?'

Junior staff shared thoughts too. In the spring of 2013 an
engineer named Ryan Patterson posted a note to tell colleagues
that '*this week marks the beginning of my 4th year at Facebook.*'
By the standards of the company, that made him a veteran. So
he decided to offer advice to new recruits. '*As a hacker, having*
agency over your world is critical to fully explore the boundaries
of problems and find how to best leverage your solutions. . . . I'm
referring both to the code that you write and to the interactions
you have within the company. . . . Take ownership over the entire
company. Find a random person with whom you haven't worked
in months and have a quick chat with them. It can provide a fresh
insight.'[40]

ON AN EARLY SUMMER evening in May 2013, several hundred
young(ish) men and women wearing sneakers, jeans, and
T-shirts assembled around the yellow crane in Hacker Square.
The sun was dipping below the horizon, leaving pink streams

in the luminescent blue sky. A man on stilts bounded across the square. Another waved an old-fashioned boogie box throbbing with dance music. A third man, bearded, wearing a blue mask and indigo Zorro-style cape, jumped onto the base of a crane. The Facebook engineers had stumbled across this hunk of machinery at another office a few years earlier, entirely by chance, and become attached to it. They used it for office meetings and pranks. So when the company moved to the new campus at Menlo Park, the engineers insisted on moving it too, as a ceremonial prop and symbol of their origins. The company had only been in existence for a decade. However, the Facebook engineers had already forged a multitude of group rituals and founding legends. The pattern would have looked familiar to an anthropologist such as Bronislaw Malinowski, the Polish academic who studied the Trobriand Islanders in the 1930s and pioneered the idea of 'participant observation.' The ceremonies at Facebook, like the Kula exchanges in the Trobriand Islands, had an important function; they were helping to glue the wider social group together by forging a common sense of identity.

'Friends, Romans, Hackers! Lend me your ears!' the man in the cape shouted. The crowd temporarily fell silent. Pedram Keyani, the nominal leader of the Hackathon group, stepped forward. 'You know the form!' shouted out Keyani, sporting jeans and an olive green T-shirt. 'If you are still here at 5 a.m. there will be breakfast! And Chinese later!' The crowd laughed again. Hackathons always started on the yellow crane, and then moved to another room where the engineers always ate exactly the same Chinese takeout several hours later, in the middle of the night.

Zuckerberg had first started buying food from this particular Chinese restaurant when he created Facebook a decade before. By 2013, the restaurant was no longer a remotely convenient place to order from, since it was a long way from Hacker Way. But nobody wanted to mess with that ritual by ordering from somewhere else.

'Is there anyone here who has not been to a hackathon before?' Keyani shouted to the crowd. A few hands waved. 'Well that's awesome! The only rule is – go enjoy yourself, go mingle, go have fun! And just remember our hackathons are not like anyone else's hackathons. Enjoy! Let's write some code!' The gang of hoodie-wearing engineers dispersed in small groups and walked to a large conference room studded with inspirational slogans: *Move fast, and break things! Done is better than perfect! What would you do if you were not afraid?* 'Posters are one of the biggest culture carrier at Facebook,' observed Sandberg. 'We will be in a meeting and someone will quote something to somebody else like "Make Great Decisions." That's the type of company we are. A lot of the initial cultural ideas came from Mark, but we are very aligned as a group. You cannot impose this from the top. It has to grow from below too.'

COULD THESE LESSONS BE transplanted into other companies? From time to time, Sandberg and the other executives would ask themselves that. By 2013, other companies across Silicon Valley were using variants of the same silo-busting tactics that Facebook had developed. At Google and Apple the employees staged hackathons, and rotated staff. The idea of conducting common induction and training programs for new recruits was spreading. The concept of using architecture as a tool to promote employee collisions and collaborations was also widespread, both inside and outside the technology world. 3M, the manufacturing group, prided itself on running research laboratories that deliberately mixed different specialists up. Google had imaginatively designed facilities that enabled staff to collide.

Numerous other entities were using social media sites to promote better employee communication. Over in Europe, the consumer company Unilever installed an internal social media platform that had been developed by Salesforce, the cloud computing group, to promote cross-company horizontal communication. This system, called Chatter, was initially created to enable the top managers to disseminate messages to everyone else. But then the Unilever executives realized it also could be used to break down silos inside the company. 'Chatter has helped us to connect all our global groups and teams, share ideas, news items and latest developments and minimise the chances for unnecessary repetition in markets,' chief scientist Kim Crilly says.

But what made the managers at Facebook unusual was the degree to which they kept turning the lens back on themselves and trying new iterative experiments in social engineering. Having built a successful business by using computing ideas to analyze human friendships, they remained endlessly fascinated by how they all interacted with each other. 'I never used to think about this social stuff. It didn't seem that important,' confessed Schrep. 'But then, when I came to Facebook, I realized just how much it matters. That's a real change! And now I cannot stop thinking about it.'

The Facebook managers had another reason for introspection: they knew that they were surrounded by competitive threats. There were dozens of smaller, more nimble start-ups who were eager to challenge Facebook, and technology was changing at a furious pace. When Zuckerberg had first created Facebook in the early years of the twenty-first century, he built the business for desktop computers and personal computing screens. Facebook was so successful in exploiting that niche, that it was slow to adapt to mobile technology. The Facebook engineers made the mistake of assuming that they could simply take the web product and put it onto mobile. But web products did not translate well onto a tiny mobile phone. 'It's pretty well documented that we were not very good at mobile [initially] – terrible, in fact,' Goldfein admitted in the spring of 2014. 'I joined Facebook in the summer of 2010, and at that point Facebook's mobile team was like four guys in the basement. [For the web] there was a News Feed team; there was a Messenger team; there was a Photos team. ... Collectively there were 100 or 200 engineers building all of these features [for the web], and then you had this one tiny team that was trying to keep feature parity with all of that in the iOS app. And I won't even talk about how we were approaching Android because it was just embarrassing.'[41]

When Zuckerberg and the others eventually realized their terrible mistake, they scrambled to respond. Facebook bought Instagram, the photo-sharing site, and other mobile companies.[42] Goldfein and the other engineers were shuffled around, to focus

on mobile technologies instead of the web. 'What we learned to
do is start with the [mobile] platform and make the best possible
application for it and to the extent that the web has things that
are useful to bring them over – but don't start from the web and
try to bring them over. Start from mobile, and take what's good
from the web,' she observed. By 2014, this switch in strategy
seemed to be working. The company's mobile app was gaining
traction, and the company was harnessing advertising revenue
from this mobile platform, alongside its more traditional PC-
based product. Indeed, when Facebook reported its results for
the 2014 calendar year, these showed that revenues had jumped
$12.47 billion, 57 percent higher than a year earlier, largely due
to a sudden surge in mobile advertising.[43]

But nobody inside the company felt complacent. The bigger
the company became – and more successful – the more nervous they felt about the threat from nimble, small rivals. When
Facebook conducted a successful IPO in late 2013, which valued
the company at an eye-popping $100 billion, this expansion
seemed to increase, not decrease, the unease. 'I don't think we
are in any danger [of getting silos] in the next two years, but for
all companies it's a question of scale,' Goldfein observed. 'But
social problems are like computer problems: you have to keep
asking if the same approach that handles 1,000 users be applied
to 100,000.'

There was another, more subtle challenge. One notable feature of Facebook was that its employees were homogenous. The
engineers were mostly trained in the same set of computer skills
and were in their twenties or early thirties. Most wore a common

'uniform,' sneakers and jeans, and had a similar outlook on life. That made it easier to foster a common group identity and break down silos *inside* the company. Moving the engineers between teams was not so hard, because they were so similar. But as the employees inside Facebook became defined as a social group, with a sense of their own identity, this created a new risk: in the future the company could end up acting like a gigantic social silo of its own.

That danger was not unique to Facebook. The boom in Silicon Valley was giving birth to a wildly successfully technology elite. The wealthier these techies became, the greater their sense of confidence, if not arrogance. Like the bankers a decade before, the techies risked becoming detached from less successful mortals around them, not just in terms of wealth, but education and outlook. To anyone outside the tech world, it was almost impossible to understand exactly what computer engineers at places such as Facebook did. The algorithms were as impenetrable as financial jargon. And the techies sometimes lost perspective of what outsiders thought of them. There was a risk of becoming a techie ghetto.

But the engineers who congregated in the orange conference room at Facebook during the hackathon on that warm May night were not too worried about those *future* dangers. The present seemed too exciting. They just wanted to write code, and push the frontiers of computing science, as the managers kept producing new ideas about social engineering. 'We think we have a system that works, which breaks down silos,' said Keyani as he looked across the groups of engineers as they did their hackathon, huddled together in clusters around computers. 'But we need to keep experimenting all the time.' It was the spirit of the 'hacker way' – and perhaps the most crucial weapon in Facebook's fight to avoid the fate of Sony.

7

FLIPPING THE LENS

How Doctors Tried Not to Behave Like Economists

'I like to turn things upside down, to watch pictures and situations from another perspective ... [and] see how things behave if you change the point of view.'

—Ursus Wehrli. Swiss comedian and artist

THE MOOD IN THE LECTURE THEATER AT HARVARD BUSINESS SCHOOL WAS earnest and respectful. Sitting in the rows of seats, arranged in a horseshoe shape around a dais, were some of the most ambitious young people in the world. Attending Harvard Business School typically costs at least $100,000, and competition to win places is fierce.[1] The students have sky-high expectations of themselves and speakers who visit that famed lecture hall. And the man chosen to address the students on that day in early autumn 2006 was dazzling.[2]

A tall, imposing figure with a craggy face and big ears, Toby

Cosgrove, sixty-five,[3] was one of most famous heart surgeons in world. During the first few decades of his career, he had shot to glory in the medical world as a pioneering cardiothoracic surgeon who had operated on more than 22,000 patients and filed thirty patents for medical innovations.[4] But in 2004 Cosgrove was appointed CEO of the mighty Cleveland Clinic in Ohio, one of the biggest medical centers in America, with an operating budget of $6 billion and staff of 40,000.[5] The clinic was ranked among the best in America in numerous fields, including Cosgrove's speciality of heart surgery. It offered cutting-edge treatments at prices that were better than those of most competitors. People from around the world flocked to use its services. It was, in short, a model of how a twenty-first-century hospital should operate, at least in the eyes of Harvard Business School.

So the students listened with awe as Cosgrove explained how Cleveland Clinic worked. He was a good speaker, who exuded firm, natural authority, leavened by flashes of dry, self-deprecating wit. What most people did not know was that Cosgrove was also dyslexic. In his teens and early twenties he had struggled at school. But he had battled through this handi-cap to become a surgeon by virtue of ferocious willpower and a photographic memory. 'Dr Cosgrove is a brilliant man, the most ambitious person in the world since Alexander the Great,' Bruce Lytle, a fellow heart surgeon at Cleveland Clinic sometimes joked. 'That is good – you need those people to change the world.'

After Cosgrove finished his speech to the Harvard students, he took questions. The first few were admiring. But then a young, slim brunette woman named Kara Medoff Barnett, who was sitting in the second row of the auditorium, stood up. 'Dr Cosgrove, my father needed mitral valve surgery. We knew about Clevelend Clinic and the excellent results you have. But we decided *not* to go there because we heard you had no empathy. We went to another hospital instead, even though it wasn't as highly ranked as yours.'[6]

There was a startled pause. Barnett pressed on, looking Cosgrove in the eye. 'Dr Cosgrove, do you teach empathy at Cleveland Clinic?'[7]

Empathy? Cosgrove was a loss. During his decades-long battle to become a star surgeon against fierce odds, Cosgrove had spent numerous days honing his technical skills. But he had never given much thought to empathy. It sounded hippie, if not self-indulgent. 'Not really,' he mumbled vaguely, and switched the subject.

The next day he left Boston, and tried to brush the incident off. But that odd little encounter kept buzzing through his mind. *Dr Cosgrove, do you teach empathy?* Ten days later, it popped into his head again, in the unlikely setting of Saudi Arabia. The top managers of Cleveland Clinic were keen to expand in the Middle East, since it had a pool of wealthy clients. So Cosgrove decided to attend the official opening of a new hospital in Jeddah. To mark the occasion, the Saudi king and crown prince hosted a ceremony, along with many local dignitaries, and the new head of the hospital gave a passionate speech.[8] 'This hospital is dedicated to the body, spirit and soul of the patient,' he declared.[9] As he spoke, Cosgrove glanced across to the Saudi king and noticed, to his complete surprise, that tears were rolling down his face.[10] He felt a frisson. *We're really missing something here.* He was used to thinking about medicine in dry, technical terms, or a delineated bundle of specialist skills. He did not usually think about the whole 'soul.'

But were specialist skills really enough? The question kept buzzing around in his mind. On paper, Cosgrove knew that Cleveland Clinic was an excellent medical center, or at least it was if you looked at it using the type of mental map that doctors used. There were world-class surgeons, physicians, nurses, psychologists, and physiotherapists; there were divisions of Anesthesiology, Pediatrics, Medicine, Surgery, Pathology and Laboratory Medicine, Post-Acute Care, Regional Medical Practice, Nursing, and Education. To name but a few of the specialist teams.

But was this what sick people *really* wanted? Was it the best, most effective, or cheapest way to do medicine? Cosgrove was starting to have doubts. Doctors visualized medicine as a collection of technical skills. Patients did not. When people were sick they did not say 'I need a cardiothoracic surgeon' or 'Take me to a cardiologist.' Instead they would declare 'My chest hurts,' or 'I am having a seizure,' or 'I can't breathe,' or 'My stomach is in pain,' or simply 'I feel unwell.'

In some sense, that differences in perception exist about medicine should come as no surprise. When anthropologists first started to study non-Western cultures in the late nineteenth century, they realized that different societies view the body and define sickness and health in subtly varying ways. Then, as anthropology expanded in the twentieth century, a sub-discipline emerged called 'medical anthropology,' which examines how health is perceived, experienced, and implemented in different communities around the world. This discipline, which is one of the fastest growing areas of anthropology, argues that health is not really a matter of biology, or not *just* science. It is a cultural phenomenon too. Our physiology might be universal. But concepts of 'sickness' can vary between different cultures, and within the same society.

In the last two decades, this idea has had a growing impact on the development and assistance work that multilateral development institutions and nongovernmental organiations do in poor parts of the world. Jim Yong Kim, the head of the World Bank, is a medical anthropologist who has a doctorate in anthropology but is also a qualified physician. He has used these two different skill sets to develop research into the spread of diseases in poor communities, and promoted this interdisciplinary approach at the World Bank. Kim's colleague and friend Paul Farmer, another medical anthropologist, has pioneered health care experiments in places such as Africa with the group Partners in Health. He has also tried to promote this idea in elite American universities such as Harvard, where he is a professor. Numerous other examples exist in different corners of the developing world.

However, medical anthropology has hitherto had less impact on the core of Western medicine. Medical anthropologists have tended to work in a corner of academia, or silo, that is far removed from high-flying surgeons such as Cosgrove. But as Cosgrove pondered his encounter in the Harvard lecture theater, he began to play around with some ideas that are the core of medical anthropology. What would happen, he wondered, if he tried to 'flip the lens,' and defined medicine as *patients*, not doctors, experienced it? What might that mean for how a hospital was organized? In the years before Cosgrove's encounter at Harvard, some doctors in Cleveland Clinic had already been discussing making tweaks to their hospital structure. Innovations in medicine were breaking down the traditional distinctions between surgeons and physicians, and many doctors at the hospital thought that it was time to rethink the structure of some of the departments. But Cosgrove did not just want to fiddle with the organizational chart. He wanted to rethink medicine in a more fundamental sense and question the very foundations of doctors' specialist silos. In essence, he wanted to do what the bankers and economists that I described in Chapters Three and Four respectively, had *not* done, namely examine the classification systems that skilled professionals use to arrange the world.

He knew it would be difficult. Doctors (like economists) spend years training in specialist fields and wield power precisely because few nonspecialists understand what they do. 'There is a whole guild system that defines who doctors are, and that guild system is very strong,' Cosgrove later observed with a dry laugh. That is true of most professions. At the Bank of England and Federal Reserve before 2008, economists had stayed inside their specialist silos and assumed that the business of regulating nonbank financial groups was an activity that lay outside the economics sphere. Similar patterns are seen in numerous other corners of business life, particularly when the activity is so technically complex that it is difficult for outsiders to understand what is going on, far less challenge it. The elite of any society rarely have any incentive to challenge the status quo, or the taxonomy.

But Cosgrove was a determined man. So, a few months after his fateful encounter in Boston with Barnett, Cleveland Clinic embarked on an experiment. It was an initiative that ended up being somewhat controversial in the medical world, capturing the attention of Washington's White House. But it also had implications that extend well beyond the medical world. What the Cleveland Clinic story shows is that if you want to combat the problem of silos, you do not always need to shuffle people around between different departments, organize corporate retreats, or encourage people to take radical career breaks (as I have described in the last two chapters). Another way to tackle the issue is to encourage people to reflect on their classification systems and how they organize the world, or to even turn those taxonomies upside down. Mental reorganization can sometimes be almost as effective as structural change, particularly if those two shifts go hand in hand. And that lesson has big implications not just for doctors, but for economists, bankers, manufacturers, journalists, and numerous other skilled professionals. Not to mention sick people who just want to find a doctor with empathy.

IN SOME RESPECTS, CLEVELAND Clinic is the perfect place for somebody to launch silo-busting experiments. The hospital has always had something of an unorthodox spirit. Its origins go back to the 1880s when Frank J. Weed, a successful surgeon, hired Frank Bunts and George Washington Crile, two newly qualified doctors, to create a small medical practice to serve the then booming market of Cleveland.[11] In 1891 Weed died of pneumonia, aged forty-five, and the remaining men paid $1,778 to buy Weed's offices, along with three horses, buggies, snow sleighs, and medical equipment such as '3 Nasal saws, 2 Intestinal clasps, 3 Bullet forceps, 1 Horse shoe turnica.,' according to the estate.[12] The men then hired a third surgeon, William Lower, and the practice swelled, to become a thriving medical center in the Osborn Building in downtown Cleveland.[13]

By 1914 the surgeons were at 'a point in their careers when most physicians might be begin planning their retirement,' as the official history notes. But that year World War I broke out and Dr Crile went to work in the United States Army Lakeside Hospital Unit in France.[14] The two other surgeons also volunteered, and that experience changed their views on life and medicine.[15] At that time, almost all doctors in American civilian life operated on a commercial, profit-seeking basis, where each doctor was an individual entrepreneur. But the army forced doctors to work in multidisciplinary teams in the military hospitals. And after tasting that approach, the three men became convinced that acting 'as a unit' was not just sensible in war, but in peacetime as well. So when they returned to civilian life in Cleveland, the three surgeons reopened their clinic on a new model. Instead of operating as individual doctors, they arranged themselves as a partnership, sharing a fixed salary, and thus acting as a unit.[16]

Cleveland Clinic was not the only American hospital that operated like that. Over in Rochester, Minnesota, two brothers, William and Charles Mayo, had established a similar hospital as far back in 1889.[17] However, this approach was rare, since most

American doctors disliked this system. 'The founders of the early group practices were not popular with the medical establishment of their day,' Cosgrove observes. 'They were called "medical Soviets," "Bolsheviks," and "communistic" [sic]. Professional associations railed against what they termed "the corporate practice of medicine" [and] when some physicians in Palo Alto attempted to form a group practice they were barred from their local medical association.'[18]

But the clinic expanded, with an eager pool of patients. In the nineteenth century, Cleveland was one of America's wealthiest cities, with a thriving industrial and agricultural base, and while the wealth was declining in the early twentieth century, the city still had many well-to-do professionals.[19] In 1929, the hospital was hit by two blows. On May 15 of that year a pile of X-ray film that was being stored in the basement of the hospital caught fire. An explosion sent a cloud of toxic gas through the building, killing 123 people, including John Phillips, the head of medicine at the hospital.[20] Five months later, the stock market crashed. The doctors slashed everyone's salaries, took out loans financed by the surgeons' own life insurance policies, and the doctors all worked overtime. By then, the septuagenarian Dr Crile, one of the original founders, was almost blind with glaucoma. But after disaster struck, he returned to service and kept conducting operations, feeling his way around the patients by touch. By 1941 Cleveland Clinic had paid off its debts, and started to recruit again.[21]

After World War II the hospital expanded. To do this it had to be inventive, since Cleveland was a city in decline. Early in the twentieth century Cleveland had been so wealthy that it had a famed Millionaire's Row.[22] By the 1960s, however, the city was blighted with such extreme industrial and economic decline that riots broke out in the downtown area around the clinic. Cars were burned, angry mobs roamed the street firing guns and throwing bricks. Indeed, the violence was so bad that Cleveland Clinic was used as a staging area for the National Guard tanks and military personnel called in to suppress the riots.[23] But the clinic did not abandon the city. It remained in its original location, on the corner of 93rd Street and Euclid Avenue,[24] and once the riots had subsided the doctors started buying up the newly vacant plots of land and looked for ways to grow.

Then a crucial breakthrough occurred: René Favaloro, one of the clinic's star surgeons, performed the world's first coronary artery bypass.[25] That attracted global attention and acclaim. As the coronary surgery unit expanded, the other areas, ranging from radiology to urology to gastroenterology, swelled too, attracting doctors and patients from across the world.

In the 1970s, the hospital spread its wings beyond Cleveland. It established medical centers across the rest of Ohio, and brought nine regional hospitals into its orbit.[26] In the 1980s it expanded into places such as Florida, where there was a big, wealthy, aging population in need of health care. The growth was so dizzy that by 1988 the hospital had become the city's largest employer, with 9,134 staff, outstripping Ford Motor Company and LTV steel.[27] By the end of the twentieth century, the roster had risen to 40,000.[28] That made the hospital not just the largest employer in Cleveland, but the second biggest employer in the whole state of Ohio, exceeded only by Walmart.[29] It was a stunning testament

to how the fortunes of Ohio had changed, as its traditional main-
stays of industry and agriculture had declined. But it was also a
striking sign of how the whole business of medicine was changing. A century earlier, when the doctors such as Crile, Bunts, and
Lower had created Cleveland Clinic, it had been easy to run the
hospital as a unit. The operations were so small that everyone
could cooperate with everyone else, face-to-face. It was possible
to run a group of doctors by using 'social grooming,' to cite the
phrase beloved by the psychologist Robin Dunbar and Facebook.
By 2000, however, Cleveland Clinic had become a vast, complex,
bureaucratic behemoth. The Dunbar threshold of 150 had been
breached many times over.

To cope, the managers of Cleveland Clinic installed cutting-
edge logistics. A network of elevated covered walkways enabled
staff to move between the different buildings, even in the baking
summer heat of Ohio – or the freezing winters, when snow
blanketed the state. Suction pipes were installed between the
buildings to enable radiology scans, X-rays, and other documents to fly between departments via tubes. When digitization
took hold in the 1990s, the suction tubes were supplemented
with a vast web of electronic networks that passed messages
around the building, tracking the operations of the hospital,
and informing doctors, nurses, orderlies, and machines what
needed to be done.[30] Underneath the buildings, the hospital
managers constructed a complex network of tunnels, along
which unmanned trucks moved along tracks carrying essential
supplies. The managers even created a vast fleet of unmanned
robots in the tunnels programmed to ferry supplies between the

different buildings. These robots were so sophisticated that they could restock items, keeping the systems running smoothly, with little human intervention. 'Cleveland Clinic is a hospital trying to be a Toyota factory,' a *Newsweek* article declared in 2009.[31] Or as a child might have said, Cleveland Clinic resembled the Willy Wonka Chocolate Factory in Roald Dahl's book; a place dedicated to seamless connections, knitted together with a vast, byzantine web of suction pipes, robots, tubes, connecting machines, and IT systems.

But while the logistics and robots looked impressive, there was a darker side to this success: the more complex that the technology *and* the bureaucracy became, the more the institution was in danger of succumbing to silos. In some sense, there was nothing intrinsically wrong with that. On the contrary, specialization is essential when operations are vast and complex. And Cleveland Clinic seemed to be working well. 'In the *U.S. News & World Report* annual evaluation of hospitals, Cleveland Clinic had been recognized among the top 10 hospitals in the country every year the survey had been done,' the official history of the hospital noted in 2004, adding that 'singled out for special recognition were cardiology (tops in the nation each year from 1995 to 2003), urology, gastroenterology, neurology, otolaryngology, rheumatology, gynecology, and orthopedics.'[32] But because those specialist silos were so successful, they were *also* becoming more entrenched. In that respect, then, the hospital looked like numerous other large institutions basking in a period of success. Or it did until Cosgrove took over.

*

IN JANUARY 2004, THE chief executive of Cleveland Clinic, Floyd Loop, a renowned heart surgeon, announced that he was stepping down after fifteen years. There was fierce competition to succeed him.[33] But in June that year, after it had 'deliberated hundreds of hours,' the trustees finally announced that Cosgrove (or Dr Delos 'Toby' Cosgrove, as he had been christened) was appointed the new CEO.[34]

When the news was announced the next day to senior staff, it sparked 'spontaneous applause and a standing ovation,' the *Plain Dealer* reported.[35] Cosgrove had a glittering career in medicine, and was running a twelve-strong team of surgeons at the thoracic and cardiovascular surgery unit. This department was producing a third of the hospital's revenue. 'He's run one of the most successful cardiac departments in the world,' as John Castor, a University of Maryland cardiologist, observed.[36] Cosgrove was also admired for having a legendary work ethic. Born in 1940, he grew up in Watertown, a small town on the edge of Lake Ontario in upstate New York. He had a comfortable childhood: Delos (he acquired the nickname 'Toby' as a child) was the son of a lawyer and grew up obsessed with sailing. (Decades later, when he moved to Cleveland, he kept a boat in Nantucket off the coast of Massachusetts.)[37] But at the age of eight, Cosgrove made friends with a local surgeon and this instilled a passion for medicine. Becoming a doctor, though, was a bitter struggle. He worked hard at school, but never achieved good grades and in his first semester in college (Williams) he scored Ds. It was not until the age of thirty-one that he understood why: dyslexia. 'My learning problem was identified by a girl I was dating at the time ... who was a teacher,' he later recalled. 'I was trying to read her selected stories from *The New York Times* and struggling with phrases. She said to me: "Toby, you're dyslexic." A light went on.'[38]

Cosgrove eventually was accepted to the University of Virginia medical school, and once he got into the practical world of medicine he blossomed. He did a medical internship at the University of Rochester.[39] He then served in Vietnam where he worked at the Air Force's Casualty Staging Flight Center, an evacuation hospital on the perimeter of Da Nang, which shipped back over 22,000 wounded soldiers to the United States in the course of just five months. 'Not a day goes by when I don't think of Vietnam,' he said. 'Many things bring it back, like when I hear a helicopter fly by or a loud noise. It changed all of us.'[40]

On his return, Cosgrove worked at Massachusetts General, then in 1975 he got his big break: a chance to join the team of cardiac surgeons at Cleveland Clinic.[41] Although Cosgrove could have moved to Harvard, he chose the Midwest because of his admiration for René Favaloro and his coronary bypass techniques.[42] He also liked the concept of working as a unit. 'In the military I learned all about collaboration,' he liked to say. 'So naturally I wondered why the rest of medicine wasn't organized in the same way.'

In the next two decades, Cosgrove worked ferociously hard and earned a legendary reputation as a surgeon. His colleagues did not always like him. Surgeons are infamous for being arrogant and Cosgrove often matched the stereotype. He was a man prone to strong judgments. 'He had one of those 360 degree evaluations when he was department chair and people wrote that "he is very effective except when he becomes angry and loses control and then he loses all of us",' observed Eric Klein, a fellow surgeon who ran the urology department. But Cosgrove could also, on occasion, be self-deprecating and kind. And he was as harsh on himself as others. 'What is really unusual about Toby is that he has the capacity to change and learn from mistakes, and he *has* really changed over the years in terms of how he handles people,' Klein added. He was also willing to take unorthodox risks.

Soon after he arrived at Cleveland Clinic he decided that he was fed up with the way that heart surgeons were repairing patients' heart valves. At the time, surgeons were typically using either a mechanical unit or valve taken from a pig to fix the human heart; these were stitched into a human valve in a solid ring to act as a collar.[43] However, this solid ring was so inflexible that it did not move with the beat of that human heart, and surgeons did not know how to fix that. But one day, by chance, Cosgrove saw an old-fashioned embroidery hoop, of the sort that nineteenth-century seamstresses had once used to make dresses, and decided to adapt it for surgery. It was an odd leap of thought. 'Heart surgery and embroidery [are phrases] that don't usually appear in the same sentence,' Cosgrove said.[44] But the innovation was a success. In subsequent years Cosgrove filed thirty patents for other inventions, many of which were equally offbeat.

Later in life, he often attributed his ability to produce unconventional ideas to his dyslexia. Not being able to read had forced him to develop a photographic mind, and find his own solutions to problems. 'This condition has proved to be a blessing in disguise,' he observed. 'Because of the limitations it imposed, I never fell prey to the herd mentality. I had to forge my own way of learning about and understanding what went on around me.'[45] He believed that his dyslexia had taught him a second lesson too: the key to being innovative was to challenge boundaries. Creativity tended to erupt when people mixed up ideas from different sources. 'Many of my ... ideas were inspired by comparisons and objects outside heart surgery that required the collaboration of professionals in other disciplines,' he observed.[46] 'Innovation happens at the margins, where one discipline rubs up against another.'[47] Or, as it were, where silos break down.

A COUPLE OF YEARS after his appointment, Cosgrove convened a meeting of the board of governors and told them that he wanted to change how the hospital was run. On one level, his colleagues were not surprised. They knew that Cosgrove was an ambitious man who was determined to create a legacy, and the senior staff had already been engaged in a wider, lively debate about whether the hospital should reorganize the department boundaries. 'We were all talking a lot about change,' Bruce Lytle, the head of surgery, observed.[48] However, the scale of Cosgrove's ambitions took his colleagues aback. Rather than shuffling a few departments, Cosgrove declared that he wanted to implement two big revolutions. First, he announced that it was time for the hospital's now 43,000 staff to rip up their existing taxonomy for defining a 'doctor' or 'nurse.' Instead of simply defining this in purely medical terms, all of the staff would now be considered 'caregivers' and responsible for treating not just the physical ailments but the spirit and emotions as well.[49] Second, Cosgrove wanted to change how the hospital was organized.

Until then, the hospital's organizational tree had been based on the tools and procedures that doctors used. One of the most crucial distinctions was that 'surgery' (or cutting people open) was considered distinct from 'medicine' (or treating people's bodies). Numerous subdivisions existed within those categories that reflected how doctors had been trained. But Cosgrove wanted to turn this map upside down. In a sense, he hoped to replicate in medical terms what Ursus Wehrli, the contemporary Swiss artist and comedian, does with paintings and performances: namely reshuffle the way that things are normally organized, to give everyone a new way to think.[50] Thus, instead of organizing Cleveland Clinic's departments on the basis of doctor labels, Cosgrove wanted to define it around the patients and their illnesses. In essence this meant creating new multidisciplinary institutes that handled *diseases* (such as cancer) or body *systems* (say, the brain) – and thus forced surgeons, physicians, and others to work together in treating patients.[51]

'When I got here, there were cardiac surgeons on one side of the hall and cardiologists on the other side of the hall and the only place we met was the waiting room,' Cosgrove liked to say. 'I had nothing in common with most of the other surgeons [I was supposed to be with] since they were rectum surgeons or whatever. But I had everything in common with cardiologists because we were all working on the heart – even though they were in a different department of medicine.'

The news caused shock. Compared to most of the other

hospitals in America, the staff at Cleveland Clinic already operated in an unusually collaborative manner, or as a unit, as its
founders had liked to say. In most parts of the American system,
doctors tend to work specialist units, divided from each other,
and are paid according to what they earn as separate individuals.
In that sense, the medical systems echoes the 'eat what you kill'
approach seen in many parts of the financial world (although in
medicine it might be better described as 'eat what you treat'). But
at Cleveland Clinic doctors got paid a fixed salary, rather than
earning fees on the basis of each separate procedure. While the
doctors could get bonuses, these tended to be paid out on a *shared*
basis, rather than on an 'eat what you treat' system.[52] This model
was (and is) standard practice in much of Europe; the British
National Health Service is entirely run on a salaried, collective
basis. But it was an outlier in the United States: according to
government data about half of the 800,000 doctors in America
operate as self-standing entrepreneurs and most of the rest work
in teams that are self-standing units in financial terms, even if
they are attached to a big hospital.[53] In 2005 just 4.5 percent of
American doctors worked in a unit of more than fifty people with
a collective, salaried system.[54]

That made Cleveland Clinic unusual. However, it still split
its operations into departments, and these departments did
not always cooperate that well, partly because there were subtle
and not-so-subtle status distinctions that created a quasi–caste
structure. Cardiac surgeons, such as Cosgrove, sat at the top of
this status system, commanding high salaries and ultra-high
status. General practitioners sat in a different niche, with lower

salaries. Groups such as radiologists or anesthesiologists were on another notch of the ladder again, and nurses even lower down. Often these groups collaborated. But sometimes the different departments could end up duplicating each other, particularly when new technologies or diseases cut across department lines.

Heart catheters encapsulated the challenge. In the first half of the twentieth century, catheters were primarily used for issues such as bladder problems, and handled by physicians who practiced medicine, *not* surgeons. Inserting a catheter did not involve cutting into human tissue, so it was not defined as a surgeon's job. But at the end of the century, physicians started cutting people to insert catheters and surgeons used catheters during heart surgery. 'There was a blurring of the lines between medicine and surgery,' Bruce Lytle, explained. 'You started to see cardiologists doing things with catheters which were interventions, but that was what surgeons were supposed to do! Then vascular surgeons started using more catheters – these guys were all trained to do open operations, but they shifted to the catheter area.' This sparked tension. 'As lines blurred, we were facing more and more conflicts about money and pride,' Lytle admitted. Or as Eric Klein, the kidney expert, observed: 'When Toby took over, you had five different [departments] doing carotid stents – cardiology, neurology, neurosurgery, neuro radiology, and vascular surgery.' Logic suggested that the teams should consolidate, since replicating these procedures was a huge waste of resources. But none of the departments wanted to cede ground. 'We tried to get those groups on the same stage to work together and share databases and protocols, but we couldn't do it,' Klein admitted. 'They were different cost centers.'

So Cosgrove announced a radical step: he summoned the two men who held the plum posts of Head of Medicine and Head of Surgery into his office, James Young and Kenneth Ouriel, and told them that he planned to abolish the departments of medicine and surgery, taking away their jobs.[55] In most hospitals those two posts are considered sacrosanct. However Cosgrove was determined to rip up the traditional model. Instead of having departments divided into surgeons and medical doctors, he wanted to create multidisciplinary institutes instead. 'I said to them both: "I value you but we need to change,"' he explained. To soften the blow, he offered Ouriel the chance to run the satellite operation in Abu Dhabi. The genial Young simply stayed on at the hospital, and ceded his top job. 'At other places, there might have been a huge fight. Abolishing this division would be unimaginable at most hospitals!' Young recalled. 'But I could see the sense of what he was suggesting.'

The next step was to imagine medicine *without* the sharp distinctions between physicians and surgeons. When Cosgrove and the other doctors listened to patients talk about their illnesses, they noticed that sick people tended to describe their experiences in terms of body parts or broad ailments. They would say that their skin was sore, or their head hurt, or they had broken a leg, or feared they had cancer. This suggested that it made more sense to organize the hospital around multidisciplinary centers based on those body parts or broad ailments, rather than the old distinctions between surgeons and physicians, Cosgrove argued.

He was not sure how this might play out in practice. But in June 2006, the chairman of the hospital's Department of Neurosurgery stepped down, so Cosgrove launched an experiment.[56] The board announced plans to create a 'Neurological Institute' that would combine the departments or neurology and psychology (from the world of medicine) with neurological surgery (from the division of surgery), and other brain-linked services as well. 'If someone has a headache, they just want to get it fixed,' Cosgrove observed. 'They don't know if they need a neurologist, neuroradiologist or whatever, so it makes sense to put it altogether.'

Getting someone to run this experiment was not easy. Initially Cosgrove wanted a well-known medical star to lead the institute. The committee duly found a brilliant neurosurgeon who was working at another hospital. But when the proposed candidate realized the unorthodox nature of Cosgrove's ideas, he backed out. Most high-status surgeons hated working on the same level as medical doctors or psychiatrists. It bucked all the usual medical conventions. 'Toby told the search committee "Go out and find Nobel Prize level leadership!" So we were looking for someone with enormous academic credentials,' recalled bearded neuroradiologist Mike Modic. 'But it was a disaster.' So, the search committee put Modic himself in charge.[57] It was another unorthodox move, since radiologists usually sit well below surgeons in terms of status. But Modic had nothing to lose. So he set about smashing down the boundaries, grouping together all the different types of medical activity and experts that were linked to the brain. 'Take the spine,' he liked to explain. 'People have been working on the spine for years in separate departments like psychiatry, psychology, imaging, psychiatry, orthopedic surgery, rheumatology, and so on. But we thought we made sense to put all these people together.'

Cosgrove looked for other ways to redefine the medical map. A special 'Institutes Planning Group' was created, with all the top doctors, to create a timetable for reform.[58] But as stories about the revolution in the neurology department spread across the hospital network, employees in other departments were becoming scared. Many surgeons feared losing status. Nonsurgeons worried that the reforms would concentrate all the power in surgeons' hands. 'The concern was that the medical departments [like us] would be subsumed under surgical ones,' admitted Abby Abelson,[59] chair of the department of rheumatology.

As fear mounted, some of the doctors asked Cosgrove to scale back the reforms. He refused. He doubled down and announced that the hospital would press ahead with all the planned reforms in one go. He knew it was an ambitious undertaking. By then there were 43,000 people working at the Cleveland Clinic, in different departments, and each of these units had their own mode of treating patients, billing for procedures, and promoting staff. But he also suspected that if he waited any longer, reforms would likely be blocked. 'People were getting nervous, they were asking who am I going to report to, who is my boss?' he later explained.

On January 1, 2008, Cleveland announced its 'Big Bang' revolution: twenty-seven new 'institutes' were created with labels such as 'Dermatology and Plastic Surgery Institute,' 'Digestive Disease Institute,' 'Urological and Kidney Institute,' Head and Neck Institute,' 'Heart and Vascular Institute,' 'Cancer Institute.'[60] In some sections, the reforms involved nothing more than moving teams into new, joint offices: At the Urological and Kidney Institute surgeons who were skilled in operating on kidneys simply moved their computers into offices next to nephrologists, the medical doctors who worked with diseases of the kidney. In other sections, it was harder to glue the new teams together. 'When the reorganization was announced, the rheumatologists were on one floor and orthopedics on another floor. We knew we were all going to work together and went around the buildings for ages looking for somewhere that we could all sit together,' Abelson recalled. 'In the end we decided to stay where we are.' But irrespective of where they were sitting, the message delivered to the doctors was the same: surgeons and physicians had to stop thinking about medicine purely in terms of their own specialist field or distinct offices – and start collaborating.

When the American Board of Surgery and American Board of Medical Specialities found out what was going on, they were baffled and alarmed. These two bodies certify the process of doctor training in America and operate on the assumption that hospitals are always split between physicians and surgeons. They had never seen a hospital that tried to break these boundaries before, and complained that losing these hallowed distinctions would make it hard for Cleveland Clinic to train its doctors. 'They were not happy. It took a lot of explaining,' Cosgrove admitted. To placate them, the hospital managers eventually agreed to keep a shadow organizational structure based on the old departments that cut across the multidisciplinary centers. 'The outside world is divided up into these specialities and so we had to keep that in play for [training] residencies and things,' Modic explained. Some of the insurance companies that dealt with Cleveland also demanded that the hospital continue to arrange payments along department, not institute, lines. The insurance groups' computing systems were not flexible enough to cope with this multidisciplinary vision of medicine. That meant the final structure for the hospital was complex, since the shadow departments cut across some of the new centers. But Cosgrove reasoned that this was a price worth paying, not least because this overlapping matrix delivered an unexpected benefit: every time doctors practiced their craft, they were reminded that there was more than one way to define and classify medicine, and forced to move between different taxonomies. A neurosurgeon might be defined as a surgeon, part of that elite tribe. Or they might be just one person working on a brain, on a par with other medical staff who defined themselves as brain experts. It all depended on what perspective you took.

IN THE SPRING OF 2008, a few months after the reforms had started, Cosgrove addressed all the staff at a town hall meeting. He brought along Kara Medoff Barnett, the young woman who had first challenged him on the stage at Harvard. 'So Kara, tell me why your father did not go to Cleveland Clinic for his operation?' Cosgrove asked in a genial manner as he sat on stage. During the first few months of his tenure as CEO, Cosgrove's speeches to staff had been stiff and stern; he did not find it easy to exude a natural air. By 2008, however, he had learned to become more approachable, and was wearing jauntier ties. 'What didn't your family like about Cleveland?'

Burnett, who had graduated Harvard a year earlier[61] and was then working in New York, cited her criticisms: the hospital had excellent technology and skills but lacked empathy. Cosgrove nodded humbly. 'So we are at fault here – we need to change!' he declared.

This public exchange startled Cosgrove's colleagues. 'People who knew Toby before would not have expected him to *ever* talk about empathy,' observed Seth Podolsky, a doctor who worked in the Emergency Services Institute.[62] Surgeons worked in such a high-pressure, competitive field that they rarely admitted to any weaknesses or emotion. 'I started as a medical student in Boston [in the 1960s]. In those days medicine was a very different world in terms of our skills. We sometimes lost five children [on the operating table] in one day,' Cosgrove explained. 'It's hard to do that and come back to work if you are thinking about emotions. Patients didn't expect a hug. They were just happy to have survived.'

But Cosgrove had taken Barnett's message to heart. In his view, talking about empathy was not just a touchy-feely issue. It represented another aspect of his desire to break down silos. Instead of looking at health in terms of biology *or* emotion, Cosgrove wanted the doctors to look at the two issues in tandem. That, after all, was how patients experienced medicine; unlike doctors, most sick people did not draw distinctions between science and feelings. 'Very few patients can judge the quality of clinical work – even if they watch me they wouldn't know if I was a great surgeon or not,' Cosgrove observed. 'But they do know how they were treated.'

So Cosgrove appointed James Merlino, a colorectal surgeon, to act as a 'chief experience officer,'[63] or CXO. All of the 43,000 staff were told to attend a half-day training course on empathy.[64] Some surgeons objected. 'When I heard about the office of patient experience I said "what is this?" Klein, the urology surgeon, said. 'I said: "We are not a hotel – we don't need to meet and greet people and check them into their room and check they have the right pillows!"' But Cosgrove and Merlino insisted that everybody who worked at Cleveland had to attend the course, on the same terms, in mixed teams. Some surgeons and doctors were also sent to Disneyland for lessons in customer service.

Architecture was used as another tool of reform; although Cosgrove had never heard of Pierre Bourdieu's concept of habitus, he was convinced that it was crucial to understand how culture reflected physical space, and vice versa. In earlier decades, the hospital buildings at Cleveland Clinic, like most of those in America, had been decorated with heavy oil portraits, dark wood panels, and carpets. But in the 1990s the hospital started to adopt a simpler, cleaner design, and under Cosgrove this trend intensified. Modern art was placed throughout the buildings.[65] Dress designer Diane von Furstenberg remodeled the patients' gowns.[66] To encourage people to feel relaxed in the hospital lobby, a giant hologram of a tree was installed, designed by artist Jennifer Steinkamp.[67] A piano was also placed in the lobby to be used by patients or (on occasion) professional musicians. Three dozen 'Red Coats,' or concierge-style porters, were hired to meet and greet patients in a cheerful way and provide a calming influence.[68] 'This originally started because Cleveland

Clinic was having so much construction work that we needed to find a way to direct patients to where they needed to go,' Cosgrove explained. 'But then we realized it worked really well to have the Red Coats. The patients like them.' Cosgrove's piece de résistànce, though, was the hospital entrance. In the early years of the twenty-first century, the managers of Cleveland Clinic had decided to overhaul the front of the building as part of another expansion plan. Initially they planned to install a fountain. But Cosgrove vetoed that idea: spurting water would create images of blood, he declared. Instead, he asked the architects to create a Zen pool of still water, to project serenity and the all-important mood of empathy.

The hospital architects looked at the corridors too. A vast web of interlinked, elevated covered walkways had initially been installed in the 1970s to ensure that patients and nurses could move between the buildings easily, even during winter blizzards. They seemed purely functional, if not dull. But as the doctors discussed how they interacted with each other, they realized that these walkways had an unexpected side benefit: because patients and medical staff were forced to walk along these long corridors each day, channeled into a small space, the hospital had inadvertently created a way to force medical staff to constantly collide with people from other teams. So the architects made them bright and airy, decorated with inspirational art and slogans, to encourage people to linger and chat.[69] As with Facebook, physical space was being used to encourage people to silo-bust. Moreover, the corridors – like Facebook's Hacker Square – often forced interaction as effectively as any formal town hall. 'You set off walking to do one thing, and next thing you know, you end up seeing people and talking to them,' explained Modic. 'Getting anywhere can take a long time. But you get ideas, and news, so it isn't really a waste of time at all.'

IN LATE 2013, COSGROVE received a cheering accolade. A survey of patient satisfaction, as measured by *U.S. News & World Report*, showed that Cleveland Clinic was the top-ranked hospital in America in terms of patient satisfaction. It was a startling turn-about. A decade earlier, when Cosgrove had been challenged at Harvard Business School about his lack of empathy, Cleveland had been at the bottom of patient satisfaction tables. But in the decade that Cosgrove had overseen the hospital, its position in the league tables had improved dramatically; indeed, by 2012 the hospital was consistently ranked among the best in the country in terms every survey of patient sentiment.[70]

There was other good news too. The *U.S. News & World* report ranked Cleveland Clinic in the top three positions in almost every medical speciality in terms of technical skill. However, insofar as there was comparative data available for the cost of care at different hospitals (and national statistics on this are shockingly poor), Cleveland Clinic's seemed lower than those of many rivals.[71] Cosgrove attributed that to incentives. In the usual 'eat what you kill' system used in most American hospitals, the cost of treatment has been (and is) high because each specialist team has an incentive to order as much medical care as possible. That, after all, is how they get paid. But the Cleveland structure, which gives doctors a fixed salary, removes some of the incentives to prescribe overlapping treatments. 'Let's take prostate cancer,' Klein, the head of the urological unit, liked to explain. 'There are five ways you can manage that in the early stages – surveillance, open surgery, robot surgery, brachytherapy, or external beam radiation therapy. In other hospitals, the specialists will push whatever they are specialists in – the one that costs the most is external beam radiation therapy, and other hospitals will often push that. But since we all work together we offer all five [treatments] equally. We have data on brachytherapy which suggests that cure rates are better there, and costs are dramatically lower, so we tend to use that.'

Indeed, the results were so striking that they won praise from President Obama. In a speech about American health care he championed Cleveland Clinic as a place 'where patients' care is the number-one concern, not bureaucracy.'[72] Or as he observed in a national radio broadcast, talking about his own health care plan: 'Some of these costs [in health today] are the result of unwarranted profiteering that has no place in our health care system . . . and yet we know that there are places like the Mayo Clinic in Minnesota, Cleveland Clinic in Ohio and other institutions that offer some of the highest quality of care in the nation at some of the lowest costs in the nation.'[73] Not everyone inside and outside the hospital was as enthusiastic as the president about some of Cosgrove's reforms. Like Cleveland, the Mayo Clinic operated with a partnership structure. But unlike Cleveland, the doctors at Mayo continued to work out of the traditional departments, not institutes, and they did not see any reason to reorganize themselves. 'You can get dysfunctional silos in institutes, as much as departments,' one senior Mayo doctor argued. 'You don't need institutes to get more collaboration or lower costs.'

However, Cosgrove and his team remained defiant – and proud. They believed that breaking down the traditional silos had not only encouraged them to take a more holistic approach to medicine, but it had also made them more innovative. The way that doctors handled muscular and joint problems was an example. Traditionally, these illnesses had been dealt with different teams of rheumatologist and orthopedic surgeons. But after the new Orthopedic and Rheumatology Institute was created, orthopedic surgeons had teamed up with rheumatologists for the first time, and discovered – to their surprise – that if they jointly monitored levels of calcium after surgery it produced better results. 'Orthopods have never checked the calcium metabolism of people with fractured hips before, but then the rheumatologists suggested that they should look at calcium and it made a big difference,' Cosgrove explained. Or as Abby Abelson, the new institute head, observed: 'Before, we had patients getting osteo-porotic fractures but didn't realize why. Now we collaborate in post-fracture management.'

Similarly, in the Urological and Kidney Institute, surgeons had started working with nephrologists for the first time to understand how metabolic balance could affect the formation of kidney stones. They hoped this would enable doctors to develop nonsurgical (and cheaper) ways to control kidney stones and cancers.[74] 'Most patients with early-stage kidney cancer are seen by urologists but now we discuss all these cases together and we have developed protocols to just take out part of the kidney, not all of it,' Klein explained. 'We haven't broken down every silo, but it works differently than before,' Bruce Lytle, the head of the Heart and Vascular Institute, observed. 'Do we have problems? Yes, all the time! But there is a mechanism for resolving those problems. Every Tuesday morning we have a meeting of the department chairs and myself and we deal with the issues as a group.'

One of the most striking changes of all, however, had taken place in the Emergency Services Institute. At most American hospitals, doctors working in Emergency Services are not allowed to admit patients into specific hospital departments without the permission of the specialists there. This delays treatment. However, specialists tend to insist on having control over the process, since it affects how they will be remunerated. But in 2012, Cleveland turned the system upside down. Emergency department doctors were given admission rights. So were some ambulance medics and paramedics. It was a controversial move. 'We had been wanting this change for years, but thought we would never ever see it!' Bradford Borden, a doctor at the Emergency Services Institute recalled. The new system did not always work as planned. 'We get the patient to the right clinical specialist within the hospital about 93 percent of the time, according to our research,' Borden reported. 'But if we get the patient to the wrong clinical specialist, we fix it the next morning.' The changes produced some tangible results. Before 2012, the Emergency Services teams had typically taken around two hours and forty minutes to admit a patient to the hospital; by the spring of 2013 that had fallen to two hours. 'What is going on here is about a change in operation and a change in culture,' Seth Podolsky, another Emergency

Services doctor, observed. 'It doesn't happen overnight. But it is now changing.'

Could the experiments be taken further? Could they be replicated elsewhere? It was a question that the doctors themselves often wondered. They did not have clear answers. They knew that the circumstances in which their experiment had been born was somewhat unusual. After all, Cleveland Clinic had always had a relatively collectivist ethos, relative to other American hospitals. It also had a more experimental spirit to start with. 'Pay matters hugely. Our system of pay is one reason we were able to break down silos. You cannot do this with a fee-for-service model,' Lytle said. 'Long-held allegiances and habits only change when they *have* to change. Harvard doesn't have to change – they are Harvard, with a long history and the largest endowed institute in the world. But we are a not-for-profit institution in a Rust Belt city on the shores of Lake Erie with a declining population. We *have* to be better and more creative.'

But the crucial point about Cleveland Clinic, the doctors argued, was that it showed the value of thinking about classification systems. When people inside businesses or government departments were encouraged to reimagine the world – say, by looking at the world from the perspective of consumers, not producers – they could often become more innovative and effective. If journalists were to start organizing their work according to how readers (not reporters) perceived the world, how would that change the media? Or if manufacturers started organizing their departments based on what customers (not salespeople or designers) thought was important, would they sell the same things? The key point, in other words, was that looking at business processes or services upside-down, or back-to-front, could change an institution's perspective. Or it could if everybody was willing to take a risk, even without knowing where that mental exercise might lead. 'A couple of years ago at Cleveland Clinic we thought we could develop a consultancy business by exporting our model – but then we realized that was a stupid idea,' Modic, the head of the Neurological Institute, observed as he sat in his office in May 2013. 'The point is that you cannot *buy* our system for breaking down silos. You have to build it yourself. It is the process of building a new system and talking about it that transforms you.'

8
BUCKET-BUSTING

How Breaking Down Silos Can Produce Profits

'One man's loss is another man's gain.'

ON MAY 11, 2012, JUST AFTER THE FINANCIAL MARKETS HAD CLOSED IN New York, Jamie Dimon, the chief executive officer of JPMorgan Chase, called an impromptu telephone conference with investment analysts. For several weeks, rumors had circulated that the mighty American bank had suffered massive losses as a result of badly judged trades made by its London traders in the credit derivatives markets. That development had come as a surprise to many observers, since JPMorgan had 'consistently portrayed itself as an expert in risk management,' as a Senate report noted.[1] It weathered the credit crisis of 2007 and 2008 better than most of its peers, and Dimon was well regarded on Wall Street, known for being a control freak who tried to monitor all the risks that the bank was running. When the rumors had first emerged about the losses, Dimon dismissed the speculation as a mere 'tempest in a teapot.'

But on May 11, Dimon was forced into a humiliating U-turn. In a curt statement, he admitted that the bank had lost several billion dollars, due to unwise trades made by a group of its traders that included men such as Bruno Iksil, operating in a unit of the bank called the Chief Investment Office. The hitherto unknown Iksil had placed a series of massive bets in the credit markets about the health of a collection of American and European companies. But he had *not* done this by buying bonds issued by those companies, or even by purchasing derivatives linked to those separate companies' bonds. Instead, he bought trading positions on an index known in the market as IG9. This product was a derivative (called a credit default swap) that essentially provided bundled insurance on the debts issued by 125 different American companies, such as Macy's, Walmart, Wells Fargo, and MBIA. Iksil also placed bets with similar instruments linked to European companies. This was normally considered to be an obscure backwater of finance. However, Iksil and his colleagues in the Chief Investment Office department had made such massive investments that the team had earned the dark nickname of 'the London Whale.' When prices turned, his losses tallied at least $6.2 billion.[2]

When the news erupted, this sparked huge recriminations both inside and outside JPMorgan. In many ways, the tale seemed uncannily reminiscent of the problems that had plagued the big banks such as UBS and Citigroup during the financial crisis. Back then, as I described in Chapter Three, managers at banks such as UBS failed to spot the problems with mortgage-linked CDOs because traders were working as self-contained desks, or silos, and they were trading instruments that were so technically complex that they were hard for outsiders to understand. This time around, the losses had been on credit derivatives linked to *companies*, not subprime mortgages. But, as with UBS, few people had realized the risks that were being taken. The unit dabbling in these dangerous bets was widely perceived to be risk-averse and thus safe. The Chief Investment Office team was a self-enclosed group, semi-detached from other units such as the investment bank. And the IG9 index sounded like gobbledygook to nonbankers (and many mainstream bankers too). Once again, the curse of silos had reared its head.[3, 4]

As the recriminations flew around, there was a second aspect to the London Whale story, which attracted less attention. This revolved around the question of who was sitting on the *other* side of JPMorgan's trade. It is a long-standing adage of markets that trading is a zero sum game: whenever somebody loses money, somebody else wins. Often it is hard to identify the winners and losers, since the gain and pain can be dispersed across the system over many years. But in the case of the trades that CIO's office had made (which were later dubbed the 'whale trades' by bankers and government officials)[5] it was possible to identify some winners. One was a $20 billion hedge fund called BlueMountain Capital. In the months before Iksil's whale trades became public knowledge, traders at BlueMountain had quietly taken the other side of his positions, placing bets in the opposite direction. Initially, they lost money. But when the markets turned in the spring of 2012, BlueMountain's trade produced a profit, and the fund was later asked to help JPMorgan sell its losing positions. Indeed, the fund eventually earned an estimated $300 million from all its different dealings with JPMorgan over the whale trades.

When the story about BlueMountain's gain broke, most observers assumed this was simply a case of a canny hedge fund running rings around a bank, using its expertise to opportunistically chase profits. The staff of BlueMountain Capital included several traders who had once worked at JPMorgan. The cofounder of the fund – an intense, cerebral dark-haired man named Andrew Feldstein – had been part of a team that had created the credit derivatives business at JPMorgan back in the 1990s.[6] His traders knew all about the obscure IG9 index and the way that credit derivatives were priced.

But in reality, there was a second, even more fascinating, aspect to this story that was almost entirely unknown. The reason BlueMountain made its winning trade was not simply that its traders were experts in the technical details of credit derivatives.[7] They were *also* fascinated by silos, or what Feldstein liked to describe as 'buckets.' Feldstein had built his hedge fund by studying how big Wall Street banks organized their operations into rigid teams and trading flows, and then trying to find ways to take advantage of the shortcomings that these classification systems created. Indeed, he analyzed the ecosystem with as much intensity as an anthropologist might study kinship groups or religious rituals. However, Feldstein and his colleagues were not driven merely by a spirit of abstract intellectual enquiry. They believed that when rigid silos emerged in the world of finance, they often distorted markets and prices. That created opportunities for canny traders to make profits. Studying classification systems – and silos – was part of their trading strategy. And this often paid off dramatically, as in the case of their *anti*-whale trades.

In some senses, this is not surprising. If you dig into the trading strategies of most successful investors, you will often find a tale of boundary-hopping and silo-busting. As John Seely Brown, the scientist and organizational theorist, has observed: 'It is at the edge that most innovation occurs and where we can discern patterns that indicate new kinds of opportunities and challenges.'[8] When individuals jump across boundaries in business, people are often more creative. Similarly in finance, the richest profits are often found when traders manage to hop between different markets, asset classes, or institutions and question the normal borders. But while the story of BlueMountain is far from unique – and not necessarily the most successful example of this phenomenon – it is interesting because of the bigger lesson it shows. In the first half of the book I described how silos can make people inside institutions behave foolishly. In the previous three chapters I have offered ideas about how companies and institutions can avoid falling prey to some of the problems associated with silos. However, silo-busting is not just a defensive move. It can be offensive too. When people think about the classification systems that their society uses, this can give them a competitive edge compared to rivals. If one institution is hobbled by silos, that can open up opportunities for somebody else. In the case of Sony, a failure to take a coordinated approach toward developing a digital Walkman opened the way for Apple to dominate the market with the iPod. A similar pattern has played out in numerous business spheres. So too with finance. The story of BlueMountain, in other words, is a powerful counterpoint to the tale of how silos damaged UBS, or undermined the prediction of economists at the Bank of England. In that sense, then, it is almost cheering. 'We love silos,' Feldstein observed shortly after the dust settled from JPMorgan's whale trades. 'Or at least we love other peoples' silos. They enable us to make money.'

THE TALE OF BLUEMOUNTAIN Capital has always been entwined with that of the Wall Street behemoths; the hedge fund, like many of its ilk, operates as the yin to the yang of the big banks. The group was first founded back in 2001, when Feldstein, then thirty-eight, teamed up with a longtime friend and classmate from Harvard Law School, Stephen Siderow, thirty-six, to create a tiny trading operation. Feldstein had spent the previous decade at JPMorgan Bank, where he had been part of a team that helped develop the concept of credit derivatives (or securities that let investors bet whether a loan will turn sour or not) before later rising to a senior management position. Back in the 1990s, as I explained in another book,[9] JPMorgan had been a creative place to work, at least to young financiers such as Feldstein. Most employees spent a long period with the bank, and junior bankers often rotated between different departments. That created a slightly more unified culture than was found at many other banks, particularly since some of the leaders of the bank, such as Peter Hancock (who, years later, in 2014, ended up running AIG, the giant insurance group), took pride in using innovative management experiments designed to create a spirit of collaboration and silo-busting.

However, during the early years of the twenty-first century the atmosphere of the bank changed. In 2000, it merged with another big bank, Chase Manhattan, and became larger and more bureaucratic. This change led to more internal rivalry. And while the pattern was never quite as fragmented or dysfunctional as it was at rivals such as Citigroup or UBS, it frustrated many of the original JPMorgan credit derivatives team, particularly those who had clustered around Hancock.

In 2001, Feldstein left JPMorgan. He joined forces with Siderow, who had been working as a management consultant at McKinsey, to set up a small hedge fund, tucked into a small, windowless office in Midtown Manhattan. Just like Sony in its early days, when it was founded by entrepreneurs in the bombed-out basement of a department store in Tokyo, or Facebook when Mark Zuckerberg created the group in a cheap, rented Palo Alto house, BlueMountain started out as a flat, freewheeling, informal group. It was easy to swap ideas, and brainstorm financial trades, since everyone was sitting next to everyone else. But Feldstein did not take that unified culture for granted. His years working at JPMorgan had shown him that when financial institutions swelled, they tended to become plagued with bureaucracy and fragmentation. Feldstein believed that caused people to behave in potentially stupid ways, making irrational trades. Or, more accurately, the silos inside big banks created perverse incentives, that often encouraged traders to do things that made sense on a micro level (in terms of the interests of individual desks), but which looked very foolish from a macro-level perspective (or for the bank as a whole).

When Feldstein talked about this problem, he did not usually express it with the language of social sciences. He had grown up in Arizona, the son of a urologist, and he studied economics as an undergraduate. He later studied law at Harvard, as a classmate of Barack Obama, and excelled in it, since he had a precise, clear mind and good quantitative skills. But along the way, he also acquired an interest in cultural and social systems. When he talked to his colleagues about markets, he tended to see them not just as mathematical models or legal documents, but as cultural *patterns* that were part of a wider ecosystem. He was fascinated by the social problems created by complexity. So much so that he later became a governor of the Santa Fe Institute, an interdisciplinary group based in New Mexico that studies the science of complex systems. This was started by physicists but is now run by an anthropologist. Feldstein was particularly interested in how people used classification systems to organize their world – particularly when these taxonomies are flawed. A common theme of anthropological research is that the way we classify the world never really matches the reality of our environments. People might draw neat diagrams of their kinship structures and family trees, but there are often ambiguities, overlaps, and underlaps. Things fall between the cracks. Life does not always fit into the official descriptions of what people are *supposed* to do. Much of the time we ignore these messy realities. It feels easier to stick with the neat classification systems we have than constantly rewrite them, be that in the sphere of kinship, religion, domestic life, or anything else.

But Feldstein thought that these messy gaps between rhetoric and reality mattered deeply. When he looked around at the financial system, he could see numerous pieces of the banking sector or markets that did not quite fit into neat boundaries, or the rigid bureaucratic structures of banks. Most bankers tended to ignore those elements, or turn a blind eye. Indeed, financiers generally did not look at financial flows in a particularly wide context. As the tale of UBS in Chapter Three shows, bankers in large organizations are often trained and incentivized to only focus on the bits of finance that sit directly under their noses (and for which they are likely to be paid). But Feldstein, like many savvy hedge fund traders, looked at the entire ecosystem of finance and saw the patterns in a bigger context. He was not only fascinated by the 'dancers,' to use the Bourdieu metaphor, but *non*-dancers too, or the blank spaces on a map that other people did not discuss. He thought these often generated the richest trading opportunities of all.

One of the first of places where BlueMountain turned this analysis into a strategy was in relation to the type of collateralized debt obligation packages – CDOs – that banks such as UBS started to create at the start of the twenty-first century. At the big banks, as I explained in Chapter Three, these products were typically handled by dedicated desks, or departments. These tended to operate in a very fragmented manner, beset by all manner of different rules. Sometimes the desks at one bank were allowed to deal with entire *bundles* of loans and derivatives, such as a completed CDO, but were not allowed to trade the individual pieces of that bundle, such as the underlying derivatives, bonds, or loans. Sometimes the desks could only handle the individual derivatives, bonds, or loans, but not trade the entire CDO. Similarly, desks might be allowed to buy assets that carried AAA ratings from the credit rating agencies, but not touch items with other ratings. The patterns varied. It was the financial equivalent of a retail store in which the assistants on one floor were only allowed to sell entire suits, but others could only deal with individual jackets and pants.

These rigid rules meant that there was uneven demand for different types of financial assets. It was not an open, free, or consistent marketplace. That distorted prices. In addition to that, the different banks each had different, internal models to value the CDOs, or the CDO tranches (as the different pieces of CDOs were known). As a result, the same chunk of credit risk could be given entirely different prices in different corners of the markets, or the silos of the banks. Finance theory suggests that when bankers bundle together diverse packages of bonds and credit derivatives, the price for the entire bundle should reflect the price of the separate constituent parts. The total sum of all the different tranches of a CDO should be similar to the value of the entire CDO. But in reality, because of all these distorted incentives and silos, the price of the entire CDO often diverged from that of the tranches, at least for a period of time.

So Feldstein's group tried to analyze the patterns of segmentation in the financial system and the different incentives this created, and then they looked at how this affected prices. Then, in the manner of any trader, they tried to exploit the places where prices seemed to be distorted, by buying low and selling high. Sometimes they used almost childishly simple tactics to do this, buying and selling different pieces of debt to different counterparties. In other cases, though, the tactics were more sophisticated. The BlueMountain team would, for example, sell a few pieces of debt to test the market prices for a particular type of loan, bond, or derivative, and then deliberately create CDOs, or other bundles of credit derivatives, to meet that demand. Then, if they saw that demand was shifting, they would sell other CDO tranches. Either way, as they set about exploiting these price discrepancies, they tended to assume that eventually financial gravity – or economic logic – would win out. Prices for different pieces of credit might be distorted for a period due to the silos. But eventually they tended to revert to the mean, reflecting the fundamental value of the credit risk. The trick, the BlueMountain traders believed, was to buy when debt was distorted – and then pocket the profit when the markets corrected themselves. This was not a remotely glamorous trade. At other hedge funds, traders have sometimes earned great renown by making bold, visible bets on the direction of the economy, a currency, or a company. The hedge fund run by George Soros, for example, bet in the early 1990s that sterling would be devalued, and then made a huge profit when that high-stakes trade turned out to be correct. Bill Ackman's fund Pershing Square placed a similarly pugnacious bet before the 2007 credit crisis that insurance companies such as MBIA were wrongly valued, which also turned out to be correct. Similarly, John Paulson, another fund manager, created a trading strategy before 2007 that predicted the demise of the subprime mortgage market. However, what BlueMountain Capital was doing was very different from those funds. It was *not* placing big, glamorous bets on the direction of the economy or a company, but simply making predictions about how the different pieces of credit risk would move relative to each other. Feldstein did not care if markets went up or down. Nor did his traders focus on the chance of a particular company going bankrupt. Or not in isolation. Instead, they looked for discrepancies in value between different securities. It was a technical, often obscure, type of trade. 'If there was a mismatch in pricing, we could take advantage of it,' Feldstein explained.* But precisely because it seemed to be so obscure and geeky, the strategy was 'uncrowded,' as traders like to say. Or, in plain English, there were relatively few other funds trying to do what BlueMountain did, which made it easier for Feldstein and others to make profits.

Sometimes Feldstein and his colleagues would wonder why the banks did not try to trade away the price discrepancies themselves. The bankers sitting inside banks were usually bright and

---

* Feldstein's strategy, above all, was to make trades linked to how the prices of the different tranches (or slices) of the CDOs were moving in the markets. This was linked to the ratings that they were being given by the credit-rating agencies.

many could often see the peculiarities of their own rules. But they were trapped in the system, and the distorted incentives this created. What mattered to the traders was whether the deals they were cutting would boost the profits of their individual team, or silo, not whether it made sense for the entire bank or system. Classic financial theory or orthodox economics did not usually take much account of these micro-level incentives or social structures. Instead, mainstream economists tend to assume that markets are efficient and that mathematical models can explain almost everything. But in reality the complex social structures inside the banks influenced how almost all assets were priced. They even shaped how bankers applied the mathematical models that were supposed to be universal and thus free of any cultural bias.

And the impact of these social patterns could be surprising. In the first decade of the twenty-first century, for example, Donald MacKenzie, a professor of sociology at Edinburgh University, conducted a study of the financial mathematical models that banks were using to measure the value of their complex instruments. Common sense would suggest that these models should not vary between different banks or asset classes; numbers are numbers across the world. But when MacKenzie did his analysis, he discovered that the way that bankers used the models to measure the value of assets could vary significantly even in similar asset classes. Bankers involved in a corner of the market that traded mortgage-backed CDOs, for example, produced different results with their models than desks that handled asset-backed securities, a related branch of finance. This 'led to the same instrument or same risk being valued differently,' MacKenzie observed. 'In consequence, it [was sometimes] possible to sell the instrument or risk to one market participant while buying it more cheaply from another, with the difference in prices being riskless profit.'[10] For BlueMountain that was the sweet spot.

BY 2009, BLUEMOUNTAIN CAPITAL had grown so fast that it had switched location. It abandoned the tiny, windowless office where it had started and moved into a smart set of offices in an imposing skyscraper on Park Avenue. Fittingly, or perhaps ironically, this location was tucked very close to JPMorgan's headquarters. It was also near one of the main American offices of UBS. If you looked through the windows on BlueMountain's trading floor, you could even see the scarlet logo of the Swiss bank on the other side of the street.

The vista was highly symbolic: a large part of BlueMountain's strategy was focused on the goal of trying to exploit the mistakes of the big banks such as UBS, particularly in CDOs. Indeed, BlueMounain had become such a powerhouse in the world of credit trading that when Goldman Sachs was forced to list its biggest counterparties in the credit derivatives sector for a Senate investigation, it named BlueMountain as the fourth largest counterparty to its trades in the run-up to the credit crisis, ahead of many big banks.[11] 'Many credit market participants operate with very broad-based restrictions. That includes anything from insurance company's ratings regulations to mandates on mutual funds that restrict them to a particular asset duration, geography, credit quality or industry sector,' Siderow told a journalist when he was asked about the fund's trading strategies.[12] '[That means] markets often price the same risk differently depending on the form and the micro story – and these mispricings often take a while to correct.'

But as time passed, BlueMountain's tactics shifted in subtle ways. Between 2003 and 2007, the group had become best known for trading bundles of credit, bonds, and derivatives. It had other activities too, such as a side operation that traded equity derivatives. However, what it was really respected for was how it handled the CDO tranches that groups such as UBS were creating. That generated returns of about 10 percent a year, a level that was not dazzling compared to some other funds, but perfectly respectable.

However, the financial crisis of 2007 and 2008 delivered a painful jolt. As the credit markets gyrated wildly, the CDO business ground to a sudden halt, and BlueMountain suffered big losses on some of its holdings. In 2008 its flagship fund, Credit Alternatives, lost 6 percent of its value. Some investors withdrew their money. The following year, though, BlueMountain rebounded. In 2009 the wounded Credit Alternatives Fund rose by 37.4 percent,[13] which bolstered client confidence and attracted new investment flows. The firm started to grow rapidly again and by late 2009 it had amassed around $5 billion in assets under management.

However, in the post-crisis world, the tactics that BlueMountain had used before 2007 no longer worked so well; or not in relation to CDO tranches. Banks such as UBS had lost so much money with CDO deals that they had little appetite to create new products again. Terms such as 'securitization' and 'super senior CDO' had become virtually taboo, and the markets trading them were drying up, reducing the amount of opportunities to exploit price gaps. So the BlueMountain team looked for other opportunities to exploit. First, they gobbled up some of the bonds and derivatives banks needed to sell at knock-down prices in the aftermath of the financial crisis. In 2011, for example, Crédit Agricole, the French bank, sold a $14 billion portfolio of assets to BlueMountain. The deal was an attractive one for the hedge fund. However it also benefited the French bank, since it needed to cut its balance sheet to comply with new regulatory rules.[14] 'It was a win-win situation,' David Rubenstein, the hedge fund's European CEO, declared. 'We transferred the risk to BlueMountain and helped Crédit Agricole's balance sheet become more efficient from a risk-weighted perspective.'[15]

Then the BlueMountain traders hunted for discrepancies in other parts of the credit derivatives sector. In the summer of 2011, Feldstein and others noticed that something odd was happening to the price of the IG9 index, a specialised credit derivative product. Outside the world of specialist derivatives trading, not many investors knew much about the IG9 index, or the numerous other similar series that existed for different types of European and American corporate derivatives. But the reason that the IG9 index existed was that it enabled investors to have a simple way to place a bet on the health of corporate America, in much the same way that somebody might buy a security linked to the Dow

Jones index of company stock prices, or the FTSE. Investors did not necessarily need to use the IG9 index to take that bet. They could also buy single name credit derivatives linked to debt issued by individual companies. If they just wanted to place a bet on the debt-worthiness of Macy's say, or the American retailers in general, they could buy credit derivatives attached to those two specific companies. If they bought the IG9 index, they were taking a bet on 125 different companies – of which Macy's was merely one (although technically there were only 121 companies in the index in 2010, since four the companies had gone into default since the launch of the IG9 in 2007). But many investors found it easier to deal with an index, rather than separate derivatives linked to different companies, since it offered a one-stop bet that appeared to be easy to trade. And it was widely presumed in the market that the price of the IG9 was roughly equivalent to the average price of all the different credit derivatives inside the index.

But by the summer of 2011, that assumption was starting to break down. Normally, the price of an index of derivatives should move broadly in line with the price of the constituent parts, or so finance theory might suggest. The value of the whole should equal the sum of the parts. But in reality that logic did not always play out. Just as the price of a complete CDO might diverge from the value of its component tranches, the price of a derivatives index sometimes diverged from the underling derivatives. And in the autumn of 2011, these discrepancies were becoming unusually large for the IG9 product.

The BlueMountain traders set to work trying to understand

why this pattern had occurred. So did a few other traders in the credit markets. After conducting some detective work, the traders at BlueMountain realized that JPMorgan's Chief Investment Office team was placing heavy bets with the IG9 index and other structured credit instruments. This reflected a subtle, but important, shift in policy that had taken place deep in the bowels of JPMorgan. Traditionally, the CIO's office had been considered one of the most boring parts of the bank. It was charged with preserving the value of the money that JPMorgan held and supporting its treasury function. As part of that, the CIO team had started investing in structured credit back in 2006, supposedly to hedge the bank's wider credit risk, and by 2008, the CIO team was running a full-fledged structured credit portfolio. Initially this was modest, totaling just $4 billion or so. However, during the course of 2011, the trading book exploded in size to $51 billion, as a team of traders in London started to take massive bets on the health of American and European companies. However, they did not generally do this by buying individual derivatives. Instead, they overwhelmingly purchased index products, such as positions in the IG9. And as the year drew to an end, their positions kept swelling in size. Indeed, by the first quarter of 2012, the CIO office's holding of credit derivatives products had further swelled to $157 billion in size, with $84 billion worth of positions in American index products, and the rest in European indices.

It was not clear to Feldstein, or the others, exactly why these bets were taking place. Some market observers thought that the CIO's office was trying to use its massive size to squeeze the market or overwhelm other traders to such a degree that prices would move in a certain direction, allowing the CIO to profit. As 2011 drew to a close, for example, the CIO group 'bankrolled a $1 billion dollar credit derivatives trading bet that produced a gain of approximately $400m,' as a Senate report later observed.[16] However, the uneven trading pattern also reflected some of the peculiarities of the rules governing the CIO. Since this department was only supposed to engage in safe trades, it was not permitted to invest in individual company credit derivatives on a large scale, since these were deemed risky. The CIO's office was, however, allowed to invest in index products, since these were considered fairly safe. Indeed, when the CIO officials talked about the index trades, they often presented them as a hedge for the bank, or a way of insuring against losses. This created an uneven pattern for demand, since the CIO office was buying the index, but not its constituent parts. And that, in turn, was helping to distort prices. Once again, artificial boundaries and rules were creating a dislocated market.

For several months, the BlueMountain traders watched the prices in the market diverge with a growing sense of amazement. Outside JPMorgan, almost nobody knew about the scale of bets that the small team of London traders in the Chief Investment Office were placing. However, relatively few people inside JPMorgan knew about them either. These were not usually mentioned in any official risk reports, let alone company accounts. 'Prior to [April 2012] the synthetic credit portfolio had not been mentioned by name in any JPMorgan Chase public filings,' as the Senate report pointed out.[17] Some traders in the investment bank suspected that the CIO office was taking large bets, and they feared that these whale trades were distorting the IG9. However, they did not intervene. There had traditionally been a high level of rivalry between the CIO and the investment bank, and the CIO team did not take kindly to external interference. Meanwhile, the CIO office did not see any reason to tell the rest of the bank what was going on, even though the size of the whale trades started to breach internal risk limits by the start of 2012. 'The [structured credit portfolio group's] many breaches were routinely reported to JPMorgan Chase and CIO management, risk personnel and traders,' the Senate report damningly noted. 'The breaches did not, however, spark an in-depth review ... or require immediate remedial action to lower risk. Instead, the breaches were largely ignored or ended by raising the relevant risk limit.'[18] As with UBS, a tiny silo inside the mighty JPMorgan was running wild.

As weeks passed, the price distortions became more extreme. During the summer of 2011, BlueMountain had taken the other side of the whale trades, betting that economic logic would prevail – and the index move back in line with financial fundamentals fairly soon. But by January 2012, that had notably not occurred: the discrepancies between the price of the indexes and individual credit derivatives kept swelling, leaving BlueMountain sitting on big paper losses. Feldstein debated with his colleagues what to do. They could not believe that the discrepancies could keep growing indefinitely. But they did not quite understand what was going on, and they were worried about the scale of risk that their hedge fund was running. So, although other funds were starting to jump into the anti-whale trade too, or doubling down on their bets, Feldstein and his colleagues decided against raising their stake. Their position – and their potential losses – was already large. Instead they nervously sat tight and hoped that eventually the trade would reverse.

The next few weeks were tense. BlueMountain's paper losses kept mounting. Meawhile, JPMorgan's Chief Investment Office kept putting more muscle – and money – behind its whales trades. But then, in the spring, news of the trades suddenly leaked into the mainstream media.[19] Suddenly this once-obscure corner of the markets started to attract a wave of scrutiny, and a set of opportunistic new investors dived in, taking the opposite side to the whale trade. That caused the price of the index to finally snap back, and as momentum built in the markets, this turned JPMorgan's paper gain into a massive loss.

For a period, the CIO team tried to keep the scale of the damage a secret from the outside world. The traders in London changed the way that they valued the positions to minimize their reported losses. The senior managers at JPMorgan tried to brush off market speculation about the scale of the losses.[20] But eventually, the damage could no longer be contained. A full-scale inquiry was launched, and the traders at the CIO who had been linked to the whale trades were all removed. Then the JPMorgan risk managers set about combing through the books. They quickly discovered that the losses were dramatically bigger than anyone had guessed. Indeed, they eventually swelled to more than $6 billion. That partly reflected the fact that the prices kept moving against JPMorgan as the scandal became widely known. But there was another problem too: when the auditors went in, they discovered that the CIO office had been valuing its holdings of credit derivatives in a different way from the investment bank – even when the different parts of the bank were holding exactly the same types of credit derivatives instruments on their books. Just as the sociologist Donald Mackenzie had described, different banking teams, or silos, were measuring complex products in different ways – even when they were supposed to be using the same models.[21]

Horrified, Dimon insisted that the investment bank take over the CIO department's whale trades and then get rid of them. In the new post-crisis regulatory climate the bank could not afford to have a stain sitting on its balance sheet. So the JPMorgan investment bank officials eventually asked BlueMountain to unwind the bank's credit derivatives positions – for a fat fee. For the JPMorgan bankers it seemed to be an easy way to quickly and quietly resolve the whole saga: since they already knew Feldstein well, they trusted his fund and knew that it was big enough to swiftly get the whale trades off the bank's books. But for BlueMountain the deal was doubly sweet. It had already made money by betting against the whale trades. Now it was being paid again; indeed the fees that BlueMountain earned by helping JPMorgan to get rid of its embarrassing problem actually ended up being larger than the profit it earned on the anti-whale trades. It was a striking sign of how the power balance on Wall Street was shifting and how nimble hedge funds could some-times get the upper hand over the mighty banks. And a year later BlueMountain enjoyed another symbolic coup: Jes Staley, the head of JPMorgan investment bank and a man who had been viewed a possible successor to Dimon, left the bank to join BlueMoutain – and work alongside Feldstein.

AS TIME PASSED, THE BlueMountain team moved into other fields, looking for new ways to apply their bucket-busting ideas in other corners of the market where prices were being distorted by artificial or rigid boundaries. They became increasingly interested, for example, in how institutions divide financial flows into separate asset classes, such as equities, bonds, and loans. Investors normally take these distinctions for granted and assume they are almost inevitable, if not natural. Shares, after all, have fundamentally different features from bonds, say, and as a result these different products tend to be handled by entirely different teams of traders and analysts inside banks and investment companies. But what would happen, Feldstein and Siderow wondered, if you tried to look beyond those different boundaries? If you analyzed bonds and shares as a whole, instead of using the fragmented pattern that normally shaped how investors analyzed financial assets, would investments look different? Was it possible to look across the *entire* 'capital structure' (to use the term that bankers typically employ when they describe the totality of the financial channels that companies use to raise money)?

Some banks had tried to combine categories in that way. Back in the early years of the twenty-first century, Candace Browning, then the head of securities analysis at Merrill Lynch, announced that she wanted to break down the long-standing split between analysts who studied equity markets and those who looked at bonds. She tried to force the U.S. bank's 500-odd analysts working in the different specialist fields of equity and fixed income to collaborate with each other. 'We just worked in our various silos [and] I consciously wanted to change that,' she explained. '[I thought] if we all start communicating and sharing our resources better, not only would we be more efficient but we would give our clients a better product and employees would feel more connected.'[22] Or as Yaw Debrah, an analyst who worked in the team that dealt with convertible bonds, observed: 'At Merrill Lynch and probably at other large firms ... equity [analysts] worked in equity, debt worked in debt, derivatives worked in derivatives, et cetera. People did not do much cross-asset-class research because it was very difficult to coordinate.'[23]

In 2005, the Merrill Lynch research team produced several pieces of analysis on companies in the American auto and cable industries that combined insights from equity and bonds specialists. They were groundbreaking. Some individual teams started collaborating on a day-to-day basis. In London, one group produced what they called a 'Dequity report,' a pioneering research report that compared the price of high-yield bonds, derivatives, and equities. This was popular among hedge funds, since the initiative started at a time the leveraged buy-out business was booming in European markets, causing the price of companies' bonds and shares to swing in some unusual ways. 'Because of these [LBO] dynamics, both equity and credit people in sales, trading and research at the firm started to seek out each others' inputs,' observed Jon Gunnar Jonsson, then a young Merrill Lynch analyst who worked on the Dequity report. 'On the CDS side, we started building frameworks that could identify mispricing between the shares and bonds (or CDS) of the same company. Corporate finance theory was of little help to us, so we had to invent everything.'

But these collaboration initiatives soon foundered. The different analysts were so specialized in their areas of knowledge that it was time-consuming for them to communicate, and to translate their concepts and methods. 'Many very bright equity analysts don't know a lot about the fixed-income side. They've been able to do their jobs well without ever really having to get their hands dirty with the rest of the capital structure,' Michael Herzig, head of Merrill's equity research marketing, observed. 'They'll know what the bond rating is and they'll know how much debt there is, but will they know the complexity of the underlying products?'[24] The mental split went hand in hand with a physical separation. 'It's really quite hard to work with someone on an ongoing basis if they sit on a different floor from you,' said equity analyst Jonathan Arnold. 'I sit next to a retail analyst on one side and have an airline person outside my door, [but] the debt guys are on a different floor.'[25]

The biggest obstacle to collaboration, though, was the pay structure. Analysts were only incentivized to promote trading in their particular corner of the markets, since bonuses were paid according to how each product group performed. The clients of the bank, such as pension funds, were organized into rigid silos too. In theory, the idea of collaboration sounded sensible for the

Merrill Lynch analysts; in practice, few people had much incentive to make it work on a long-term basis.

However, Feldstein and Siderow thought – or hoped – that *precisely* because the silos at banks were so rigid, they might find some good opportunities by taking the opposite tack and adopting a diverse perspective. From its inception BlueMountain had employed researchers and portfolio managers who looked at bonds, loans, credit derivatives, and equity derivatives. However, in 2010, the hedge fund made a more concerted effort to expand into equities. They hired new equity experts and asked them to sit with the credit team and swap ideas about trading strategies and investment opportunities. 'We gather everyone into a room together, and by drawing on diverse perspectives we get to a richer research process and generation of ideas,' explained Marina Lutova, a credit portfolio manager at BlueMountain. Or as David Zorub, an equity portfolio manager, who sat near her, echoed: 'The idea is to generate investment opportunities that you will not necessarily see if you were just evaluating them from an equity or credit perspective. We are agnostic about which piece of the capital structure we invest in – equities, bonds, and loans. It is just a question of the fundamental view, and of relative price.'

To reinforce that cooperation, the managers at BlueMountain insisted that all the investment ideas be put onto a common database. They also decided that the traders and analysts would receive a significant part of their compensation based *not* just on the individual investments they had worked on, but the results of the entire team and firm. This collaborative system was very different from the more common 'eat what you kill' model at most banks and hedge funds. 'We have a distinctive culture, and it doesn't work for everyone,' Feldstein explained. 'But if someone wants to work here, then they need to know that we are taking a team-based approach.'

ONE EXAMPLE OF THIS collaborative bucket-busting approach involved an investment in HanesBrands, a North Carolina–based company that produces 'everyday apparel,' as its website says. In plain English, this means underwear. The range includes the Wonderbra, Playtex products, as well as brands such as Champion, Maidenform, and Gear for Sports. 'In the United States, we sell more units of intimate apparel, male underwear, socks, shapewear, hosiery and T-shirts than any other company,' the official HanesBrand website declares.[26] Four fifths of all households in America have at least one of its products.

In 2011, the company caught the eye of credit portfolio manager Lutova. To her, the company looked like what traders sometimes describe as a 'potential bond short,' or the type of company that it was worth betting against, since the price of its bonds looked likely to decline in the future. One reason she thought it might make a bond short trade was that the price of HanesBrands' bonds were relatively high, even though the company had a high level of debt. Since bond investors typically pay a great deal of attention to the debt profile of companies (because they want to know if they will get repaid), that high leverage level rang a warning bell. Worse still, HaneBrands' trading margins were falling as a result of a recent increase in the cotton price, which was used in many of the underwear products. The company's sales of printed T-shirts were suffering too because another company known as Gildan was grabbing market share. Those two factors threatened to undermine another factor that bond investors typically watch very closely: the cash flows of the company.

So Lutova set to work analyzing the company to see whether it could be a bond short, working with colleague Ami Dogra, who was the senior retail analyst at BlueMountain. But as they dug into the numbers together, their perspective started to change. Most analysts who looked at HanesBrand assumed it was a 'leveraged cyclical retailer,' or a company that had lots of debt and whose fortunes were likely to go up and down in line with the wider macroeconomic cycle. This designation put it into a particular mental box in the eyes of many investors, since it meant that analysts would compare it to other companies in that definitional box, to work out whether it was a good investment or not. Once a company has been placed into a certain mental box in the investment world, it is often hard for investors to question that; our taxonomies tend to be subject to inertia.

But as Dogra looked more closely at HanesBrands, she started to question the usual definition. She thought it was not really a leveraged cyclical retailer but should be viewed instead as a 'stable consumer products' business. After all, Dogra pointed out to her colleagues, HanesBrands dominated the world of American underwear, and was the largest or second largest player in many of the different underwear and clothing niches. Moreover, shoppers tended to buy underwear at a fairly steady rate, irrespective of the economic cycle. That meant that the company's profits and cash flows were relatively stable – and, crucially, much more consistent than most leveraged cyclical retailers such as fashion outlets. And although these cash flows and margins had been dented by the rise in cotton prices, Dogra thought that HanesBrand would be able to pass the cotton price increases onto shoppers. She also thought that the company could generate new inflows of cash by reducing its working capital. Indeed, when Dogra took note of these factors, she calculated that the company should soon have cash flows worth more than $400 million a year. That made HanesBrands seem like a dramatically more attractive investment bet – particularly since the company was also planning to cut its capital expenditure and move out of the struggling printed T-shirt market. Better still, Dogra argued, although HanesBrands had a lot of leverage the management had promised to cut that debt burden significantly, from 3.6 times the level of earnings before interest, tax, depreciation, and amortization to just twice EBITDA. That alone promised to raise the company's earnings by 18 percent. So Lutova and Dogra changed their mind: instead of betting against the company with a bond short, they decided they wanted to place a positive bet, or go long.

That conclusion still begged a crucial question: how? An obvious choice would have been to buy the bonds. But Lutova did not think that strategy made sense, since the bonds were structured in a manner that made it hard for investors to benefit from future earnings growth. But what about the shares? Normally, credit portfolio managers such as Lutova would not move into that field.

But she asked for advice from David Zorub, an equity portfolio manager. He had already made investments linked to Gildan, the company that was grabbing business from HanesBrand in the printed T-shirt sector, and Zorub's team knew about the dynamics of the cotton market. That left them initially skeptical about investing in HanesBrands, particularly because its debt burden seemed so high and its trading margins had been falling. But Lutova and Dogra showed Zorub that if you looked at the company as a stable consumer products group, and analyzed its cash flows using the tools that *credit* – not equity – investors typically used, the picture looked different.

Back and forth, the group tossed their ideas around, testing out Dogra's thesis. Could the company recover its business margins given the dynamics of the cotton market? Would customers swallow price increases? What would happen to the cash flows and the debt? But eventually a consensus emerged around the idea that HanesBrands should be traded in the markets like a consumer products company, *not* leveraged cyclical retailer, since its cash flows were stable. That conclusion had a big implication for what a fair value of HanesBrands' share price should be, since consumer staples were typically deemed more valuable, relative to earnings, than risky cyclicals. Indeed, when the BlueMountain analysts looked at the prospect for HanesBrands' earnings, and its plans to pay down debt, they predicted that the share price should be twice as high.

So they put their idea to work. In early 2012, Lutova and Zorub started to buy HanesBrands' shares on a large scale, betting that their analysis was correct. By the summer of 2013, the stock had indeed doubled – just as they had hoped. 'It was a very profitable strategy,' Lutova later commented. Or as Zorub observed: 'We wouldn't have done this if we hadn't had the type of joint collaboration that BlueMountain makes possible. That was what made the investment work.'

ON FEBRUARY 5, 2014, BlueMountain held a conference for about 100 of its investors at the Council on Foreign Relations building in New York. It was an elegant, opulent setting: the council headquarters are tucked into a gracious tree-lined street next to Manhattan's exclusive Park Avenue. The conference room reeks of history and gravitas. However, the hedge fund's organizers were not content with using the normal background of dark wood panels or curtains. Instead they cut a collection of gigantic silver buckets in half and fixed these to the council's conference wall. These emitted a ghostly flow under the stage spotlights. The installation would have blended well into the displays in the Museum of Modern Art.

'What we do at BlueMountain is bucket-bust,' Andrew Feldstein explained from the podium to the assembled crowd, gesturing at the big silver buckets. 'The financial system is divided into buckets and these are often very artificial. We like to break those boundaries down.' Stephen Siderow was in the room with Feldstein. So was Jes Staley, the man who had formerly run the JPMorgan investment bank. As the audience listened, Siderow, Staley, and Feldstein explained their philosophy and investing approach. They talked about their bet on HanesBrands. Then BlueMountain analysts described how they had combined equity and debt analysis to invest in companies such as NRG Energy, Valero (another energy group), Eastman Kodak, Lexmark, and Scripps (publishing and television). Not all of these investments had paid off as handsomely as HanesBrands or the whale trades. Indeed some had barely produced gains. But the direction was clear. 'The financial system is divided into buckets and these are often very artificial,' Feldstein declared. 'We like to break those boundaries down.'

The audience listened respectfully. Some observers seemed to be impressed. By 2014, the ideas being advanced by BlueMountain were starting to find favor elsewhere. On the other side of the world, groups such as the New Zealand Superannuation Fund (a sovereign wealth group) and the Government of Singapore Investment Corporation (another sovereign wealth fund) were investigating similar ideas about mixing up bond and equity analysis, both in terms of how they organized themselves and handed money to outside investors. Canada's Pension Plan Investment Board was moving in that direction too. And as these mighty sovereign wealth funds jumped into this sphere, it was starting to provoke more interest among smaller groups.

But not everyone was impressed. On the contrary, some of the investors who were sitting in the Council on Foreign Relations room, staring at the ghostly display of silver buckets, seemed distinctly wary, if not baffled, by what they saw. Many of these came from traditional asset management groups, such as pension funds, small endowments, or local government offices. Like big banks, these investors lived in a bureaucratic world, where there were clear rules about how anyone could invest money. They generally expected and wanted neat, familiar labels to be attached to trades and institutions. When they decided which hedge funds to invest in, they usually did so by measuring these funds against a box of similar funds. They did not know how to judge success in a world without clear boundaries, or the categories that seemed familiar. The type of bucket-busting that BlueMountain was pitching made them feel lost.

'This all sounds very clever, but it's harder to see how it all works in practice,' one pension fund manager in the audience observed. Or as Feldstein admitted: 'People don't know what to make of us, because we just don't conform to what they expect. They ask us if we are a fixed income fund, or an equity fund, or something else. When we try to explain our strategy, some get confused.'

In one sense, this presented a problem for BlueMountain. Precisely because the idea of bucket-busting was so alien, the hedge fund sometimes struggled to attract as many new clients as it would like. In a world of boxes, it was easier to pitch your wares to investors if you fit into the usual categories. Potential clients might applaud the results in theory. But some were not willing to take the plunge. But in another sense, the fact that BlueMountain was an outlier was also the secret of its success. The more that silos were ingrained in the other parts of the financial system, the more opportunity that created for institutions that *were* willing to challenge the artificial boundaries. Time and again, price distortions kept appearing in the markets because different teams of financiers had peculiar patterns of incentives or simply did not talk to each other or swap information.

Organizational boundaries were rigid, but money was not. And that created a never-ending set of opportunities to make profits, not just for BlueMountain but for any investor who was smart enough to look at the system as a whole. Or, more accurately, for any financier who was able to think about finance not merely in terms of statistics and spreadsheets, but through the lens of social patterns – and silos – too.

Conclusion

CONNECTING THE DOTS

'The real voyage of discovery consists not in seeking new landscapes but in having new eyes.'

—Marcel Proust[1]

IN LATE 2014, AS I WAS FINISHING THIS BOOK, I MET AGAIN WITH MIKE Flowers, the lawyer-turned-computer-geek who had pioneered the big data experiments at Michael Bloomberg's City Hall. By then his life had moved on in several ways. At the start of that year, Bloomberg's term as mayor had come to an end, and he had been replaced by Bill de Blasio. That had sparked an overhaul of the senior staff at City Hall and Flowers had left for new pastures. So, as Flowers and I sat in a cheap Italian neighborhood café in downtown Manhattan, he told me he was working at New York University, teaching data science and government to a new generation of kids. He liked to think of it as another type of silo-busting, trying to bridge the gap between the public sector and academia. He was also working with an open data start-up, Enigma, and offering advice to other governments who wanted to create their own silo-busting skunkworks. Soon after our lunch he headed to Paris to work with French officials there.

By then he had lots of juicy stories about silo-busting to tell his students, the French, or anyone else. There was the tale of how City Hall had reduced the scourge of yellow grease dumps. There was the saga of the struggle to spot deadly fire traps. But one of Flowers's favorite stories about silo-busting revolved around ambulances. Soon after Flowers joined City Hall, the Health Department had noticed that there was a wide variety in the length of time that it took ambulance crews to respond to 911 emergency calls. So Flowers asked his skunkworks team to look at the issue, and they stumbled on something odd: in New York, like most American regions, there were no fewer than *six* different bureaucratic systems involved in handling 911 emergency calls. Nobody had ever tried to connect the data behind these separate structures to get an effective overview of how the process worked, which made it impossible to monitor the system. So one of the skunkworks kids, Lauren Talbot, tried to link the statistics. After a long and painful struggle she created a central monitoring process that prompted city officials to change the scripts that telephone operators use when they handle 911 calls. That shaved several seconds off the response times.[2]

'This kind of thing makes my job worthwhile,' Flowers explained over lunch. 'It didn't require big changes. We just had to bring the data together. And think.'

As I listened, I realized that this is the essence of what this book is about. Most of us have an uneasy sense that our world is marred by silos. We might not use that specific word to describe the problem. However, we encounter it all the time: in bureaucracies where one department does not talk to another; at companies where teams are fighting each other or hoarding information; in societies where rich and poor or different ethnic and political groups live in separate social and intellectual ghettos, side by side. Technology should help break these barriers down. In theory, the Internet could connect us all. However, social media will not do this automatically, or even easily. Silos exist in cyberspace too. We live in a world that is hyper-connected, yet often we barely know what is happening around us.

That begs the question: what can we do? We cannot entirely abolish silos, any more than we could abolish electricity and maintain our modern lifestyles. We need to have specialists in the twenty-first-century world to create order in the face of extreme complexity and an ever-swelling deluge of data. Facebook could not operate as a company if everybody was trying to write the same piece of code all the time. Some autonomy and accountability is essential. Similarly, Cleveland Clinic would not be an effective hospital if everybody tried to treat the same patients. Central banks would not be able to conduct their monetary policy operations unless somebody inside the institution knew how economic models worked. Silos, if you define this concept as narrow, specialist groups, are inevitable.

But as this book shows, when our classification systems become excessively rigid, and silos dangerously entrenched, this can leave us blind to risks *and* exciting opportunities. The story of Sony, in Chapter Two, shows those perils. So does the tale of UBS, or the story of the economics profession before 2007. These stories are not necessarily the worst examples out there: silos have caused problems at numerous other institutions, such as Microsoft, General Motors, the White House, Britain's National Health Service, the BBC, BP. To name but a few.

So is there anything we can do to mitigate this problem? I believe there is. In the second half of this book, I presented some stories where ordinary people have tried to master their silos, instead of being mastered by them. These stories should not be viewed as finished, neat success stories. Mastering silos is not a task that is ever truly completed. It is always a work in progress. But the stories in the second half of this book do, I hope, offer some varied ideas about what we can do to ameliorate the silo syndrome. One lesson is that it pays to keep the boundaries of teams in big organizations flexible and fluid, as Facebook has done. Rotating staff between different departments, as in the Hackamonth program, makes sense. Creating places and programs where people from different teams can collide and bond is also a good idea, be that through hackathons, off-sites, or other types of social collisions. It can also be beneficial to design physical spaces that funnel people into the same area, forcing constant, unplanned interactions. The corridors at Cleveland Clinic do this well. So do the squares at Facebook. Either way, people need to be mixed together to stop them becoming inward-looking and defensive.

A second lesson is that organizations need to think about pay and incentives. When employees are rewarded purely on the basis of how their group performs, and when groups are competing with each other internally, they are unlikely to collaborate – no matter how many expensive off-sites an institution holds, or open plan offices it creates. A key reason why UBS was so fragmented, as I described in Chapter Three, was that it had an 'eat what you kill' incentive structure. The same problem besets most large financial groups. It also affects medicine, where the 'eat what you treat' approach has raised health care costs in America. Collaborative pay systems, of the sort seen at Cleveland Clinic or BlueMountain Capital, are needed – at least in part – if people are going to think as a group.

A third lesson is that information flows matter too. The stories of UBS or Sony show that when departments hug information to themselves, huge risks can build up. One solution to this is for everybody to share more data, and modern computing technology now makes that much easier. However, it should be stressed that you cannot combat silos simply by opening the data spigot and letting information spill out. What is equally important is to create a culture that enables everyone to *interpret* information – and let different interpretations be heard. This is not easy to do when there are teams of experts who use complex technical language that only they understand, or when they refuse to listen to alternative ideas. Or as Paul Tucker (formerly of the Bank of England) points out, what big institutions really need are 'cultural translators,' people who are able to move between specialist silos and explain to those sitting inside one department what is happening elsewhere. 'You don't need everyone to be a cultural translator – perhaps

just 10 percent of the staff, or so. Most people can be specialists, and you need different types of specialists,' argues Tucker.
'But any large organization needs to have somebody, or some
people, who can play that translation role because they are lit-
erate in a number of specialisms.' Mutual respect for different
'languages' – be that economics jargon, trader-speak, or anything else – is important too. 'It is about epistemology, about
what counts as knowledge. If someone is saying something in
a different language from the one you use, that does not mean
you should just ignore it.'

A fourth lesson is that it pays if people can periodically try to
reimagine the taxonomies they use to reorganize the world, or
even experiment with alternatives. Most of the time, most of us
simply accept the classification systems we have inherited. But
these are almost never ideal: they can become outdated, or end
up serving just narrow interest groups. At Sony, the engineers
did not question their silos, and ended up missing huge opportunities to innovate as a result. The economics profession before
2008 suffered a similar flaw, and as a result economists failed to
see the scale of leverage that was developing in the system. But
at Cleveland Clinic, doctors have tried to flip their mental maps
of how medicine should be organized upside down, to visualize
the world around how the patient experiences health, rather than
how a doctor is trained. The same principle could be applied to
numerous other businesses. Media groups, for example, are often
arranged into departments defined according to how journalists
have traditionally organized themselves (as, say, 'political reporters' or 'banking reporters' or 'sub-editors' or 'writers') rather than

how consumers experience the news. Banks tend to offer their financial products in departments defined by bankers, not investors or savers. Industrial companies often organize themselves according to how products were made fifty or a hundred years ago, or the different skills that engineers have, rather than around the problems that their modern customers want to solve. If those patterns are rigid, they risk becoming outmoded or clumsy and cause people to do foolish things. Changing them can spark innovation or, at the very least, a broader perspective.

And a fifth lesson is that it can also pay to use technology to challenge our silos. Computers do not automatically remove silos from our lives. Far from it. The sheer volume of digital data that now exists in our system forces us to constantly keep creating new systems to organize data, which inevitably forces us – or, more accurately, prompts computers – to put information into specific buckets. But the beauty of computers is that they are not born with indelible mental biases. They can be programmed to rearrange information in different ways and test out different ways of organizing data. Indeed, it is usually dramatically faster and easier to rearrange computer bytes than people, particularly given the power of data processing in modern computing systems (and the fact that data, unlike real-life people, cannot rebel against an order or foot-drag). The story of the New York skunkworks shows how effective this process of data reorganization can sometimes be in driving subtle, but potentially important, policy shifts. So does the tale of Brett Goldstein's battle to cut the murder rate in Chicago. But these stories also reveal an important caveat. Data does not reorganize itself, or break down silos by itself; somebody needs to program the computers. What is needed above all is a big dose of human imagination. Like that displayed by Mike Flowers.

SO HOW WE GET that all-important sense of imagination that enables us to challenge classification systems, be that in cyberspace or real life? One potential tool is to borrow some of the principles of anthropology. This does not mean studying far-flung exotic cultures, lurid rituals, or dusty bones. As I explained in Chapter One, these days anthropologists are as likely to work in complex industrialized settings as non-Western cultures. Moreover, the discipline is not really defined by the types of people that anthropologists happen to study (be they Berber nomads, Swiss bankers, or anyone else). Instead anthropology is best viewed as a *mind-set*, or a way of looking on the world. It has several defining traits. First, anthropologists tend to take a bottom-up view of life. They usually get out of their offices and experience life on the ground, trying to understand micro-level patterns to make sense of the macro picture. Second, they listen and look with an open mind and try to see how all the different pieces of a social group or system interconnect. They tend to be flies on the wall. Third, because anthropologists try to look at the totality of what they see, they end up examining the parts of life that people do not want to talk about, because they are considered taboo, dull, or boring. They are fascinated by social silences. Fourth, they listen carefully to what people say about their life, and then compare it to what people actually do. Anthropologists are obsessed with the gap between rhetoric and reality.

Fifth, anthropologists often compare different societies and cultures and systems. A key reason they do this is because comparison can help illuminate the underlying patterns of different social groups. That is useful when looking at another culture. It is also invaluable if we want to understand our own society. When we immerse ourselves in another world, we not only learn about the 'other' but can look back on our *own* lives with fresh eyes and a clearer perspective. We become insider-outsiders.

The sixth and most important point about anthropology, though, is that the discipline celebrates the idea that there is more than one valid way for humans to live. That sounds obvious. But humans in any society tend to assume that their own culture is natural. Our own social rules and classification systems feel so normal, if not inevitable, that we rarely devote much effort to thinking about them at all. But anthropologists know that the classification systems we use to organize our worlds and minds are *not* inevitable; they are usually a function of nurture not nature. We can change our cultural patterns if we really want to do that. We can also change the formal and informal rules that we use to organize the world. Or we can if we stop and think.

These six principles from anthropology can offer a good perspective for thinking about silos. As I have argued repeatedly in this book, we cannot live without silos in the modern world. But we can avoid succumbing to the problems they pose. Looking at how we organize the world with an insider-outsider perspective – as anthropologists do – is one way to combat the risks. Being an insider-outsider enables us to see our classification systems in context. It also helps us to see the overlaps, the underlaps, the issues that fall between the cracks of our taxonomies, or the ways that our boundaries have become dangerously rigid or outdated. Being an insider-outsider helps us see the risks of sclerotic boundaries. And it can also give us the imagination to mix up our borders, imagine a different world, and seek innovation 'on the edge' of our classification systems and organizations, as John Seely Brown, the scientist, has observed.[3]

You do not need to be an anthropologist to get that insider-outsider view. Having that training certainly helps (and I think that many organizations could benefit enormously from hiring an anthropologist to look at how they operate). However, some people get that all-important insider-outsider perspective on life because they have been tossed across borders, or moved between different worlds. Sometimes this is accidental. Mike Flowers never expected to learn about data mixing in Baghdad. Sometimes the journey is deliberate. When Brett Goldstein, in Chapter Five, plunged into the police department, he was voluntarily jumping out of one cozy world into a much less familiar one, in a manner that later enabled him to break down silos in an innovative way. But change does not always need to involve a dramatic switch in career. We can temporarily jump into a different world by changing the information and news we consume, moving our location, talking to different people and trying to imagine how life might look through their eyes. 'I think we need to do a mental exercise sometimes, and imagine that we are at the optician's, with those old-fashioned eye frames that they used to drop different lens into,' suggests Bob Steel, the former deputy mayor of New York. 'I sometimes try to imagine slotting a different lens into my glasses and asking what I would see. How the world would look through somebody else's eyes.' We can also travel to collide with new people and ideas. 'The Internet provides priceless access to a world of ideas and information. But even the Internet is no substitute for "innovation trips" and safaris to strange places to encounter new ideas "in the wild,"' argues Cleveland Clinic's Toby Cosgrove, who urges his doctors to travel to conferences, other hospitals, and nonmedical sites. 'Ambitious individuals in every field need to close their laptops, get out of their chairs, and take trips to explore new places and meet people who are doing things differently.' Above all, we need to leave ourselves open to collisions with people and ideas outside whatever silo we inhabit. If we make space in our lives to collide with the unexpected, we often end up changing our cultural lens.

THE CURSE OF EFFICIENCY

Of course, there is at least one big obstacle to this goal: it takes time and energy to make enough space to collide with the unexpected, roam around the world, and gain an insider-outsider perspective. Staying in a silo, or just accepting the boundaries we inherit, often appears a lot easier. After all, we live in a world where people are expected to streamline their careers and become specialists. Our schools and universities put students into boxes at a young age, and academic departments are fragmented. As Fareed Zakaria, the American journalist, points out, the main thrust of educational policy in America today is to support specialized technical subjects, not generalist courses like liberal arts degrees, where students jump between different topics.[4] We tend to assume that people will be penalized if they jump between professions or jobs. The people running institutions also face pressure to make these as efficient as they can by cutting out waste. Specialization and focus is considered desirable in the modern world. That makes it hard to justify time-consuming activities that do not deliver instant results, such as talking to people from other departments, rotating people across departments, or sending people out on innovation safaris. 'Running something like Hackamonth takes a lot of time,' as Michael Schroepfer of Facebook, observed. 'You have to have some slack in the system, or it won't work, so it's wasteful in a way.' Letting people 'roam' in an undirected way tends to seem like a self-indulgent luxury. So is the idea of creating cultural translators, conducting social analysis, or – dare I say it – looking at life through an anthropologist's lens. There is a constant tendency for people to organize themselves into silos in the name of hyper efficiency, accountability, and effectiveness.

But if there is one key message from this book, it is that our world does not function effectively if it is always rigidly streamlined. Living in specialized silos might make life seem more efficient in the short-term. But a world that is always divided into a fragmented and specialist pattern is a place of missed risks and opportunities. If we become blind creatures of habit – or habitus, as the anthropologist Pierre Bourdieu liked to say – our lives are poorer as a result.

Or to put it another way, in today's complex twenty-first-century world we are all faced with a subtle challenge: we can either be mastered by our mental and structural silos or we can try to master them instead. The choice lies with us. And the first step to mastering our silos is the most basic one of all: to think how we all unthinkingly classify the world around us each day.

And then try to imagine an alternative.

Acknowledgments

THIS BOOK AROSE OUT OF VARIOUS SILO-BUSTING JOURNEYS I HAVE experienced in my own life: since the age of eighteen, I have lived on several different continents, moved from the world of academic anthropology into a career in journalism, and written about numerous different topics, ranging from finance to politics to culture to economics and wars. Along the way, I have collected the intellectual threads that are woven into the tapestry of this manuscript, and I am deeply grateful to everyone who has deliberately or inadvertently offered me these ideas, sometimes through extensive debate, but usually simply through an offhand comment, chance meeting, or unplanned collision.

One particularly big thank-you must go to the anthropology department at Cambridge University, where Ernest Gellner (my former PhD supervisor), Caroline Humphreys, and Keith Hart all provided great inspiration. Subsequently, anthropologists such as Douglas Holmes, Martha Poon, Gitti Jordan, and Craig Calhoun have offered valuable insights, as has the work of the ReD consultancy in New York. Another source of inspiration has come from my colleagues at the *Financial Times*, where Lionel Barber (editor) and John Thornhill (deputy editor) have been endlessly supportive, not least by letting me take time off to write this book. Many *FT* colleagues also kindly read early drafts of different chapters and offered helpful comments; one joy of the *FT* is that my colleagues are not just smart but very collegiate. Particular thanks must go to Andrew Edgecliffe Johnson, Richard Waters, Hannah Kuchler, Tom Braithwaite, Greg Meyer, and Cardiff Garcia.

In the last two years, a plethora of people outside the *FT* have provided inspiration, discussed the book with me, or read different parts of it. In that respect I am particularly grateful to William Janeway, William Haseltine, Rana Faroohar, Hugh Van Steemis, Carlos de la Cruz, Richard Blum, John Seely Brown, Hans Helmut-Kotz, Andy Haldane, Sandy Pentland, Rolf Renders, Donald Marron, Daniel Glazer, Biz Stone, Merryn Somerset Webb, Mark Ein, Ben Hardy, Scott Malkin, Andrew McCaffee, Daniel Goroff, Jon Ledecky, Thomas Snitch, Gary Gensler, Peter Hancock, Adam Glick, and Laura Nolen. Jon was very supportive and a source of many great ideas; Gary provided constant intellectual challenge, and without his diligent, patient input the book would be far weaker. Amanda Urban, my agent at ICM, has been a tireless champion and friend. Ben Loehnen, my book editor at Simon & Schuster, did a stunning job of overseeing the project, constantly pushing me to improve my ideas, challenging my thesis, and then tightening up the writing. Tim Whiting of Little, Brown has also been very helpful. Emily Loose, the first editor with whom I discussed this book at Simon & Schuster, also deserves great thanks for having faith in the project. Joy Crane was a fabulous researcher for the book and a fount of ideas and laughter.

I am also deeply grateful to everyone who agreed to be interviewed for this book; many of them were very generous with their time and comments, even when my questions were apt to be irritating or inconvenient. If I have misunderstood what they were trying to say, the fault is entirely mine.

I am very grateful to my brother and father, Richard and Peter Tett, for all the help they have offered me over the years. A huge thank-you goes to Joshua Brockner, for bringing joy, fun, and order and making me see beyond my own mental silos. But, the biggest thanks of all go to my two wonderful daughters, Analiese and Helen. They are at the center of my heart and remind me every day why it is important to live a holistic life, to celebrate and explore the world in all its dimensions.

Notes

In the course of writing this book I conducted numerous interviews with the people mentioned in the narrative. Some of these were done explicitly for my book. Others were carried out for the *Financial Times*. Unless otherwise stipulated, the quotes in this book are taken from author interviews. Any mistakes in interpretation are mine.

NOTE FROM THE AUTHOR

1. Daniel Kahneman, *Thinking, Fast and Slow* (New York: Farrar, Straus & Giroux, 2013).
2. Gillian Tett, *Fool's Gold: The Inside Story of J.P. Morgan and How Wall Street Greed Corrupted Its Bold Dream and Created a Financial Catastrophe* (New York: Free Press, 2010).
3. Gillian Tett, 'Ambiguous Alliances; Marriage and Identity in a Muslim Village in Soviet Tajikistan' (PhD diss., Cambridge University, 1996). See also Gillian Tett, 'Guardians of the Faith, Gender and Religion in an (Ex) Soviet Tajik Village,' *Muslim Women's Choices; Religious Belief and Social Reality*, C. F. El-Solh and J Mabro, eds. (Providence, RI), pp. 128–51.

INTRODUCTION: BLOOMBERG'S SKUNKWORKS

1. Daniel Kahneman, *Thinking, Fast and Slow* (New York: Farrar, Straus & Giroux, 2013).
2. New York Senate files, Jeffrey D. Klein, 'A Survey of Bank Owned Properties in New York City,' July 2011.

3. 'Bronx House Fire Kills Boy, 12, and His Parents,' *New York Times*, April 25, 2011.

4. '3 Killed in Monday Morning Bronx Fire,' *CBS New York*, April 25, 2011.

5. Klein, 'A Survey of Bank Owned Properties in New York City.'

6. Barry Paddock, John Lauinger and Corky Siemaszko, 'Drug Dealers in First Floor of Illegal Bronx Apt. Building Barred City Inspectors,' New York *Daily News*, April 27, 2011.

7. 'Out of Control, Out of Sight,' Citizens Housing Planning Council Report, May 2, 2011.

8. Klein, 'A Survey of Bank Owned Properties in New York City.'

9. Barry Paddock, John Lauinger, and Corky Siemanzko, 'No Way Out for Tragic Family,' New York *Daily News*, April 27, 2011.

10. Fire Department Citywide Statistics, Performance Indicators.

11. City of New York press release, 'Bloomberg and Fire Commissioner Cassano Announce 2012 Sets All-Time Record for Fewest Fire Fatalities in New York City History,' January 2, 2013.

12. Benjamin Lesser and Brian Kates, 'Hidden Deathtraps: After Flushing Fire and 200k Complaints, Divided Apartments Still Run Rampant,' New York *Daily News*, November 14, 2009.

13. Data from City Hall and Mike Flowers's presentations.

14. 'Top 25 Employers in New York City in 2013,' *Crain's New York Business*, March 21, 2014.

15. Paul Davidson, 'Compatible Radio Systems Would Cost Billions,' *USA Today*, December 28, 2005.

16. 'Big Data in the Big Apple,' *Slate*, March 6, 2013.

17. See Bloomberg's tweets on www.twitter.com; also Commencement Speech by Michael Bloomberg to Johns Hopkins University, 2010.

18. Michael M. Grynbaum, 'The Reporters of City Hall Return to Their Old Perch,' *New York Times*, May 24, 2012.

19. Code for America Summit 2012, Mike Flowers, Day 1, October 4, 2012.

20. Thor Olavsrud, 'How Big Data Saves Lives in New York City,' *CIO*, October 25, 2012.

21. To see the Primary Land Use Tax Lot Output file (PLUTO), see http://www.nyc.gov/html/dcp/html/bytes/applbyte.shtml.

22. Kenneth Cukier and Viktor Mayer-Schoenberger, 'The Rise of Big Data,' *Foreign Affairs*, May 1, 2013. See also Cukier and Mayer-Schoenberger, *Big Data: A Revolution That Will Transform How We Live, Work, and Think* (Eamon Dolan: Mariner, 2014).

23. Interview with Mike Flowers, http://radar.oreilly.com/2012/06/predictive-data-analytics-big-data-nyc.html.

24. Alex Howard, 'Predictive Data Analytics in Saving Lives and Taxpayer Dollars in New York City,' *Radar Online*, June 26, 2012; 'Mayor Moves Against Drugs,' *Wall Street Journal*, December 13, 2011.

25. Ian Goldin and Mike Mariathasan, *The Butterfly Defect: How Globalization Creates Systemic Risks and What to Do About It* (Princeton: Princeton University Press, 2014).

26. https://www.imf.org/external/np/speeches/2014/020314.htm.

27. *Oxford English Dictionary*.

28. Ibid.

29. Ibid.

30. Adam Smith, *An Inquiry into the Nature and Causes of the Wealth of Nations*, Part 1 (Indianapolis: Liberty Fund, 1982) (from 1776 manuscript).

31. See the official report on the BP oil spill: National Commission on the BP Deepwater Horizon Oil Spill and Offshore Drilling, 'Deep Water; The Gulf Oil Disaster and the Future of Offshore Drilling. Report to the President,' January 2011, http://www.gpo.gov. Also: Peter Elkind and David Whitford with Doris Burke, 'BP: An Accident Waiting to Happen,' *Fortune*, January 24, 2011, and Ed Crooks, 'US report spells out BP failures in Gulf,' *Financial Times*, September 15, 2011.

32. See the damning report by Anton Valukas on the GM scandal: 'General Motors Company: Regarding Ignition Switch Recalls,' May 29 2014, by Anton R. Valukas, Jenner & Block LLC, http://s3.documentcloud.org/documents/1183508/g-m-internal-investigation-report.pdf.

33. See the Mary Barra town hall on June 5, 2014, http://media.gm.com/

media/us/en/gm/news.detail.html/content/Pages/news/us/en/2014/Jun/060514-ignition-report.html.

34. 9/11 Commission Report Executive Summary, 'Management' subsection, http://www.gpo.gov/fdsys/pkg/GPO-911REPORT/pdf/GPO-911REPORT.pdf.

35. Denis Campbell, 'NHS Told to Abandon Delayed IT Project,' *The Guardian*, September 21, 2011.

36. Stephen Hugh-Jones, 'The Symbolic and the Real,' Cambridge University Lectures, Lent term 2005, http://www.alanmacfarlane.com/hugh_jones/abstract.htm.

1: THE NONDANCERS

1. Pierre Bourdieu, *Outline of a Theory of Practice* (Cambridge: Cambridge University Press, 1977).

2. Pierre Bourdieu, *The Bachelor's Ball: The Crisis of Peasant Society in Bâearn* (Chicago: University of Chicago Press, 2008). Translated from *Le bal des celibataires* (Bourdieu: Edition de Sevil, 2002).

3. Taken from Bourdieu's essay 'La dimension de la domination economique,' *Etudes Rurales* 113–114 (January–June 1989), pp. 15–36. Reproduced in Bourdieu, *The Batchelor's Ball*, pp. v1–vll.

4. Pierre Bourdieu, *Sketch for Self-Analysis* (Boston: Polity, 2008), p. 63.

5. Ibid.

6. George A. Miller, '*The Magical Number Seven, Plus or Minus Two: Some Limits on Our Capacity for Processing Information,*' *Psychological Review* 63 (2) (1956), pp. 81–97.

7. Ibid.

8. Daniel Kahneman, *Thinking, Fast and Slow* (New York: Farrar, Straus & Giroux, 2013).

9. Luc de Brabandere and Alan Iny, *Thinking in New Boxes: A New Paradigm for Business Creativity* (New York: Random House, 2013).

10. René Descartes, *Discourse on Method and Meditations on First Philosophy*, Donald A. Cress, trans. (Indianapolis: Hackett, 1999).

11. Brent Berlin and Paul Kay, *Basic Color Terms: Their Universality and Evolution* (University of California Press, 1969).

12. Caroline M. Eastman and Robin M. Carter, 'Anthropological Perspectives on Classification Systems,' 1994. Eastman, C. (1994). 5th ASIS SIG/CR Classification Research Workshop, 69–78, doi:10.7152/acro.v5i1.13777.

13. Jared Diamond, *The World Until Yesterday: What Can We Learn from Traditional Societies?* (New York: Penguin, 2013).

14. Bourdieu, *Sketch for Self-Analysis*, p. 5.

15. Ibid., p. 97.

16. Ibid., p. 91.

17. Ibid., p. 38.

18. Ibid.

19. Ibid., p. 40.

20. Robert Layton, *An Introduction to Theory in Anthropology* (Cambridge: Cambridge University Press, 1999), p. 1.

21. David Hume, *Treatise on Human Nature* (1738; U.S.: CreateSpace Independent Publishing, 2013).

22. Ernest Gellner, *The Concept of Kinship* (London: Blackwell, 1973), p. vii.

23. Ibid., pp. vii, viii.

24. Bronislaw Malinowksi, *Argonauts of the Western Pacific* (Long Grove, IL: Waveland Press, 1984; rpt. of 1922 edition).

25. Claude Lévi-Strauss, *Myth and Meaning* (Germany: Schocken, 1995; rpt. of 1978 edition).

26. Claude Lévi-Strauss, *The Elementary Structures of Kinship* (Boston: Beacon, 1971); Claude Lévi-Strauss, *Tristes Tropiques* (New York: Penguin, 2012; rpt.; Claude Lévi-Strauss, *The Savage Mind* (Chicago: University of Chicago Press, 1966).

27. Bourdieu, *Sketch for Self-Analysis*, p. 40.

28. An excellent description of this period of Bourdieu's life can be gathered from the photographic account of his work in Algeria, gathered by one of his former students, Craig Calhoun: Pierre Bourdieu and Craig Calhoun, ed., *Picturing Algeria* (New York: Columbia University Press, 2012).

29. Bourdieu, *Sketch for Self-Analysis*, p. 48.

30. Ibid., p. 53.

31. Ibid., p. 47.

32. Ibid., p. 61. See also Bourdieu, *The Batchelor's Ball*, p. 3.

33. Ibid., p. 67.

34. Bourdieu, *Outline of a Theory of Practice*, p. 170.

35. Kate Fox, *Watching the English* (London: Hodder & Stoughton, 2005), p. 6.

36. Ibid., p. 13.

37. Karen Ho, *Liquidated: An Ethnography of Wall Street* (Durham, NC: Duke University Press, 2009).

38. Caitin Zaloom, *Out of the Pits: Traders and Technology from Chicago to London* (Chicago: University of Chicago Press, 2006).

39. Alexandra Ouroussoff, *Wall Street at War: The Secret Struggle for the Global Economy* (Boston: Polity, 2010).

40. Douglas Holmes, *Economy of Words: Communicative Imperatives in Central Banks* (Chicago: University of Chicago Press, 2013).

41. Annelise Riles, *Collateral Knowledge: Legal Reasoning in the Global Financial Markets* (Chicago: University of Chicago Press, 2011).

42. Danah Boyd, *It's Complicated: The Social Life of Networked Teens* (New Haven: Yale University Press, 2014).

43. Margaret Mead (1950, p. xxvi) cited in: Tom Boellstorff, *Coming of Age in Second Life: An Anthropologist Explores the Virtually Human* (Princeton, NJ: Princeton University Press, 2010), p. 71.

2: OCTOPUS POTS

1. Lou Gerstner, *Who Says Elephants Can't Dance? Inside IBM's Historic Turnaround*. (Waterville, ME: Thorndike Press, 2002).

2. Sony video by Comdex, http://groupx.com/ourwork/launch/sony.html.

3. Paul Thurott, 'Fall Comdex 1999 Reviewed,' http://winsupersite.com/product-review/fall-comdex-1999-reviewed.

4. Martyn Williams, 'George Lucas, Playstation 2 Highlight Sony Keynote at Comdex,' CNN, November 16, 1999.

5. http://www.zdnet.com/news/star-wars-creator-gives-sony-thumbs-up/104118; http://www.ign.com/articles/1999/11/17/comdex-1999-sony-aims-high-with-playstation-2.

6. Martyn Williams, 'George Lucas, Playstation 2 Highlight Sony Keynote at Comdex,' CNN, November 16 1999.

7. 'Sony Global – Sony History,' November 2006, http://web.archive.org/web/20061128064313/http://www.sony.net/Fun/SH/1-1/h2.html.

8. 'Masaru Ibuka,' PBS Online 1999, ScienCentral, and the American Institute of Physics. 'Akio Morita,' PBS Online 1999, ScienCentral, and the American Institute of Physics.

9. 'Akio Morita: Gadget Guru,' *Entrepreneur*, October 10, 2008.

10. Akio Morita, *Made in Japan: Akio Morita and Sony* (New York: E. P. Dutton, 1986), p. 56.

11. Ibid., p. 65.

12. Ibid., pp. 79–81.

13. Meaghan Haire, 'A Brief History of the Walkman,' *Time*, July 1, 2009.

14. Morita, *Made in Japan*, p. 82.

15. Steve Lohr, 'Norio Ohga, Who Led Sony Beyond Electronics, Dies at 81,' *New York Times*, April 24, 2011.

16. Sea-Jin Chang, *Sony vs. Samsung: The Inside Story of the Electronics Giants' Battle for Global Supremacy* (Hoboken, NJ: Wiley, 2008).

17. John Nathan, *Sony: Private Life* (Boston: Mariner, 2001), p. 315.

18. Sony Corporate Information, Chapter 24: Diversification, www.sony.net.

19. Karl Taro Greenfeld, 'Saving Sony: CEO Howard Stringer Plans to Focus on 3-D TV,' *Wired*. March 22, 2010.

20. Walter Isaacson, *Steve Jobs* (New York: Simon & Schuster, 2011), p. 408.

21. Ibid., p. 362.

22. Sony 2005 Financial Year Fiscal Report, www.sony.net.

23. Andrew Ross Sorkin and Saul Hansel, 'Shakeup at Sony Puts Westerner in Leader's Role,' *New York Times*, March 7, 2005.

24. Mark Gunther, 'The Welshman, the Walkman and the Salarymen,' *Fortune*, June 1, 2006.

25. For an account of this see: Lou Gerstner, 'Who Says Elephants Can't Dance?' *Harper Business*, 2002; Lisa DiCarlo, 'How Lou Gerstner Got IBM to Dance,' *Forbes*, November 11, 2002; 'IBM Corp Turnaround,'

Harvard Business School Case Study, March 14, 2000; Lynda Applegate and Elizabeth Collins, 'IBM's Decade of Transformation; Turnaround to Growth,' Harvard Business School Case Study, April 2005.

26. 'A Word from Howard: Breaking Down Silos,' Sony United newsletter, January 2, 2006.

27. Martin Fackler, 'Sony Plans 10,000 Job Cuts,' *New York Times*, September 23, 2005.

28. Daisuke Takato, 'Sony to Cut 10,000 Jobs, Product Models to End Losses,' Bloomberg News, September 22, 2005.

29. David Macdonald, 'Sony Tries to Get Its Mojo Back,' *Asia Times*, February 7, 2006.

30. Martin Fackler, 'Cutting Sony, a Corporate Octopus, Back to a Rational Size,' *New York Times*, May 29, 2006.

31. Sony corporate announcement, September 2005, www.sony.net.

32. Ibid.

33. Ginny Parker Woods, 'Sony's Picture Is Looking Brighter,' *Wall Street Journal*, February 3, 2006.

34. Mark Gunter, 'The Welshman, the Walkman and the Salarymen,' *Fortune*, June 1 2006.

35. *Who Says Elephants Can't Dance?* Harper Business, 2002; see also Lisa diCarlo, 'How Louis Gerstner Got IBM to Dance,' *Forbes*, November 11, 2002.

36. Mark Gunther, 'The Welshman, the Walkman and The Salarymen,' *Fortune*, June 1, 2006.

37. Tim Ferguson, 'Samsung v Sony – The Growing "2000" Divide,' *Forbes*, April 30, 2012.

38. Andrew Ross Sorkin and Michael De La Merced, 'American Investor Targets Sony for a Breakup,' *New York Times*, May 14, 2013.

39. Mike Fleming, 'George Clooney to Hedge Fund Honcho Daniel Loeb: Stop Spreading Fear at Sony,' *Deadline Hollywood*, August 2, 2013.

40. For an account of the challenges at Microsoft and the company's response see: Monica Langley, 'Reboot at Microsoft: Impatient Board Sped Ballmer's Exit,' *Wall Street Journal*, 2013; 'Microsoft Tears Down

Walls to Open Up Future,' *St Augustine Record*, July 13, 2013; Thom Forbes, 'Microsoft Blows up Its Silos,' *Marketing Daily*, July 12, 2013; 'Microsoft Transforms But Will It Leave Its Past Behind?' Voice of America, October 25, 2013.

3: WHEN GNOMES GO BLIND

1. Upton Sinclair, *I, Candidate for Governor: And How I Got Licked* (Berkeley: University of California Press, 1994), p. 109.
2. FINMA (Swiss Financial Market Supervisory Authority), 'Financial Market Crisis and Financial Market Supervision,' September 14, 2009, p. 22. (Hereinafter FINMA report.)
3. Tobias Straumann, 'The UBS Crisis in Historical Perspective,' University of Zurich Empirical Research in Economics, September 2010, p. 5.
4. FINMA report, p. 21.
5. Ibid.
6. Ibid., p. 22.
7. Ibid.
8. Shareholder Report on UBS's Write-Down, April 18, 2008, p. 6, http://maths-fi.com/ubs-shareholder-report.pdf.
9. Ibid., p. 6.
10. Stephanie Baker-Said and Elena Logutenkova, 'The Mess at UBS,' *Bloomberg Markets*, July 2008.
11. Mark Landler, 'UBS Sells Stake After Write-Down,' *New York Times*, December 10, 2007.
12. Ibid.
13. UBS Shareholder Report, 2008, p. 6; Statement to Shareholders, December 2008.
14. UBS Shareholder Report, 2008, p. 7.
15. Baker-Said and Logutenkova, 'The Mess at UBS.'
16. 'Switzerland Unveils UBS Bail-out,' BBC World News, October 16, 2008.
17. UBS Shareholder Report, 2008, p. 6.
18. Nick Mathiason, 'UBS and US Government Reach Deal over Tax Evasion Dispute,' *The Guardian*, July 31, 2009.

19. Straumann, 'The UBS Crisis in Historical Perspective,' p. 3.
20. Ibid.
21. Ibid., p. 6.
22. Ibid.
23. John Tagliabue, '2 of the Big 3 Swiss Banks to Join to Seek Global Heft,' *New York Times*, December 9, 1997.
24. Adrian Cox, 'Costas Sees UBS Eclipsing Goldman, Citigroup as Top Fee Earner,' *Bloomberg Magazine*, March 1, 2004.
25. 'Swiss Bank to Acquire Chase Investment Unit,' Associated Press, reprinted in *New York Times*, February 22, 1991.
26. 'Has UBS Found Its Way Out of the Woods?,' *BusinessWeek*, March 29, 1999.
27. FINMA report, p. 25, footnote.
28. John Tagliabue, 'Swiss Banks Calling Wall St. Home,' *New York Times*, August 31, 2000.
29. Riva D. Atlas, 'How Banks Chased a Mirage,' *New York Times*, May 26, 2002.
30. Michael Corkery, 'Health Scare: Calculating UBS's Loss of Banker Benjamin Lorello,' *Wall Street Journal*, June 26, 2009.
31. 'Top UBS Banker Founds Private Equity Firm,' *Financial News*, June 29, 2007.
32. 'Jefferies Nabs One-time Critic from UBS,' *Dow Jones Financial News*, June 25, 2009.
33. Cox, 'Costas Sees UBS Eclipsing Goldman, Citigroup as Top Fee Earner.'
34. Uta Harnischfeger, 'UBS Faults Blinds Ambition for Subprime Miscues,' *New York Times*, April 22, 2008.
35. The usual definition of securitization is that it is enables bankers to create and issue 'tradable securities, such as bonds, that are backed by the income generated by an asset, a loan, a public works project or other revenue source,' to cite the *Financial Times* lexicon, http://lexicon.ft.com/Term?term=securitisation, Or as Investopedia says: 'Securitization is the process of taking an illiquid asset, or group of assets, and through financial engineering, transforming them into

a security. A typical example of securitization is a mortgage-backed security (MBS), which is a type of asset-backed security that is secured by a collection of mortgages.' This occurs in several stages. To quote Investopedia again: 'First, a regulated and authorized financial institution originates numerous mortgages, which are secured by claims against the various properties the mortgagors' purchase. Then, all of the individual mortgages are bundled together into a mortgage pool, which is held in trust as the collateral for an MBS. The MBS can be issued by a third-party financial company, such as a large investment banking firm, or by the same bank that originated the mortgages in the first place. Mortgage-backed securities are also issued by aggregators such as Fannie Mae or Freddie Mac. Regardless, the result is the same: a new security is created, backed up by the claims against the mortgagors' assets. This security can be sold to participants in the secondary mortgage market.' http://www.investopedia.com/ask/answers/07/securitization.asp.

36. Stephanie Baker-Said and Elena Logutenkova, 'UBS $100 Billion Wager Prompted $24 Billion Loss in Nine Months,' *Bloomberg News*, May 18, 2008.

37. Straumann, 'The UBS Crisis in Historical Perspective,' p. 17.

38. UBS Shareholder Report, 2008, p. 18.

39. Nelzon Schwartz, 'The Mortgage Bust Goes Global,' *New York Times*, April 6, 2008.

40. Baker-Said and Logutenkova, 'UBS $100 Billion Wager Prompted $24 Billion Loss in Nine Months.'

41. Karen Ho, *Liquidated: An Ethnography of Wall Street* (Durham, NC: Duke University Press, 2009).

42. FINMA report, p. 25.

43. Greg Ip, Susan Pullam, Scott Thurm, and Ruth Simon, 'How the Internet Bubble Broke Records, Rules, and Bank Accounts,' *Wall Street Journal*, July 14, 2000.

44. UBS Transparency Report to Shareholders, 2010, p. 18.

45. Ibid., p. 27.

46. UBS Shareholder Report, 2008, p. 9.

47. Ibid., p. 15.

48. Ibid., p. 16.

49. Chris Hughes, Haig Simonian, and Peter Thal Larsen, 'Corroded to the Core: How a Staid Swiss Bank Let Ambitions Lead It into Folly,' *Financial Times*, April 21, 2008.

50. UBS Shareholder Report, 2008, p. 4.

51. 'Brady W. Dougan,' Official Bio Credit Suisse Group AG website, https://www.credit-suisse.com/governance/en/pop_s_cv_dougan.jsp.

52. Haig Simonian and Peter Thal Larsen, 'UBS Reveals Top Level Shake-up,' *Financial Times*, July 1, 2005.

53. FINMA report, p. 28.

54. UBS Transparency Report, 2010, p. 21.

55. Sinclair, p. 109.

56. FINMA report, p. 27.

57. Ibid., p. 22.

58. Ibid.

59. UBS Transparency Report, 2010, p. 35.

60. Ibid., p. 5. On August 8 the chairman's office and the Group Executive Board were informed as to the extent of the problems.

61. Straumann, 'The UBS Crisis in Historical Perspective,' p. 9.

62. Hughes, Simonian, and Larsen, 'Corroded to the Core How a Staid Swiss Bank Let Ambitions Lead it into Folly.'

63. Gillian Tett, 'Silos and Silences,' *Banque de France Financial Stability Review*, July 2010, p. 126.

64. FINMA report, p. 26.

65. 'Executive Profile: Joseph Scoby,' http:.//www.bloomberg.com/research/stocks.

66. UBS Shareholder Report, 2008, p. 6.

67. Megan Murphy and Haig Simonian, 'Banking: Lightning Strikes Twice,' *Financial Times*, October 3, 2011.

68. Straumann, 'The UBS Crisis in Historical Perspective,' p. 8.

69. Ibid., pp. 4–5.

70. Haig Simonian, 'UBS Board Makes Formal Appointment,' *Financial Times*, December 8, 2009.

71. UBS Transparency Report, 2010, p. 7.

72. Lofts was appointed chief risk officer in 2008. He then left but was subsequently reappointed in 2011.

73. 'Christian Wiesendanger Executive Profile,' Bloomberg, www.bloomberg.net.

74. Megan Murphy, Kate Burgess, Sam Jones, and Haig Simonian, 'UBS Trader Adoboli Held over $2bn Loss,' *Financial Times*, September 15, 2011.

75. Tony Shearer, 'The Banks Are Simply Too Big to Be Managed,' letter to the head of business, *Daily Telegraph*, September, 19 2011.

4: RUSSIAN DOLLS

1. This account is based on an interview with Luis Garicano. See also Andrew Pierce, 'The Queen Asks Why No One Saw the Credit Crunch Coming,' *Daily Telegraph*, November 5, 2008; Chris Giles, 'The Economic Forecasters' Failing Vision,' *Financial Times*, November 25, 2008.

2. Etymological origins of 'Economy': *The American Heritage Dictionary of the English Language*, 4th ed. (New York: Houghton Mifflin, 2009).

3. Chris Hann and Keith Hart, *Economic Anthropology* (Boston: Polity, 2011), p. 34.

4. 'News release: Paul Tucker to Leave the Bank of England,' Bank of England website, June 14, 2013, www.bankofengland.co.uk.

5. Bill Janeway, *Doing Capitalism In the Innovation Economy: Markets, Speculation and the State* (Cambridge:Cambridge University Press, 2012), p. 163.

6. Axel Leijonhufvud, 'Life Among the Econ,' *Western Economic Journal*, 11:3 (September 1973), p. 327.

7. Ibid., p. 328.

8. 'Alan Greenspan,' *Biography*, A&E, 2014.

9. Gillian Tett. 'An Interview with Alan Greenspan,' *Financial Times*, October 25, 2013.

10. '1997: Brown Sets Bank of England Free,' *On This Day in History*, www.bbc.co.uk.

11. Chris Giles, 'The Court of King Mervyn,' *Financial Times Magazine*, May 5, 2012.

12. For a discussion of how silos impacted the media and the public debate about the financial risks before the financial crisis, see: Gillian Tett, 'Silos and Silences: Why So Few People Spotted the Problems in Complex Credit and What That Implies for the Future,' *Banque de France Financial Stability Review* no. 14, July 2010. See also Gillian Tett, 'Silos and Silences: the Problem of Fractured Thought in Finance,' Speech to the American Anthropological Association, New Orleans, 2010.

13. Tyler Cowen, 'Bailout of Long-Term Capital: A Bad Precedent?,' *New York Times*, December 26, 2008.

14. 'Speech: Macro, Asset Price and Financial System Uncertainties,' Roy Bridge Memorial Lecture given by Paul Tucker, Executive Director for Markets and Monetary Policy Committee Member, Bank of England, December 11, 2006, www.bankofengland.co.uk.

15. Ibid., p. 123.

16. Ibid., p. 127.

17. Ibid., p. 128.

18. Ibid.

19. Ibid., p. 127.

20. 'A perspective on Recent Monetary and Financial System Developments,' by Paul Tucker, Executive Director for Markets and Monetary Policy Committee Member, delivered April 26, 2007, www.bankofengland.co.uk.

21. Ibid., p. 6.

22. Ibid.

23. For a discussion of this, see Tett, 'Silos and Silences.'

24. 'About the Jackson Hole Economic Policy Symposium,' Publications Page, http://www.kc.frb.org/.

25. 'Housing, Housing Finance, and Monetary Policy,' speech by Chairman Ben S. Bernanke delivered August 31, 2007, at the Federal Reserve Bank of Kansas City's Economic Symposium, Jackson Hole, Wyoming, www.federalreserve.gov, 2007 speeches.

26. 'The Shadow Banking System and Hyman Minsky's Economic Journey,' *PIMCO Global Central Bank Focus*, newsletter, May 2009.

27. 'PIMCO Expert Bios: Paul A. McCulley,' PIMCO website.

28. Krishna Guha, 'Credit Turmoil Has Hallmarks of Bank Run,' *Financial Times*, September 2, 2007. See also Kansas Federal Federal Reserve minutes at http://www.kc.frb.org/Publicat/Sympos/2007/PDF /General Discussion6 0415.pdf.

29. Taken from the minutes of the Jackson Hole symposium, August 2007, http://www.kc.frb.org/Publicat/Sympos/2007/PDF/General Discussion 60415.pdf.

30. See Robert J Shiller, 'Bubble Trouble,' Project Syndicate. September 17, 2007, www.project-syndicate.org.commentary/bubble-trouble.

31. The specific problem with the entities such as SIVs and conduits was something known as a maturity mismatch. These vehicles had funded themselves by selling very short term notes (or bonds) in a market called the asset backed commercial paper market, and they had used that money to buy long-term assets such as mortgage bonds. The short-term bonds needed to be constantly rolled over, but the long-term assets could not be sold easily when the markets froze up. So when investors panicked and stopped giving funding to the conduits and SIVs, these faced a liquidity crunch. Since banks had extended off-balance-sheet guarantees to some of these vehicles, when the conduits and SIVs started to collapse this hit banks' balance sheets – and prompted a general sense of panic.

32. Jason Douglas and Geoffrey T. Smith, 'FSB's Carney Seeks Help to End Too-Big-to-Fail,' *Wall Street Journal*, April 11, 2014.

33. Heather Stewart, 'This Is How We Let the Credit Crunch Happen Ma'am,' *The Observer*, July 29, 2009.

34. Gillian Tett. 'An Interview with Alan Greenspan by Gillian Tett,' *Financial Times*, October 25, 2013.

35. 'Memorandum of Understanding Between the Financial Conduct Authority and the Bank of England, including the Prudential Regulation Authority,' Bank of England website, www.bankofengland.com.

36. 'One Mission. One Bank. Promoting the Good of the People of the

United Kingdom,' speech given by Mark Carney, Governor of the Bank of England, March 18, 2014, Mais Lecture at Cass Business School, City University, London.

37. Emma Charlton, 'Bank of England Creates New Unit to Crunch Economic Data,' Bloomberg news, July 1, 2014.

38. 'Financial Stability Oversight Council Created Under the Dodd-Frank Wall Street Reform and Consumer Protection Act,' October 2010, Treasury.gov.

39. Ian Katz, 'Richard Berner to Help Treasure Build Financial Research Office,' Bloomberg News, April 25, 2011.

40. Jennifer Ryan and Simon Kennedy, 'Carney Gets Chance to Reshape BOE as Tucker Plans Departure,' Bloomberg News, June 14, 2013.

5: GUN-TOTING GEEKS

1. Speech by Steve Jobs to Stanford University students, 2005, http://news.stanford.edu/news/2005/june15/jobs-061505.html.

2. For press reports on highly educated professionals volunteering for the police, see 'First NYPD Recruits Since 9/11,' *Police: The Law Enforcement Magazine*, July 9, 2002.

3. http://news.yahoo.com/chicago-murder-capital-of-america-fbi-142122290.html; http://www.foxnews.com/us/2013/09/19/fbi-chicago-officially-america-murder-capital/; http://www.huffington-post.com/2012/06/16/chicago-homicide-rate-wor_n_1602692.html.

4. For background on the culture of the Chicago police, see: Star #14931, *Chicago Cop: Tales From the Street* (CreateSpace Independent Publishing Platform, 2011); Martin Preib, *Crooked City* (CreateSpace Independent Publishing Platform, 2014); Daniel P Smith. *On the Job: Behind the Stars of the Chicago Police Department* (Chicago: Lake Claremont Press, 2008); Jim Padar and Jay Padar, *On Being a Cop: Father and Son Tales from the Streets of Chicago* (Self Published, 2013).

5. Kari Lydersen, 'In Chicago, Choice to Head Police Dept. a Controversial One,' *Washington Post*, December 2, 2007; Gary Washburn and Todd Lighty, 'New Top Cop Seeks to Fix Broken Trust: FBI Agent Aims to Soothe Police, Gain Confidence of Detractors,'

Chicago Tribune, November 30, 2007; Fran Spielman, '$310,000 for Top Cop? "Yes, It's Worth It": Daley; Weis Will Earn $93,000 More Than Mayor,' *Chicago Sun-Times*, December 5, 2007.

6. Locke Bowman, 'Will Mayor Rahm Emanuel Commit to Reforming the Chicago Police?,' *Huffington Post*, March 7 2011. www.huffing-tonpost.com.

7. For an account of the way that stove-piping has hampered the operations of intelligence and security forces in the last decade, see U.S. commission's report on 9/11: http://www.fas.org/irp/offdocs/911comm-sec13.pdf. See also the state department's report on the events in Benghazi, Libya, which echo a similar theme. http://www.state.gov/documents/organization/202446.pdf.

8. http://web.archive.org/web/20131203194757/http://www.suntimes.com/news/metro/23189930-418/grateful-for-cops-commitment.html.

9. See Chicago Police Memorial Foundation Website, Officer Of The Month – Brett Goldstein. May 2014 www.cpdmemorial.org/officer-of-the-month-brett-goldstein/.

10. Adam Lisberg, 'Chicago Buried in Murders; 2nd City Passes New York in Killing,' New York *Daily News*, November 2, 2008; Angela Rozas, 'Chicago Murder Rate Is Up 9 Percent So Far This Year,' *Chicago Tribune*, May 17, 2008.

11. David Heinzmann, 'After Scandal, a New Cop Unit: This Special Outfit Won't Be Called SOS,' *Chicago Tribune*, October 7, 2008.

12. 'Crime Is Down, but It's Still a Huge Problem,' Editorial, *Chicago Sun-Times*, August 5, 2010.

13. 'Two Lawmakers Propose National Guard Should Deal with Gun Violence and Murder in Chicago,' *NBC Nightly News*, April 26, 2010; Hal Dardick and Monique Garcia, 'Daley: Guard Isn't the Answer; Mayor, Governor, Police Union Not Fans of Proposal to Deploy Troops,' *Chicago Tribune*, April 27, 2010.

14. Lauren Etter and Douglas Belkin, 'Rash of Shootings in Chicago Leaves 8 Dead, 16 Wounded,' *Wall Street Journal*, April 17, 2010.

15. Terry Wilson, 'Top Cop Pushes Accountability as He Makes Changes in the Ranks,' *Chicago Tribune*, February 2, 2000.

16. See The Gang Book by the Chicago Crime Commission 2012 for estimates of the size and scope of the Chicago gangs: http://www.chicagocrimecommission.com. See also Peter Slevin, 'Jennifer Hudson's Nephew Found Dead,' *Washington Post*, October 28, 2008; Fran Spielman, 'A Different Beat for Weis,' *Chicago Sun-Times*, October 25, 2008.

17. Gary Slutkin and Tio Hardiman, 'The Homicide That Didn't Happen,' *Chicago Tribune*, February 9, 2011.

18. For statistics on Chicago murders, see portal.chicagopolice.org. For press reports on this decline, see William Lee, 'Decreases in Major Crime Categories, Chicago Police Say,' *Chicago Tribune*, September 8, 2010.

19. Frank Spielman and Frank Main, 'Police Supt. Weis Bails Out,' *Chicago Sun-Times*, March 2, 2011.

20. 'Weis Critical of Decision Allowing Burge To Keep Pension' CBS Chicago, January 28, 2011.

21. http://harris.uchicago.edu/directory/faculty/brett_goldstein.

6: (RE)WRITING SOCIAL CODE

1. Julia Bort, 'Facebook Engineer Jocelyn Goldfein to Women: Stop Being Scared of Computer Science,' *Business Insider*, October 2, 2012.

2. Nicholas Carlson, 'At Last – The Full Story of How Facebook Was Founded,' *Business Insider*, March 5, 2010.

3. Jessica Gurnn, 'The Grunts Are Geeks at Facebook Bootcamp,' *Los Angeles Times*, August 1, 2010.

4. Brier Dudley, 'Facebook Message: Girls, Too, Can Do Computers,' *Seattle Times*, March 11, 2012.

5. 'Audio Podcast: Deep Inside Facebook with Director of Engineering Jocelyn Goldfein,' Taken from the Entrepreneurial Thought Leaders Lecture Series, Ecorner: organized by Stanford University's Entrepeneurship Corner, May 22 2013.

6. Dudley, 'Facebook Message: Girls, Too, Can Do Computers.'

7. 'Audio Podcast: Deep Inside Facebook with Director of Engineering Jocelyn Goldfein.'

8. Nick Bilton, 'Facebook Graffiti Artist Could Be Worth $500 Million,' *New York Times*, 'Bits' blog, February 7, 2012.

9. Sarah Phillips, 'A Brief History of Facebook,' *The Guardian*, July 24, 2007.

10. Ibid.

11. 'Timeline: Key Dates in Facebook's Ten Year History,' Associated Press, February 4, 2014.

12. Tomio Geron, 'The Untold Story of Two Early Facebook Investors,' *Forbes*, February 2, 2012.

13. Ashlee Vance, 'Facebook: The Making of 1 Billion Users,' *Bloomberg Businessweek*, October 4, 2012.

14. Robin Dunbar, *Grooming, Gossip and the Evolution of Human Language* (Cambridge: Harvard University Press, 1998). See also Robin Dunbar, *How Many Friends Does One Person Need?* (Cambridge: Harvard University Press, 2010); 'Neocortex Size as a Constraint on Group Size in Primates,' *Journal of Human Evolution* 22, no. 6 (June 1992).

15. Drake Bennett, 'The Dunbar Number, from the Guru of Social Networks,' *Bloomberg Businessweek*, Technology. January 10, 2013.

16. R. I. M. Dunbar, 'Coevolution of Neocortical Size, Group Size and Language in Humans,' *Behavioral and Brain Sciences* 16, no. 4 (1993): 681–735.

17. Jessica Guynn, 'The Grunts Are Geeks at Facebook Bootcamp,' *Los Angeles Times*, August 1, 2010.

18. See the post by Andrew Bosworth on Facebook on November 19, 2009, entitled 'Facebook Engineering Bootcamp.' https://www.facebook.com/notes/facebook ... bootcamp/177577963919.

19. Mike Swift, 'A Look Inside Facebook's "Bootcamp" for New Employees,' *San Jose Mercury News*, April 18, 2012.

20. Samantha Murphy Kelly, 'The Evolution of Facebook News Feed,' *Mashable*, March 12, 2013.

21. Diberendu Ganguly, 'How Facebook's Jocelyn Goldfein Brought Magic to the Most Popular Product "Newsfeed,"' *The Economic Times*, January 25, 2013.

22. Ibid.

23. Ibid.

24. Ibid.

25. Ibid.

26. Ibid.

27. Ibid.

28. Sam Laird, 'Facebook Completes Move into New Menlo Park Headquarters,' Mashable.com, December 19, 2011.

29. Emil Protalinski, 'Facebook Wants Two Menlo Park Campuses for 9,400 Employees,' ZDnew. www.zdnet.com/.../facebook-wants-two-menlo-park-campuses August 24, 2011.

30. Megan Rose Dickey, 'Some of Facebook's Best Features Were Once Hackathon Projects,' *Business Insider,* January 9, 2013.

31. Jocelyn Goldfein, Facebook post, March 10, 2011, and March 17, 2011, www.facebook.com.

32. Ibid., September 15, 2011.

33. Ibid., April 23, 2012.

34. Ibid., January 24, 2012.

35. Ibid., June 24, 2012.

36. Ibid., April 25, 2012.

37. Mark Zuckerberg, Facebook post, June 28, 2013, www.facebook.com.

38. Ibid., August 19, 2012.

39. Mike Schoepfer, Facebook post, August, 14 2012. www.facebook.com.

40. Ryan Patterson, Facebook post, May 20, 2013, www.facebook.com.

41. Devindra Hardawar, 'Facebook Home Isn't Dead Yet and More Surprises from Engineering Director Jocelyn Goldfein,' *Venturebeat,* February 17, 2014, http://venturebeat.com/2014/02/17/facebook-home-isnt-dead-yet-more-surprises-from-mobile-engineering-director-jocelyn-goldfein.

42. Evelyn Rusli, 'Facebook Buys Instagram for $1 Billion,' *New York Times,* 'DealBook,' April 9, 2012.

43. 'Facebook Reports Fourth Quarter and Full Year 2014 Results,' January 28, 2015. www.investor.fb.com.

7: FLIPPING THE LENS

1. Financial Aid Cost Summary, Harvard Business School website.
2. Toby Cosgrove, MD, *The Cleveland Clinic Way: Lessons in Excellence from One of the World's Leading Healthcare Organizations* (New York: McGraw-Hill, 2014).
3. Diane Solov, 'From C's and D's to Clinic's Helm: At the Age of 63, Delos "Toby" Cosgrove, Surgeon, Inventor, Go-to Guy (and Dyslexic), Finds the Job and Opportunity He's Been Looking For,' Cleveland *Plain Dealer*, June 9, 2004.
4. Cosgrove, *The Cleveland Clinic Way*, p. xi.
5. *To Act as a Unit: The Story of Cleveland Clinic*, Cleveland Clinic Foundation, 2011, p. 129.
6. Cosgrove, *The Cleveland Clinic Way*, p. 109.
7. Ibid.
8. Alison Van Dusen, 'America's Top Hospitals Go Global,' Forbes.com, August 25, 2008.
9. Cosgrove, *The Cleveland Clinic Way*, p. 110.
10. 'King Abdullah to Open Jeddah's International Medical Center Tomorrow,' news release, Saudi Embassy archives, October 28, 2006.
11. 'Cleveland Clinic: A Short History,' Cleveland Clinic official website, www.clevelandclinic.org, p. 1.
12. 'Bill of Sale: From Estate of Dr Frank J. Weed to Dr Frank E. Bunts and Dr George Crile,' Cleveland Ohio, April 10, 1891, reprinted in John D. Clough, Peter G. Studer, and Steve Szilagyi, eds., *To Act as a Unit: The Story of Cleveland Clinic*. 5th ed., (Cleveland: Cleveland Clinic, 2011), p. 15.
13. Clough et al, *To Act As A Unit*, p. 16.
14. Ibid., p. 12.
15. Ibid.
16. 'Cleveland Clinic: A Short History,' p. 2.
17. Kate Roberts, 'Mayo Clinic: History,' Minnesota Historical Society website, 2007.
18. *The Cleveland Clinic Way*, p. 7.

19. Thomas Bausch et al., *Economic and Demographic Analysis for Cleveland, Ohio* (Cleveland: Cleveland Urban Observatory, 1974).

20. 'Cleveland Clinic: A Short History,' p. 5.

21. Ibid., p. 6.

22. Ibid., p. 7.

23. Ibid., p. 8.

24. Ibid., p. 7.

25. *To Act as a Unit*, pp. 168–69.

26. Ibid., p. 129.

27. 'Cleveland Clinic: A Short History,' p. 8.

28. Clough et al, *To Act as a Unit*, p. 129.

29. Ibid., p. 119.

30. Cosgrove, *The Cleveland Clinic Way*, p. 33.

31. Jerry Adler, 'What Health Reform Can Learn from Cleveland Clinic,' *Newsweek*, November 26, 2009.

32. Clough et al, *To Act as a Unit*, p. 109.

33. Ibid., p. 110.

34. Ibid.

35. Solov, 'From C's and D's to Clinic's Helm: At the Age of 63, Delos "Toby" Cosgrove, Surgeon, Inventor, Go-to Guy (and Dyslexic), Finds the Job and Opportunity He's Been Looking For.'

36. Ibid.

37. Bob Rich, *The Fishing Club: Brothers and Sisters of the Angle* (Guilford, CT: Lyons Press, 2006), pp. 220–21.

38. Ibid., pp. 222–23.

39. Ibid., pp. 225.

40. Ibid., pp. 228–29.

41. Ibid., p. 231.

42. Solov, 'From C's and D's to Clinic's Helm: At the Age of 63, Delos "Toby" Cosgrove, Surgeon, Inventor, Go-to Guy (and Dyslexic), Finds the Job and Opportunity He's Been Looking For.'

43. Cosgrove, *The Cleveland Clinic Way*, p. 90.

44. Ibid., p. 91.

45. Ibid., p. xi.

46. Ibid., p. 91.

47. Ibid.

48. Ibid.

49. Cosgrove, *The Cleveland Clinic Way*, p. 119.

50. Ursus Wehrli, 'Tidying Up Art,' Talk Video, 2006. www.ted.com. See also Penelope Green, 'The Art of Unjumbling,' *New York Times*, March 27, 2013, or Ursus Wehrli, *The Art of Clean Up; Life Made Neat and Tidy* (San Francisco: Chronicle Books, 2013).

51. Clough et al, *To Act as a Unit*, p. 132.

52. Cosgrove, *The Cleveland Clinic Way*, p. 22.

53. Accenture, 'Clinical Transformation: New Business Models for a New Era in Healthcare,' September 27, 2012.

54. Cosgrove, *The Cleveland Clinic Way*, p. 4.

55. Clough et al, *To Act as a Unit*, p. 155.

56. Ibid., p. 133.

57. Ibid., p. 134.

58. Ibid.

59. 'Abby Abelson, MD, Named Chair of Department of Rheumatology at Cleveland Clinic,' Cleveland Clinic News Service, April 6, 2011.

60. Clough et al, *To Act as a Unit*, p. 136.

61. 'A Common Purpose: Kate Medoff Barnett and Amy Belkin,' *Harvard Business School Alumni Magazine*, June 5, 2013.

62. 'Seth Podolsky, MD,' Official Biography, Cleveland Clinic website.

63. 'James Merlino, MD,' Official Biography, Cleveland Clinic website.

64. Cosgrove, *The Cleveland Clinic Way*, p. 119.

65. Ibid., p. 126.

66. ibid., p. 114.

67. Ibid., p. 124.

68. Ibid., p. 114.

69. Ibid., p. 33.

70. For data on patient satisfaction see the *US News & World Report* surveys on hospitals. 2012–2015, http://health.usnews.com/best-hospitals/rankings. See also the HCAHPS (Hospital Consumer Assessment of Healthcare Providers and Systems) survey at www.cms.gov.

71. For some comparative data on healthcare costs see 2014 Hospital Costs Reports from the American Hospital Directory at www.ahd.com.

72. Clough et al, *To Act as a Unit*, p. 127.

73. Ibid.

74. Ibid., p. 159.

8: BUCKET-BUSTING

1. See 'JPMorgan Chase Whale Trades: A Case History of Derivatives Risks and Abuses,' Majority and Minority Staff Report, Permanent Subcommittee on Investigations, United State Senate, March 15, 2013, www.hsgag.senate.gov. This provides a comprehensive account of this saga.

2. The estimates of losses are drawn from the Senate 2013 report, www.hsgag.senate.gov.

3. Anthony Effinger and Mary Childs, 'From BlueMountain's Feldstein, a Win-Win with JPMorgan; After Betting Against, and Beating, the London Whale, Feldstein Did More than Just Make Money,' Bloomberg, January 20, 2013.

4. Farah Khalique, 'The Whale,' *Financial News*, December 7, 2012; Farah Khalique, 'Unwinding the Whale Trade,' *Financial News*, December 12, 2012.

5. See 'JPMorgan Chase Whale Trades: A Case History of Derivatives Risks and Abuses,' Majority and Minority Staff Report, Permanent Subcommittee on Investigations, United State Senate, March 15, 2013, www.hsgag.senate.gov.

6. Gillian Tett, *Fool's Gold* (New York: Simon & Schuster, 2009).

7. Ibid. See also Dan McCrum and Tom Braithwaite, 'Restraint Pays Off for BlueMountain Chief,' *Financial Times*, March 14, 2013.

8. John Seely Brown, 'New Learning Environments for the 21st Century,' www.johnseelybrown.com/newlearning.

9. I explain this story in great detail in my book *Fool's Gold*.

10. Donald MacKenzie, 'The Credit Crisis as a Problem in the Sociology of Knowledge,' *American Journal of Sociology*, May 2011.

11. Ibid.

12. Jonathan Shapiro, 'Exploiting Inefficiencies,' *The Australian Financial Review*, June 6, 2013.

13. Effinger and Childs, 'From BlueMountain's Feldstein, a Win-Win with JPMorgan; After Betting Against, and Beating, the London Whale, Feldstein Did More than Just Make Money.' See also Tett, *Fool's Gold*.

14. 'The Whale,' *Financial News*, December 7, 2012.

15. David Rubenstein, BMCM, interview, *Global Investor*, September 1, 2013.

16. 'JPMorgan Chase Whale Trades: A Case History of Derivatives Risks and Abuses,' Majority and Minority Staff Report, Permanent Subcommittee on Investigations, United State Senate, March 15, 2013, p. 3.

17. Ibid., p. 260.

18. Ibid., p. 7; 'JP Morgan Chase Whale Trade: A Case History of Derivatives Risks and Abuses,' Senate committee investigation, p. 260, www.hsgag.senate.gov.

19. Stephanie Ruhle, Bradley Keoun, and Mary Childs, 'JPMorgan Trader's Positions Said to Distort Credit Index,' Bloomberg, April 6, 2012. See also Shannon D. Harrington, Bradley Keoun, and Christine Harper, 'JPMorgan Trader Iksil Fuels Prop-Trading Debate with Bets,' Bloomberg, April 9, 2012; Gregory Zuckerman and Katy Burne, 'London Whale Rattles Debt Markets,' *Wall Street Journal*, April 6, 2012.

20. 'JPMorgan Chase Whale Trades: A Case History of Derivatives Risks and Abuses,' Majority and Minority Staff Report, Permanent Subcommittee on Investigations, United State Senate, March 15, 2013. See pages 3–19 for a complete account of this.

21. MacKenzie, 'The Credit Crisis as a Problem in the Sociology of Knowledge.'

22. 'Innovation and Collaboration at Merrill Lynch,' Harvard Business School case study, March 26, 2007, p. 4.

23. Ibid., p. 7.

24. 'Innovation and Collaboration at Merrill Lynch,' p. 16.
25. Ibid., p. 19.
26. http://www.hanes.com/corporate.

CONCLUSION: CONNECTING THE DOTS

1. Marcel Proust, *Remembrance of Things Past*, Volume 5, *The Captive*, Chapter 2, trans. C. K. Scott Moncrieff (New York: Random House, 1935).
2. To see a description of this from Lauren Talbot: https://www.youtube.com/watch?v=S6EvneIRiTo.
3. Douglas Thomas and John Seely Brown, *A New Culture of Learning* (CreateSpace Independent Publishing Platform, 2011). See also www.johnseelybrown.com/newlearning.pdf.
4. Fareed Zakaria, *In Defense of a Liberal Education* (New York: W. W. Norton, 2015).

Index

To buy any of our books and to find out
more about Abacus and Little, Brown, our authors
and titles, as well as events and book clubs,
visit our website

www.littlebrown.co.uk

and follow us on Twitter

@AbacusBooks
@LittleBrownUK

To order any Abacus titles p & p free in the UK,
please contact our mail order supplier on:

+ 44 (0)1832 737525

Customers not based in the UK should contact
the same number for appropriate postage
and packing costs.